Vicente Leñero

University of Texas Studies
in Contemporary Spanish-American Fiction

Robert Brody
General Editor

Vol. 3

PETER LANG
New York • Bern • Frankfurt am Main • Paris

Danny J. Anderson

Vicente Leñero
The Novelist as Critic

Merlin –
You've been a great friend and colleague.
I appreciate your support when I was in
the "middle" of this project. I hope
that you enjoy the final product.
                                        Always,
                                        Danny

PETER LANG
New York • Bern • Frankfurt am Main • Paris

Library of Congress Cataloging-in-Publication Data

Anderson, Danny J.,
   Vicente Leñero.
   (University of Texas studies in contemporary
Spanish-American fiction ; vol. 3)
   Bibliography: p.
   Includes index.
    1. Leñero, Vicente – Fictional works. 2. Mexican
fiction – 20th century – History and criticism. I. Title.
II. Series.
PQ7297.L37Z514   1989   863   89-12152
ISBN 0-8204-0937-5   CIP
ISSN 0888-8787

CIP-Titelaufnahme der Deutschen Bibliothek

Anderson, Danny J.:
Vicente Leñero : the novelist as critic / Danny J.
Anderson. – New York; Bern; Frankfurt am
Main; Paris: Lang, 1989.
   (University of Texas Studies in Contemporary
   Spanish-American Fiction; Vol. 3)
   ISBN 0-8204-0937-5

NE: University of Texas <Austin, Tex.>:
University of Texas . . .

Printed by Weihert-Druck GmbH, Darmstadt, West Germany

for JoEd and Nancy

Contents

Preface

The novels of Vicente Leñero manifest the spirit of innovation and cultural awareness indicative of the Boom in Mexico, in particular, and generally throughout all Spanish America. Through an analysis of Leñero's novels, I have attempted to account for two aspects of his *novelística*: first, the function of the texts as implicit critiques of the potentials of the genre; and second, the use of the novel as a vehicle for exploring and producing a critical interpretation of reality. In this perspective, the following studies contribute to the critical evaluation of both Leñero's exploration of the flexibility of the novel and the general cultural and social consciousness often attributed to contemporary Spanish American novels.

The choice of Vicente Leñero's novels for such a project is not gratuitous. One of the less fortunate aspects of the Boom has been the tendency to disregard many excellent writers in favor of international superstars such as Carlos Fuentes, Mario Vargas Llosa, Gabriel García Márquez, and Julio Cortázar. Although these writers are, by all standards, worthy of such attention, many Spanish American novelists merit greater critical interest than they have received to date. Indeed, Vicente Leñero was among the first Spanish American novelists of the Boom to win an international literary prize, the *Premio Biblioteca Breve* awarded by Seix Barral in 1963 for *Los albañiles*. Nevertheless, after a momentary recognition of brilliance, Leñero, like the majority of Spanish American novelists, fell into the shadows of the more flashy and outspoken literary personalities of the day.

Since he began to write professionally in 1959, Vicente Leñero has been a source of constant stimulation and renewal for contemporary Mexican literature and journalism. Born in Guadalajara, Jalisco, in 1933, Leñero completed his studies in civil engineering in 1959 at the Universidad Nacional Autónoma de México, in Mexico City. Yet he never practiced as a professional civil engineer. He had completed a course of studies at the Escuela de

Periodismo Carlos Septién García in 1956, and immediately turned to writing as his career.

In 1958 Leñero won a prize from a university magazine for a short story. The following year he published his first book, *La polvareda y otros cuentos* (1959). Throughout the early sixties, Leñero divided his talents between writing novels and scripts for soap operas in both radio and television. *La voz adolorida* (1961) was his first novel. In addition to the prize for *Los albañiles*, during this period Leñero twice held fellowships from the Centro Mexicano de Escritores, in 1961-62 and in 1963-64. Finally, Leñero published two more novels in the sixties, *Estudio Q* (1965) and *El garabato* (1967), and a revised edition of his first novel, *A fuerza de palabras* (1967).

The late sixties, however, marked a change in Leñero's career. In 1967-1968 Leñero held a John S. Guggenheim fellowship and he directed his creative energies toward the theater. In 1968 he staged his first drama, *Pueblo rechazado*, a critical success that introduced documentary drama to contemporary Mexican theater. Throughout the late sixties and early seventies Leñero continued to dedicate his creative efforts to drama. After *Pueblo rechazado*, he wrote five major theatrical works between 1969 and 1972: *Los albañiles* (1969), an adaptation of the novel, which won the Premio Juan Ruiz de Alarcón for the best work staged in 1969; *Compañero* (1970), based on the life of "Che" Guevara; *La carpa* (1971), an adaptation of the novel *Estudio Q*; *El juicio* (1971), another documentary piece based on the trial of two religious figures, José de León Toral and Concepción Acevedo de la Llata, for the 1928 assasination of president elect, General Alvaro Obregón; and *Los hijos de Sánchez* (1972), a stage version of Oscar Lewis's anthropological text, *The Children of Sanchez*. In addition to writing these plays, Leñero was also director of the women's magazine *Claudia* from 1969 to 1972.

After 1972, Leñero served as the director of the *Revista de revistas*, a weekly publication of the newspaper *Excélsior*. From 1972 to 1976, while working for *Excélsior*, Leñero published only one novel. This novel, however, *Redil de ovejas* (1973), bears the imprint of his work with documentary drama for it explicitly depends on an experimental approach to history and novelization. Also, consonant with such interest in documentary writing, Leñero published a journalistic work, *Viaje a Cuba* (1975), an experimental report on post-revolutionary Cuba.

In 1976, however, Leñero's career once again takes a turn. The federal government of Mexico censored *Excélsior* and forced a change in official editorial policy. In effect, the government ousted the directors of the journalistic cooperative. As the result of such an experience, Leñero, together with Julio Scherer García, the ex-director of *Excélsior*, and other journalists, founded the weekly news magazine *Proceso*. Since 1976 Leñero has served as the sub-director of the magazine. As an additional reaction to the *Excélsior* incident, in 1978 Leñero published a nonfiction novel, *Los periodistas*, which chronicles the details of the episode.

Since 1978, Leñero's writing has become even more heterogeneous than before. In contemporary Mexican drama, Leñero has continually produced works of great importance: *La mudanza*, a piece staged in 1979 that contrasts the problems of marital conflicts against the larger backdrop of socio-economic inequality in contemporary Mexico, and that won the Premio Juan Ruíz de Alarcón for 1979; *Alicia, tal vez* (1980) and *La visita del ángel* (1982), two plays that demonstrate innovative use of stage space and theatrical time; *Martirio de Morelos* (1981), a polemical, historiographic-documentary drama that reconsiders the origin of a Mexican national hero; and *¡Pelearán diez rounds!* (1985), an experimental drama that portrays a boxer whose public and private life are both represented as a boxing match. Vicente Leñero's contributions as a dramatist have been fundamental in stimulating, renewing, and solidifying the theatrical tradition in contemporary Mexico.

In narrative prose writing, Leñero has been equally prolific since the end of the 1970s. He has published three more novels: *El evangelio de Lucas Gavilán* (1979), *La gota de agua* (1983), and

Asesinato: El doble crimen de los Flores Muñoz (1985). In addition to these novels, a growing interest in Leñero's work has led to the publication of anthologies of his writing in various genres: *Cajón de sastre* (1982), a collection of short stories and journalistic pieces; *Justos por pecadores* (1982), a collection of three film scripts; *Vivir del teatro* (1983), Leñero's memoirs of his experiences in contemporary Mexican theater; and *Talacha periodística* (1983), an anthology of Leñero's best journalistic writings and critiques of popular Mexican culture. Undoubtedly, Vicente Leñero is one of the major figures of contemporary Mexican literature. Although his interests vary widely, he has contributed above all to the continued growth of Mexico's novel, theater, and journalism.

In spite of Leñero's important role in Mexican literature, the critical studies dealing with his works have been relatively scant. Among the criticism concerning Leñero's novels, the dissertation by Lois S. Grossman stands out for its excellent insights. In addition, dissertations by Miguel Angel Niño, Ellen Marie McCracken, and Neil Jay Devereaux provide useful information and interpretations. The critical articles written by Iris Josefina Ludmer, Lucía Garavito, John M. Lipski, and José Luis Mártinez Morales are among the best considerations of Leñero's novelistic writings. The bibliography contains references to the aforementioned studies and includes all works cited in the endnotes.

In addition to the recognition that I have given to these readers and critics of Leñero's novels, I wish to thank several individuals who generously offered me their time and critical attention as I prepared this book. First, I am endebted to John S. Brushwood, who carefully read drafts of almost the entire manuscript and shared with me his knowledge of Mexico and the Mexican novel. Also, I thank Robert C. Spires and Michael Doudoroff for their reading and patiently commenting on large portions of this study. In addition, I thank José Rabasa and Madeline Sutherland, who generously gave of their time to read and discuss drafts of the second and sixth chapters; John Lipski and Kent Stone provided me with unpublished manuscripts on *Estudio Q* and *Los albañiles,* respectively; and Robert Brody and Naomi Lindstrom contributed greatly to this entire book with insightful editorial recommendations that I deeply appreciate. And I thank Jennifer Kennedy Anderson for years of friendship. Finally, I thank the University Research Institute of the University of Texas at Austin for funding that supported the research and writing of chapter six. And most importantly, generous support from the Endowment Association of the University of Kansas has made the publication of this book possible. Although the support of these friends, colleagues and institutions has proven invaluable, any deficiencies in this book are, of course, my own.

Introduction:
Vicente Leñero and the Contemporary Mexican Novel

Vicente Leñero has contributed immensely to growth and innovation in the novel, theater, and journalism of contemporary Mexico. Unlike many of the more outspoken or publicly renowned literary personalities of the day, however, Leñero has not received the serious critical attention that his creative efforts merit. In certain contexts, such an archival lacuna would have constituted sufficient justification for a study of the novels of Vicente Leñero. In the contemporary context, since the advent of post-structuralism, a study of the novels of Vicente Leñero can be neither as straightforward nor as simple as it might once have seemed.

An analysis of Leñero's novels, however arbitrary or simple the selection of such a corpus may appear, already invokes a complex series of relationships beginning with the phrase "Leñero's novels." As a label, the phrase classifies and differentiates Leñero's novels from all others--a possessive referring back to the author. Nevertheless, in the case of an author, such a possessive does not refer back to a "real" writer, for, as Michel Foucault writes:

> . . . unlike a proper name, which moves from the interior of a discourse to the real person outside who produced it, the name of the author remains at the contours of texts--separating their mode of existence. It points to the existence of certain groups of discourse and refers to the status of this discourse within a society and culture.[1]

Hence, the phrase "Leñero's novels" implies several pertinent relations between an author and his works. First, an account of Leñero's novels will distinguish them from other novels and demonstrate how the distinction marks their form and mode of existence. Furthermore, the singular status of the novels emerges against a socio-cultural background of other novels by other writers. And finally, the process of differentiation entails the recognition of a breach, of the discontinuity between Leñero's novels and a broader discursive practice of writing novels. Consequently, the focus of analysis shifts away from a biographical "the man and his work" approach to Leñero and locates itself in a realm of contextual interaction.

In the present study, these considerations about an author merge in my reading of Vicente Leñero, the novelist, as a critic. The critical purport of Leñero's novels requires consideration of a double context. First, in the literary context, and, more specifically, in the perspective of novel writing in Mexico, Leñero's works insistently explore the constraints and potentials of the novelistic genre as practiced at a precise cultural and historical moment. Attention to questions of genre and narrative strategies, therefore, reveals how Leñero's novels distinguish themselves from, for example, Carlos Fuentes's or Salvador Elizondo's, and, moreover, how Leñero's use of novelistic discourse critically investigates the possible uses of the genre. The second context and critical message refer, in turn, to the broader socio-historical milieu, and underscore the relation between the world and the text, that is, the worldliness of Leñero's novels. Edward W. Said notes "that texts have ways of existing that even in their most rarefied form are always enmeshed in circumstance, time, place, and society--in short, they are in the world and hence worldly."[2] In this perspective, Leñero's use of the constraints and potentials of the genre also represent some of the ways texts inscribe their worldliness or, quoting Said again, constitute a "system of tentacles . . . partly potential, partly actual: to the author, to the reader, to a historical situation, to other texts, to the past and present."[3] A circumspect examination of the worldliness of Leñero's novels, then, further refines an understanding of his critical approach to the genre and, concurrently, lays bare the social and cultural criticism conveyed through his narrative practices.

A first approximation to these contexts will define the contours and status of Leñero's novels.[4] Between 1961 and 1985 Leñero published ten novels. In the first decade of this period, the 1960s, Leñero's early novels and most Mexican novels demonstrate the general tendency toward experimental use of narrative strategies. Such experimentation has its beginnings in the changes in the novel that took place in the late 1940s and the 1950s. In Mexico, Agustín Yáñez's *Al filo del agua* (1947) closes a previous tradition and opens a new one: the final pinnacle of the novel of the Mexican Revolution and the beginning of the New Novel. Similar patterns of renewal and innovation commence throughout Spanish America from 1946 to 1949. Writing on the novels of these years, the "years of the reaffirmation of fiction," John S. Brushwood points out:

> They all deal with the Spanish American world, but they are excellent examples of the difference between personification and novelization. In other words, they are all based on objective reality but they accomplish more than the addition of life to the facts of history. They transform objective reality, create worlds within the novels.[5]

The term "novelization" may serve as a key to understanding the nature of the New Novel. As the writers of these years gain the self-confidence needed to invent worlds, the process of novelization comes to include a greater interest in and capacity for the manipulation of language and narrative structures.[6]

In the following years, novels such as Juan Rulfo's *Pedro Páramo* (1955) and Carlos Fuentes's *La región más transparente* (1958) attest to the ongoing concern with novelization. Through the careful use of language and structure Rulfo and Fuentes create worlds within their novels and provide readers with a more original and a more complex interpretation of time and reality than that found in traditional narratives. The intensification in technical experimentation after *Al filo del agua* also requires a substantial change in the nature of the act of reading. Although contemporary theories about the act of reading have demonstrated that to read is always to participate actively in a meaning-producing interaction, the New Novel is characterized by a considerably higher degree of active participation, a quality that I associate with Roland Barthes's concept of the "writerly."[7] As the New Novels become more writerly, readers experience an intensification of the demand to become the producer or writer of the text, totally removed from the realm of passively consuming an aprioristically construed meaning.

In addition, the concern with novelization manifests in a clear fashion the synthetic nature of innovation in the New Novel. The so-called newness of the novels written in Mexico after the 1940s resides in a successful combination of techniques and themes found in the opposing currents of vanguard literature, the novel of the Mexican Revolution, and the social protest literature of the 1920s and 1930s. Furthermore, the newness reflects a thorough understanding of the novel of the early twentieth century as exemplified in the writings of James Joyce, William Faulkner, Ernest Hemingway, and John Dos Passos. In many instances it is not an issue of direct influence or imitation but a comprehension, on the part of the Mexican novelists, of how these writers used language and narrative structure to create worlds, to express regional themes that in the end become universal in their significance.

In the 1960s, the writerly text occupies a privileged position in the novelistic genre in Mexico: experimental techniques in novelization are acceptable, if not expected in a "serious" novel. Fortunately, the gradual process of selection throughout the 1950s insures the quality of novels in the 1960s, permitting writers to benefit from both the mistakes and the achievements of earlier novels. Thus, when Leñero publishes his early novels, he participates in an atmosphere conducive to novelistic innovation, an historical moment in which both the quality and quantity of novels increase. Although most Mexican novelists continue and extend the emphasis on innovative narrative strategies established by landmark publications of the 1940s and 1950s, their novels in the 1960s fall into two thematic areas. Joseph Sommers has noted that first, "There are those novels which, directly or indirectly, concern themselves with aspects of Mexican reality or problems of the individual in a societal context." And second, he continues:

> There was also fiction which reflected a conscious effort to move directly toward universal themes and styles, tending away from social and national preoccupations. Entering the more abstract realms of philosophic or stylistic emphasis, these novels and short stories reduced somewhat the direct tie between literature and the major problems of the post-Revolution.[8]

Most critics of the Mexican novel have categorized Leñero in this second division, which Sommers labels "The Universalizers."[9] Upon reconsideration, however, the dual critical import of Leñero's novelistic production places him in a thematic position between the two areas delineated by Sommers.

The five novels Leñero published in the 1960s manifest the emergence of a dialectical tension between the "social" and the "universal" in his early fiction. *La voz adolorida* (1961) demonstrates Leñero's innovative skills by successfully presenting the obsessive monologue of a mentally disturbed young man, Enrique. From the outset of the novel readers detect the presence of an interlocutor, the doctor to whom Enrique speaks. The novel earns its universalizing label for dealing so exclusively with the internal torments of a single protagonist. Indeed, the universalizing tendencies of the 1960s result in "un acentuado interés por el descubrimiento de la realidad más interior y profunda."[10] Nevertheless, the novel also implicitly criticizes the various forms of social repression that have contributed to Enrique's psychological instability, especially a compulsive religiosity that cannot adapt to the demands of a rapidly changing social context.

Social criticism also underlies Leñero's second novel, *Los albañiles* (1964). This novel considers the problem of guilt in society as a detective fails to resolve a murder case. Interpretation of the detective's failure constitutes the major hermeneutic difficulty of the novel: the detective, Munguía, cannot name a single murderer in accordance with the demands of police and bureaucratic protocol; his investigation, however, succeeds in that he becomes aware of the fundamental problems of his and all human society: he recognizes that guilt is essentially social, not individual.

Although consideration of such an abstract concept as guilt may appear to be universal, the treatment of the theme in *Los albañiles* embeds it in the concrete social problems of contemporary Mexico City. The various socio-economic strata of the national capital, all portrayed in the novel, reveal the problems arising in post-Revolutionary Mexico because of the demographic shifts of unskilled provincial laborers to Mexico City in search of a better life. Indeed, this fact of national reality constitutes an integral element in *Los albañiles*: the construction site of a high-rise apartment complex is the scene of the crime, and the suspected group of construction workers includes uprooted individuals who arrived in Mexico City with neither skills nor training. Although *Los albañiles* does manifest Leñero's concern for a specific problem of national reality, it also differs from those novels that consider the historic process that produced the problems, such as Carlos Fuentes's *La muerte de Artemio Cruz* (1962). Throughout all of Leñero's novels, the urban environment of Mexico City serves as the setting; furthermore, in the represented world social problems are usually accepted as a given, sidestepping any search for their historical source.

Los albañiles also exemplifies the complexity a narrative can achieve through the careful use of language and structure. By 1964, however, complexity is no longer an exceptional quality for a Mexican novel. Rather, as Bushwood has commented, it has become a norm for novelistic production:

> Inclusive el examen más superficial de las novelas de 1964 indica que la llamada novela tradicional (es decir, la sucesión de introducción, desarrollo de la trama, crisis y resolución) ha desaparecido casi completamente. La estructura predominante usa segmentos narrativos que rompen el orden cronológico ortodoxo, comúnmente para alcanzar el efecto de simultaneidad o aprovechar múltiples voces narrativas. Frecuentemente, las técnicas requieren más explicación que los temas. Esto tiene enorme importancia, pues indica que la manera en que un autor se expresa es una parte cada vez más importante de lo que dice. Este fenómeno indica con claridad que la ficción mexicana no es ingenua, pues sabe muy bien lo que hace. El hincapié en el factor estético, sin embargo, no significa necesariamente que una novela diga menos acerca de México. Por el contrario, la apreciación de la técnica puede ser la clave esencial para comprender lo que el autor dice acerca del país.[11]

In an atmosphere of intense novelization, with a great emphasis on the aesthetics of creation, it is not surprising that novels of subsequent years turn toward the thematics of life and art, reality and fiction.

In 1965, the year following *Los albañiles*, Leñero publishes *Estudio Q*, a novel that radically dramatizes the similarities between fiction and reality as a soap opera actor loses the ability to distinguish his life from a soap opera about his life--just as readers subsequently fail to separate the two represented worlds into distinct narrative levels. Leñero is far from being the only Mexican novelist to deal with the repetitions between life and art. Many other writers invent parallel narrative structures that achieve the same effect as *Estudio Q*, if not carrying it to an even more emphatic extreme. For example, Salvador Elizondo's *Farabeuf* (1965) and *El hipogeo secreto* (1968), Carlos Fuentes's *Cambio de piel* (1967), and José Emilio Pacheco's *Morirás lejos* (1967) all strive to push the writerly novel to a self-conscious limit in which readers can no longer separate themselves from the process of creating the text, nor separate the novelized reality from the subordinate fictional reality represented within the text. In 1967 Vicente Leñero publishes another metafiction, *El garabato*, a novel within a novel within a novel. From the vantage point of the 1980s, the self-referential or metafictional tendency emerging in the mid-1960s stands as the dominant characteristic of the Mexican novel from the late 1960s into the 1970s.[12]

After *El garabato*, Leñero edits his first novel and publishes it under the title *A fuerza de palabras* (1967). The changes in the second version intensify the writerliness of the text. *A fuerza de palabras* leaves Enrique's interlocutor unidentified, represented only by the periodically recurrent pronoun *usted*. This modification, removing the verifiable presence of a therapist, complicates the represented speech act as readers assume the full burden of determining the credibility and rationality of Enrique's monologue. Thus, the changes in *A fuerza de palabras* demonstrate the same effect as that produced by the metafictions of the same years: they increase readers' participation in the *process* of the novel.

After 1967, however, Leñero's novel writing reaches a hiatus, which he does not break until 1973. According to Leñero's autobiography, the interruption of his novelistic production comes about because of the dead end he found when writing the metafictions *Estudio Q* and *El garabato*; the "presumptuous" (Leñero's word) search for originality and the distance from pertinent social problems led him to shift genres and, from 1968 to 1972, to dedicate himself, very successfully, to the theater, especially documentary drama.[13]

To summarize the tendencies of Leñero's novels from 1961 to 1967, a universalizing perspective gives rise to a set of thematic concerns that transcend the boundaries of strictly national reality. Also, revisionist criticism of Catholicism as hypocritical and repressive plays a large role in *La voz adolorida, Los albañiles, El garabato,* and *A fuerza de palabras.* The manner of producing religious revisionism, of course, varies drastically among these texts. In all of them, however, Mexican Catholicism appears as a cultural given that directly or indirectly links Leñero's works to the problems of national reality. George R. McMurray, recognizing the peculiar link between universal themes and the problems afflicting national life, observes about Mexican novelists in the mid-1960s: "Their objective is not to suggest remedies but rather to cast doubt on traditional values, alter attitudes and thus create an atmosphere conducive to change."[14] In this respect, the works Leñero published in the 1960s form a corpus of critical revisions of Mexican reality, exposing and rejecting many of the contradictions and inadequacies of national life.

In the years before Leñero resumes his novel writing, 1968 to 1972, the Mexican novel continues along the same lines of development initiated in the late 1940s and 1950s. During these years the "novel of the city" becomes simply the novel, and the group of writers a decade younger than Leñero achieves full recognition as the "onda": principally Gustavo Sainz, José Agustín, and René Avilés Fabila.[15] The writers of the "onda" in a certain sense share Leñero's rejection of national reality and his interest in experimentation with new forms of novelistic expression. Their mode of expression, however, strongly reflects a generational division that separates them from Leñero through both their youthful language and their perspective. In general terms,

Mexican novelists of the 1960s achieve a greater awareness of their craft and a sense of security about their place in a tradition that transcends national borders.[16]

The self-confidence of the Mexican novelists in their right to create worlds, and the increase in both the quantity and quality of novels is part of the larger phenomenon called the "Boom" of the Spanish American novel. The increasing quality of the Spanish American novel begins in the late 1940s with the New Novel; the Boom, on the other hand, more properly refers to the unprecedented international interest in the Spanish American novel and the considerable increase in the number of novels published.[17] In very broad terms, the Spanish American novels of the 1960s fall into two categories, as suggested by José Miguel Oviedo: first, "La línea realista que postula una historia definida en la base del relato que trata de renovar la tradición del realismo latinoamericano operando dentro de esa misma tradición," and second, the line of novels that, following the examples of Carlos Fuentes, Julio Cortázar (Argentina), and Guillermo Cabrera Infante (Cuba), "casi prescinde de la historia o la subordina a una búsqueda formalista casi exasperada"; in this second category the story is either nonexistent or used "meramente como un pretexto para sus juegos y distorsiones verbales: escribiendo novelas que quieren burlar el concepto mismo de la novela."[18]

Fernando Alegría finds profound implications in this second line of novels. According to Alegría, who calls the second category "antiliteratura," these texts attempt to destroy the unexamined social conventions that define the nature of reality. Antiliterature thus constitutes an assault against falsification in art, a search for a manner to resolve the absurdity of the human condition by accepting even its most extreme implications.[19] In this sense, the critical revisionism implicit in the rejection of national reality as seen in Mexican novels of the 1960s, even in the narcissistic metafictions, also takes part in a parallel antiliterary movement in the Spanish American Novel of the same decade.

Returning to the Mexican literary context, in the 1970s Leñero publishes two more novels, *Redil de ovejas* (1973) and *El evangelio de Lucas Gavilán* (1979), and in addition, he begins his exploration of the nonfiction novel with *Los periodistas* (1978). In the decade under consideration here, the Boom in the Mexican novel, and in the Spanish American novel in general, declines. Similarly, although the Boom in the novel declines in the 1970s, the tradition of renewal and innovation remains constant. In *Redil de ovejas* readers encounter the critical Catholic stance typical of Leñero's earlier novels. The religious theme, however, emerges more overtly and Leñero's social concerns become even more evident as the novel takes on a semi-testimonial aspect: the novelized world includes the historically verifiable extratextual referent of Catholic anticommunist movements of the early 1960s. In addition, *Redil de ovejas* manifests one of the principal characteristics of the Mexican novel between 1968 and 1982: the unstable identity of characters.[20] The novel inscribes this instability by exploring the tensions among a small group of individuals and then revealing the unexpected detail that two generations of characters bear the same names and repeat the same conflicts.

The innovation typical of all of Leñero's novels exists in quintessential form in *El evangelio de Lucas Gavilán* (1979). In contrast with the tension between documentation and invention in *Redil de ovejas*, this *tour de force* combines total fictionalization with socio-cultural criticism. In the opening prologue, Leñero's narrator, Lucas Gavilán, explains that he is rewriting the Gospel of St. Luke in a contemporary Mexican setting. The novel, however, is not a paraphrase of the Biblical Gospel in contemporary Spanish. Following the tenets of liberation theology, *El evangelio de Lucas Gavilán* presents a man, Jesucristo Gómez, who lives in present day Mexico and practices the new theology at a grass-roots level. Various characters portray different aspects of the hypocritical and repressive beliefs of Mexican Catholicism, all within the perspective of contemporary socio-economic problems and cultural prejudices. As Jesucristo Gómez's life follows a course of events parallel to those of Jesus Christ in the Gospel of St. Luke, explicit criticisms arise in reference to the practices of Christianity within Mexican culture. The language, situations, and organization of the novel produce sensitive and often humorous effects, yet comprehension of the novel must take place in the space between two texts and various interpretations: in order to understand *El evangelio de Lucas Gavilán* readers must constantly recall the Gospel of St. Luke, and concurrently recognize Leñero's text as an interpretation, a translation comprehensible only in juxtaposition to other traditional and institutional interpretations of St. Luke's Gospel. Thus, *El evangelio de Lucas Gavilán* continues the social criticism found in Leñero's other novels, intensifies the religious criticism present in all of his works, and carries experimentation with novel form to another extreme, totally different from all of his other innovations.

With respect to Leñero's novels of 1973 and 1979, it is clear that his preoccupation with renewal of the novel form never diminishes. Nevertheless, his social and religious concerns take a more prominent position than before. Even though the later novels remain within the realm of the writerly, the process becomes much more subtle: whereas *Redil de ovejas* may pose some difficulties to readers because of the unstable identity of characters, *El evangelio de Lucas Gavilán*, with its linear structure, colloquial language and clearly recognizable Biblical antecedent, make it surprisingly easy to read. Such ease notwithstanding, *El evangelio de Lucas Gavilán* exploits a writerly technique of novelization by denying the existence of meaning *within* the text itself and instead locating the process of signification in the space that readers must negotiate among the novel, society, and the Gospel of St. Luke.

In comparison with other Mexican novelists of the 1970s, Leñero gains a more distinct profile than he had in the 1960s. In Brushwood's recent study of the Mexican novel, *La novela mexicana (1968-1982)*, he points out five general characteristics that extend through the 1970s: (1) the predominance of metafictions or self-referential novels, (2) the theme and technique of unstable identities, (3) "the novel" as the novel of Mexico City, (4) the presence of an historical reaction to the tragedy of Tlatelolco, and (5) the appearance of nostalgia as both a theme and a technique in the contemporary novel.[21] Against this background, Leñero moves away from the metafictional and self-referential tendencies. Although the complexities of *Redil de ovejas* and the ingenuity of *El evangelio de Lucas Gavilán* do manifest a degree of self-evident artifice, the novels in no way subordinate theme to technique in order to contemplate their own process of creation. In relation to unstable identity, only *Redil de ovejas* employs this technique as a manner of altering readers' perception of represented reality. Also, just as unstable identity plays a small role in Leñero's later novels, the fifth characteristic of nostalgia is very minor, if at all present.[22]

In contrast, in all of Leñero's later novels Mexico City is the predominant setting. Whereas the city exists as a given in *Redil de ovejas*, it plays a much more important role in *El evangelio de Lucas Gavilán*. The Christian praxis of Jesucristo Gómez follows a circuitous route throughout the Mexican Republic, and he finally arrives at the mythic national capital for the culmination of his life. Upon entering Mexico City, however, Jesucristo Gómez visits the major *barrios*, emphasizing particularly the more declassed ones inhabited by the under- or unemployed and the sub- or lumpenproletariat. Thus, the novel represents a kind of ethnographic voyage through the other, less fortunate Mexico and Mexico City. In this light, the Mexico City of *El evangelio de Lucas Gavilán* manifests three of the principal functions of "the city" in the contemporary Mexican novel. First, within the biblical framework, Mexico City takes on both mythic and modern qualities, as in Fuentes's *La región más transparente* and Agustín Yáñez's *Ojerosa y pintada* (1959). Second, social criticism provides an element of protest to the novel. And finally, the amelioration of the protest, through tenderness, humor, and sympathy, produces

14

a poignant identification of Mexico City as a homeland.²³ In summary, *El evangelio de Lucas Gavilán* does manifest many links with other tendencies of the Mexican novel in the 1970s; however, the religious theme and biblical pre-text combine to make it *sui generis*, contrasting distinctly with other Mexican novels of the same decade.

In a different perspective, the massacre at Tlatelolco provided a "shock" for Mexican society at large. Briefly, the night of October 2, 1968, made patent the contradictions of Mexican democracy when forces under the command of president Gustavo Díaz Ordaz used unnecessary force to put an end to student demonstrations: they opened fire on university students who had gathered in protest in the Plaza de la Tres Culturas (commonly called Tlatelolco). The number of students who died that night continues to be a topic of debate. Although the reaction to this incident may serve as either a principal theme or a background element of represented reality in many novels, its consideration reveals a return to a more direct consideration of national problems. In this sense, the critical purport of Leñero's novels of the 1970s reflects a larger literary and social response to the problems of Mexican reality.

The theme of Tlatelolco never directly enters Leñero's later novels, but the literary reactions to the Tlatelolco incident constitute the backdrop for Leñero's experiments in the nonfiction novel. Elena Poniatowska's *La noche de Tlatelolco* (1971) perhaps marks the beginning of contemporary nonfiction texts in Mexican literature. In contrast to the often directly historical novels of the Mexican Revolution or Ricardo Pozas's experiment in documentary narrative, *Juan Pérez Jolote* (1952), which manifests an interest in both the Revolution and ethnographic representation, after the Tlatelolco massacre nonfiction texts tend to confront the use and abuse of power in contemporary Mexico. The case of *La noche de Tlatelolco* is one example that overtly refers to the incidents of 1968; yet, in general, the events of that year encourage a direct examination of the social construction of reality and hence the emergence of contemporary nonfiction narratives. Besides *Los periodistas* (1978), Leñero has published two more nonfiction novels, *La gota de agua* (1983), and *Asesinato: El doble crimen de los Flores Muñoz* (1985). In each case, nonfiction novelization depends on various kinds of documentation of empirical reality and exploits numerous narrative techniques to transform the world into text.

An additional consideration of the Mexican literary context must emphasize that just as Leñero's novels become more "readable" after 1973, so does the Mexican novel in general shift to a more accessible style of narration. In part, this phenomenon is related to the diminishing number of self-referential novels. Also, as the number of Mexican novels dealing with national reality and social problems increases, the need to insure the effective communication of a social message becomes greater. The greater ease in reading found in the novels of the late 1970s in no way implies that the Mexican novel has become simpler; many writers continue to employ the complex narrative strategies popular in the 1960s and early 1970s, but they do so with greater ease and less self-consciousness, with less overt emphasis on technique. As a result, reading novels of the late 1970s, on the whole, requires less of the cerebral contemplation of abstract concepts and narrative games, hence the greater "ease" in reading.[24]

Against the broader backdrop of Spanish American fiction in the 1970s, Leñero's works maintain a similar pattern of divergences and convergences. Primarily, throughout the 1970s and into the 1980s metafictional novels continue to appear in all of Spanish America. In these novels, "metafiction" becomes a term more appropriate than "self-referentiality": rather than fictions that contemplate their own process of creation, the metafictions of the 1970s exploit the unabashedly open manipulation of artifice. In Argentina, Manuel Puig's *The Buenos Aires Affair* (1973) and *El beso de la mujer araña* (1976), which rely on strong intertextualities with pop culture, demonstrate the extreme to which the role of narrator can be reduced when integrating varieties of information and discourse into the text. Using a similar artifice to achieve a different effect, *Pantaleón y las visitadoras* (1975) and *La tía Julia y el escribidor* (1977), by Mario Vargas Llosa of Perú, are composed of military reports, letters, radio announcements, and even intercalated soap-opera scripts.

In Mexico this metafictional trend remains strong in the narratives of Carlos Fuentes: *Terra nostra* (1975), *La cabeza de la hidra* (1978), and *Una familia lejana* (1982). *Terra nostra* consists of the novelization of a concept (i.e., the dialectics of history at the time of the discovery of the New World), the literary tradition of late Medieval and Golden Age Spain, and Aztec mythology. In *La cabeza de la hidra*, rather than novelizing a concept, the language of the text calls attention to itself through the intrusions of a narrator whose enigmatic identity parallels the central mystery of this novel of international espionage. Finally, *Una familia lejana*, deploys Döppelgangers, intricately framed speech acts, and fantastic elements to make the artifice of novelization self-evident.

In the case of Leñero, *El evangelio de Lucas Gavilán* and the experiments in narrative techniques in the nonfiction novels most closely approximate the metafictional trend of Spanish American fiction in the 1970s. Leñero's novels reject the "natural" appearance of a more conventional realist narration through an open exhibition of their artificial substance, just as do most metafictions of the 1970s and early 1980s.

The second tendency of the Spanish American novel during these years is the importance given to history and the transformation of it in literature.[25] Although history appears as a novelized concept in *Terra nostra*, the historical process is also a major theme of the novel. Augusto Roa Bastos's *Yo el supremo* (1974, Paraguay), Jorge Edwards's *Los convidados de piedra* (1978, Chile), and Mario Vargas Llosa's *La guerra del fin del mundo* (1981) also manifest the same epic or panoramic treatment of history as found in *Terra nostra*. On the other hand, the later novels of the 1970s tend toward a narrower consideration of history. In the second group one may place novels such as

Antonio Skármeta's *Soñé que la nieve ardía* (1975, Chile), and Gustavo Alvarez Gardeazábal's *Los míos* (1983, Colombia). *Redil de ovejas* and Leñero's nonfiction novels resemble the second trend much more than the first: the novelization of contemporary reality emphasizes the synchronic dynamics of the historical situation.

The synchronic focus on a social situation in Leñero's novels also maintains links with the resurgence of a recognizable social reality in the Spanish American novel. After the extreme narcissism of self-referential novels in the late 1960s and early 1970s, writers begin to respond to social reality in a more direct manner. The response to the Tlatelolco tragedy in Mexico is a paradigm for the reactions to social disturbances throughout Spanish America in the 1970s, especially the 1973 *coup d'état* in Chile. Similarly, the social protest and documentary value of Leñero's later novels, both fictional and nonfictional, manifest the need to portray a recognizable social reality in order to protest its injustices.

In a final consideration, it should be noted that in the latter half of the 1970s, the Spanish American novel in general follows the trend toward greater readability. In part, the gradual decline in self-referential novels in favor of metafictions based on self-evident artifice contributes to this shift. Whereas the self-referential novel depended on the cerebral contemplation of creativity, the later metafictions develop on the basis of an enigma (in appearance similar to either traditional high literature or popular literature) that, when combined with self-conscious stylization, produces the dynamics of a writerly narrative. In addition, in non-metafictional novels, the need for history to appear verisimilar and the resurgence of a recognizable social reality both depend on the representation of reality through a complex experience activated in the process of reading. Yet one must keep in mind that easier reading by no means implies the end of the New Novel; by using many of the same techniques characteristic of the 1960s, writers of the 1970s and 1980s continue the evolution of the New Novel, manipulating narrative strategies in a more subtle fashion, and thus producing more "easily" read texts.

In much broader terms, the question of "novelization" constitutes the key issue for a consideration of the Mexican novel from the late 1940s to the present. Novelization, as stated above, refers to the writer's privilege to create worlds within the novel. The numerous experiments in narrative strategies during the years of the New Novel serve as explorations in the possible organization of the signifying structures, or conventions, of the genre. The overt emphasis placed on the use of less traditional narrative strategies, however, must be considered in a larger context that primarily consists of the historically active model of nineteenth-century literary Realism, based on a logic of cause and effect, and the thematic tradition of the Mexican novel.

The logic underlying nineteenth-century Realism predominates in the Mexican novel until the late 1940s. In general terms, the forms associated with nineteenth-century Realism, soundly rooted in positivism, allowed writers to express observations of cause and effect, placing readers in the role of intellectually understanding the observation as an undeniable and true relationship: these novels manifested the desire to explain the world to readers. The reasoning implied by this impulse, both for writers and for readers, however, occurred outside the text, *a priori* to both the writing and the reading of the text; the linguistic structure of the text served as the medium in which such reasoning was inscribed for recognition. Although Realism often adopted a critical stance with regard to the selection of socially pertinent issues, it nevertheless proposed that a certain way of representing the world--a supposed scientific or objective approach--would insure the transmission of a "logical" or rational "truth."

The emergence of the New Novel in the 1940s is not, however, an altogether "new" phenomenon. Spanish American *modernismo* at the turn of the century and the *vanguardismo* of the 1920s and early 1930s both initiate varying degrees of assault on the strategies of representation associated with nineteenth-century Realism. In a first moment, *modernismo* introduces a self-conscious critical stance in Spanish American letters and an unprecedented awareness of the world-creating power of language in the literary text.[26] Later, the diverse movements and literary experiments associated with *vanguardismo* brought to the fore a different notion of the self through the discovery of the psychoanalytic concept of the unconscious. By exploring the irrational elements repressed in a more orthodox approach to culture and identity, vanguard narrative questions the image of unity, both psychological and textual, that Realist representation presupposes and defends.[27] The New Novel, viewed in this perspective, emerges with a certain history; the legacy of the attention to critical consciousness, to the world-creating power of language, and to the illusory image of psychological and textual unity instructed writers in the nature of a "logical" or "rational" truth constructed and protected by the conventions of Realist representation.

The experiments of the New Novel, then, constitute assaults on this scientific objectivity, logic, and rationalism, in fine, on the truth of Realism. At times the texts attempt to produce a more experiential perception of the novelized reality, that is, a reading process not bound by the *a priori* closure of rational orthodoxy but instead cognizant of the often repressed heterological aspects of existence. In other cases, the novels concertedly resist the teleology of linking causes and effects as a deforming constraint on the comprehension of reality. To put it another way, the New Novel fundamentally contests the worldview implicitly espoused by Realist tendencies, often by calling into play interpretations of reality that Realism must repress to insure its "truth" and, at other times, by departing from the linearity of cause-effect reasoning to emphasize that such logic rests upon its own tautology, the fallacy of a *post hoc ergo propter hoc* representation of objectivity and truth.

The thematic tradition of the Mexican novel, generally produced within and through the logic of nineteenth-century Realism until the 1940s, produced a hybrid literary artifact. Such hybridization evidences a disparity between conventional literary forms, in this case the underlying logic of European Realism imported to Mexico, and the culturally determined national thematic tradition. The moments of interest generated by *modernista* and *vanguardista* narrative, although radically revolutionary in their representational practices, were ultimately overshadowed by the ongoing tradition of Realist narrative and were often accused of neglecting national social issues. Hence the experiments of the New Novel indicate an evolutionary stage in Mexican literature. Through experimentation with narrative techniques, Mexican writers attempt to resolve the incommensurate relationship between an imported literary tradition and cultural reality, dialectically synthesizing many of the contradictions inherent in the post-Colonial tradition of Mexican letters and searching for a deeper understanding of their national identity. To novelize is to explore critically one's cultural reality, and concurrently, to test the potentials and constraints that enable and impede critical exploration through novelistic discourse.

The experiments in novelization after the late 1940s, therefore, attempt to remove the boundaries set by the logic of objective representation and to adapt the functions of the genre to local circumstances and reality. The experiential and linguistic processes of the novel become primary: meanings arise not from the tacit faith in a positivistic worldview residing beyond the text, but from the dynamic interaction among the text, readers, and the world. To this end, the innovations in narrative strategies serve to involve readers in the construction of a world, not to reconfirm *a priori* interpretations of reality exterior to the text. In other words, the New Novel strives to incite in readers the desire to participate in the creation and and construction of the world.[28]

In closing, and returning to the novels of Vicente Leñero, the preceding contexts delineate the background against which I read the novelist as critic. On the one hand, Leñero's novels participate in the larger revision of novelistic discourse characteristic of the New Novel and, simultaneously, they interrogate the enabling potentials and constraining limitations of the genre as it is collectively practiced in the Mexican context. On the other hand, and contrary to the possible implications of their "universalizing" label, the novels also critically engage reality and circumstance as part of their signifying structure and their quest for social relevance. In Leñero's novels readers find unique textual organizations that, within the context of the genre, investigate the boundaries of literary conventions and thrust readers into the active construction of a world. It is the goal of the analyses in the following chapters to examine Leñero's dynamic use of the novel form as exemplary of the experimentation characteristic of the New Novel in Mexico, and to consider the way the novels transform and create realities. In this perspective, Leñero's works function as implicit critiques of the potentials of the novel and they explore the novel form as a vehicle for producing a critical interpretation of reality. Thus, I read Vicente Leñero, the novelist, as critic of both the genre and his cultural context.

Chapter One:
Epistemology and Interpretation:
The Contradictions of Narrative in
A fuerza de palabras

Vicente Leñero's *La voz adolorida* (1961) explores the potentials of the novelistic genre to represent the experience of the self in a cultural context. In addition, it undertakes the exploration of identities and a culture's knowledge of itself. The changes and revisions for the definitive version of the text, *A fuerza de palabras* (1967), further intensify the epistemological questioning that confronts the nature of truth in identity and in the interpretation of narrative.[1] In the same years, a similar questioning of identity and knowledge flourishes throughout Mexico and Spanish America as the Boom emerges from an unprecedented interest in the novel, and the novelistic genre comes to occupy a privileged position. Just as in *A fuerza de palabras*, the emphasis on technical experimentation and the intense focus upon culture during the Boom define the novel as a vehicle for exploring knowledge, for testing the possibilities of how to represent and how to know one's self and one's culture. The Russian theorist M. M. Bakhtin has noted one trend in literary evolution that may explain a great deal about the Boom, in general, and about Leñero's first novel, in particular: "When the novel becomes the dominant genre, epistemology becomes the dominant discipline."[2]

In a strategic manner, the structure and thematics of *A fuerza de palabras* produce an epistemological dilemma for readers. In terms of structure, the novel comprises a single event: the linguistic act of the protagonist's speaking. Such a structure inscribes a radical imbalance: since only Enrique speaks throughout the entire novel, readers engage in a complex hermeneutic process without any of the authoritative or objective cues that conventionally guide interpretation. Further compounding this imbalance between text and readers, Enrique's disturbed mental state thematically disrupts the everyday norms and conventions associated with communication. Moreover, structure and thematics contribute to Leñero's dual critical intent as a novelist: while they require reading strategies that place questions of genre and interpretive conventions in the foreground, they also make problematic the referential links that embed Enrique's experience in an empirical reality, and by extension, that relate the novel to the world. A focus, then, on the radical imbalance in *A fuerza de palabras* must come to terms with the process of reading; it must attend to the nature of interpretive assumptions in novelistic narrative.

I

The structural imbalance in *A fuerza de palabras* is profoundly marked by the speech situation in the novel. Enrique assumes the *yo* of discourse and concurrently evokes the *usted* to whom he speaks, hence inscribing the situation of a dialogue.[3] Although the interlocutor never intervenes verbally, Enrique's comments repeatedly emphasize his presence. Whereas dialogue commonly implies an exchange between the participating subjects, in *A fuerza de palabras* it sets into play an absolute imbalance in the flow of information (a speaking subject, Enrique, and a listening subject, *usted*), and, nevertheless, implicitly anticipates the eventual active response of the interlocutor.[4] The analysis of this communicative asymmetry will specify several characteristics of the structural imbalance in *A fuerza de palabras*. First, every aspect of the act of speaking bears the imprint or distortion of Enrique's subjectivity, thus characterizing Enrique and his position in the dialogue.[5] Second, then, a consideration of the asymmetric speech situation must account for the role of the silent interlocutor. Throughout his discourse Enrique implicitly characterizes the *usted* who patiently listens without commenting. The most notable aspect of this implicit characterization is the power that Enrique attributes to *usted*. In brief, the asymmetry of the dialogue reveals a parallel yet inverted asymmetry in the power relationship between the participants.

From the opening lines of the text Enrique urgently invokes a capacity of comprehension in the interlocutor: "Tiene que entenderlo usted, porque es muy importante" (7).6 After this initial moral imperative Enrique frequently interrupts his narrative in order to appeal to the understanding of *usted* and to reveal his trust in *usted*:

> Siempre he sido muy reservado, usted sabe,
> solamente hablo de mis asuntos a personas que me
> inspiran confianza, y eso hasta mucho después de
> dialogar sobre otros temas. Si me doy cuenta de que
> la persona se interesa en mi charla, si descubro una
> posibilidad de auténtica comunicación, entonces
> comienzo a intimar. Poco a poco, no rápidamente,
> poco a poco nada más. Pero ya intimando, es decir,
> ya establecido ese misterioso puente de la mutua
> confianza entonces resulta que me desato y me
> suelto a hablar y hablar, sin freno, sin
> interrupciones, hasta entrar de lleno en mis
> asuntos personales. (85)

In addition to the comprehension and trust attributed to the interlocutor, Enrique's discourse recognizes that *usted* has superior physical power. Enrique makes this observation patent when he comments:

> No discuto. Elija el lugar que se le antoje. Oblígueme
> a acompañarlo. Mande llamar a sus subordinados y
> ordéneles que me lleven por la fuerza. Yo solo no
> puedo luchar contra todos y desgraciadamente no
> tengo amigos que acudan en mi auxilio. Usted tiene
> amigos y subordinados de sobra y conseguirá su

> objetivo a pesar de que la razón y la cordura estén de
> mi parte. (42-43)

In this manner, the dialogue and Enrique's act of speaking presuppose the superiority and power of *usted* in terms of physical resources, trustworthiness, and the ability to understand.

In the perpsective of such an imbalance, Enrique's choice of *usted* as a subject pronoun also suggests multiple significations. Although the use of *usted* (rather than *tú*) reflects the protocol for communication between strangers and creates appropriate social distance, it also carries the possible implication of inferiority on the part of the speaking subject who addresses the other as *usted*. Enrique confirms precisely this sense of inferiority as he nears the end of his discourse, before revealing the immediate purpose of his speaking. He asks: "¿Por qué todo me ha salido mal en la vida? ¿Por qué no he podido realizar mis planes? Dígame usted: ¿por qué siempre he necesitado de ayuda para resolver una situación?" (116).

Only in the concluding sentences of the novel does Enrique openly state his petition to *usted*:

> Y nuevamente abracé a Raúl Zetina y él me dijo que
> también usted tendría interés en colaborar de algún
> modo para borrar de la mente de mi hijo los malos
> recuerdos que tal vez haya acumulado en tantos
> años de vivir en el sótano de la casa de San Angel. Y
> estoy seguro de que usted lo ayudará. Estoy seguro
> de que usted y Raúl Zetina sacarán a mi hijo del
> sótano y harán de él un hombre sano y feliz: el
> hombre que yo pude haber sido. (138-139)

Throughout the dialogue, Enrique's communicative strategies strive to exert power over *usted* in order to guarantee the acceptance of this goal. The piecemeal exposition of this purpose, only expressing it in definite terms at the end of the dialogue, produces an enigma about what Enrique wants and why he speaks. Thus, placing the expression of purpose in the closing arguments emphasizes the paramount nature of such a request.

Leaving aside the question of the verisimilitude of Enrique's purpose, the pertinent aspects of Enrique's act of speaking and of the speech situation in general can be summarized under four observations. First, the text consists of an event: Enrique's speaking. Second, this act not only inscribes a subject but also the *usted* to whom *yo* directs the discourse, hence there is a dialogue. Third, Enrique feels inferior with respect to *usted*, in terms of both physical strength and knowledge, thus implying an unequal power relationship between the two of them. And fourth, Enrique speaks in order to reverse the power relationship and to persuade *usted* to help him achieve a goal: the freedom and mental restoration of his son. Taken together, these observations serve as a framework to explore how *A fuerza de palabras* thematically evokes and structurally resembles certain aspects of the psychoanalytic speech situation.

The orientation toward the psychoanalytic situation is in itself an inference. Although readers of *La voz adolorida* were aided by the recurring phrase *usted, doctor*, readers of *A fuerza de palabras* can only assume that Enrique is speaking to a therapist or mental health professional. Nevertheless, several details clearly point readers toward such a deduction. On the third page of the novel Enrique informs his interlocutor:

> . . . (entiéndame bien, es muy importante) me escapé del sanatorio de Puebla. Si usted quiere, todo es oscuro; admito que todo sea oscuro y que yo no entienda las ideas de los demás, que no logre razonar lógicamente; que a veces, muchas veces, no acierte al decir qué horas son, en qué mes estamos, quién es el presidente de la República, cuál es la capital de Venezuela, por qué a Juana de Arco la

> quemaron en la hoguera mientras cantaba con esa
> voz tan bonita y mientras se convertía poco a poco
> en cenizas como las cenizas de mi cigarro o las del
> cigarro de usted. (9)

Enrique's recognition of these facts combined with his speaking, interpreted as a mode of behavior, creates an image of mental imbalance. The experiences Enrique recounts, in and out of mental institutions, and his bizarrely pathetic and often unbelievable life story serve to confirm the image of psychic imbalance. Moreover, upon the suggestion of Raúl Zetina, whom one initially assumes to be normal or sane, Enrique has gone to visit *usted*. Raúl's knowledge of Enrique's problems must include recognition of the need for some sort of mental therapy. Indeed, Enrique's purpose is to solicit mental therapy from *usted*, not for himself but for his son, "para borrar de la mente de mi hijo los malos recuerdos que tal vez haya acumulado en tantos años de vivir en el sótano de la casa de San Angel" (139). *A fuerza de palabras*, in this respect, does not represent the course of a therapeutic analysis; rather, it dramatizes a moment of crisis and the appeal for professional assistance.

The factor of crisis intervention and the inferred characterization of *usted* notwithstanding, the structure and the thematic content of Enrique's discourse make pertinent certain aspects conventionally associated with the the psychoanalytic speech situation. Emile Benveniste has commented that

> . . . psychoanalysis seems to be different from all
> other disciplines. The principal difference is this:
> the analyst operates on what the subject *says* to
> him. He considers him in the discourses which he
> holds with him and examines him in his locutory or
> "fabulatory" behavior, and through the patient's
> discourses another discourse slowly takes shape for
> the analyst, one which he will endeavor to explain:

that of the complex buried in the unconscious. The success of the cure depends on bringing this complex to light, and this in turn testifies to the correctness of the induction. Thus, from patient to analyst, and from analyst to patient, the entire process operates through language.[7]

Benveniste's comments serve to characterize more precisely the roles of Enrique and *usted* and the similarity to the psychoanalytic transaction. Enrique speaks in *A fuerza de palabras*, providing a sample of his verbal behavior. Similarly, *usted*, in the position of "analyst," must interpret Enrique's discourse in order to discover the other "unconscious" discourse that motivates his actions, verbal and otherwise.

In light of these roles, the consistent silence of *usted* gains immense importance for the novel. Enrique speaks with the immediate goal of persuading *usted* to help him achieve the freedom of his son. All of Enrique's communicative strategies aim toward this end. Given the importance of *usted*, his silence emphatically dramatizes Enrique's desire for and need of a response. In other words, *usted*'s silence in *A fuerza de palabras* forcefully poses the question of what the appropriate therapeutic interpretation should be.

The text, however, offers no grounds for postulating the possible or likely responses of *usted*, his interpretation. The novel closes at the end of Enrique's discourse, leaving readers with the problem of silence, precisely at the moment when the dialogue most desires a response. In this perspective, the issue of an appropriate response from *usted* rehearses readers' interpretive role, for both *usted* and the readers must analyze and interpret on the basis of Enrique's discourse. An initial approach to the meanings of *A fuerza de palabras* involves, therefore, an identification with *usted*, readers' acceptance of their role *qua* "analysts." Such an approximation must account for the process of signification within the speech situation. Here readers must formulate deductions and inferences that explain the specific nature of Enrique's linguistic peformance and the psychological factors that disrupt and motivate his verbal behavior.

II

From the outset, to read in identification with the silent *usted* of *A fuerza de palabras* is to interpret with a specific agenda: the revelation of another discourse that motivates Enrique's verbal performance. Indeed, since only Enrique speaks in the novel, analysis of the speech situation consists of defining the various levels of patterning and repetition that constitute the specific nature of his utterance and, through this process, unmasking the other discourse that lies behind his narrative. Readers discern the other discourse gradually as they formulate deductions and inferences, revise their tentative conclusions along the way, and eventually accumulate further details and fragments of information.[8] Given Enrique's self-characterization as mentally imbalanced, readers will notice the subnormalcy of the speech situation and deduce that "expressions cannot be presumed to express fully whatever is meant to be expressed."[9] Since a subnormal speech situation presupposes "disparity between thought and expression," writes T. K. Seung, interpretation "must postulate the nature of thought that fails to be expressed in overt speech and the psychological mechanism that brings about this failure."[10] In a psychoanalytical bent, interpretation presupposes motivation and must seek to establish the prior cause of the manifest symptom, in this case Enrique's narrative.

Reading in a psychoanalytical perspective and seeking to account for the mechanism that disrupts expression is fundamentally an examination of causality. The question of causality, moreover, immediately invokes the notion of temporality, the search for the *prior* cause that manifests itself in the *present* story of suffering. In this causal and temporal perspective, the analysis of narrative depends upon two fundamental operations: on the one hand, the chronological reordering of the events recounted by Enrique in order to examine the sequential history of causes and effects, which in narratological terms consists of reconstructing the *histoire*; and on the other hand, the linear analysis of Enrique's discourse as it is offered to *usted*, observing how his speaking unfolds over time with its own peculiar progressions and associations (rather than the chronological or historical links), which corresponds to the narratological operation of explicating the *récit*.[11]

Establishing the *histoire* of Enrique's discourse serves to identify a bedrock of events that explain the etiology of his malady. The events, in turn, delineate a series of temporal sequences with causal links. In broad terms, Enrique adduces two temporal progressions: (1) escape from the sanatorium in Puebla--incidents on the highway to Mexico City--arrival home in San Angel, and (2) infancy and childhood days--adolescence and young adult life-- mental crises and eventual confinement in the sanatorium in Puebla.[12] In the *histoire* the two progressions are linked temporally and causally, since the second one ends where the first begins. Moreover, the dialogue with *usted* constitutes a third point of reference that begins following the events in the first progression. According to Enrique's account, the cause for his illness lies in the most remote temporal stratum, the events of the second progression. Given the categories of information provided throughout the text, the question of psychological motivation in the *histoire* may be explained from a variety of thematic viewpoints. For example, socio-economic, familial, and religious interpretations are all suggested, and moreover, these viewpoints all echo each other in mutually confirmatory conclusions.

Miguel Angel Niño provides a detailed examination of the *histoire* of *A fuerza de palabras/La voz adolorida* in a socio-economic perspective. Niño concludes that Enrique's problems arise from the incompatibility between his traditionalist environment and the rapid changes in Mexican society. Tradition does not provide an adequate view of reality that would permit

Enrique's successful socialization. [13] The failure to integrate into contemporary society is manifest in several details: Enrique does not know what it is like to drink coffee in a restaurant (7), he dresses differently (*pantalones guardapedos*) and does not know how to communicate with other children (21-22). Enrique textually reveals the conflict between the traditionalist world and the contemporary world when he cites his Aunt Ofelia's comments:

> Dijo que aquella situación estaba resultando insoportable. Dijo que durante muchos años San Angel había sido una colonia aristocráctica, decente, en donde las personas indecentes no se atrevían a poner un pie; se daban la vuelta y se iban a otra parte: al centro de la ciudad, a las colonias proletarias, a los basureros alejados de San Angel. Dijo que en San Angel la vida se estaba volviendo insoportable por culpa de esas mujeres llamadas prostitutas que invadían las esquinas para escandalizar a nuestra sociedad. (92-93)

Hence, with the economic decay of the traditional aristocracy, conflicts arise in adapting to the changes of contemporary society. Placing this phenomenon in a broader historical perspective, R. Díaz-Guerrero states:

> Mexico has changed profoundly with the Mexican Revolution and with recent industrialization; it is probably ill-advised to maintain norms that no longer reflect the reality of present-day Mexico. Traditions, like old maps, may well fail to represent the many newly added territories; thus they inevitably contribute to frustration and conflict and therefore to unhappiness or mental instability.[14]

Thus Enrique's mental illness is a logical result of the conflict between the traditions of the declining, old aristocracy and the socio-economic changes of contemporary society.

Comments on this socio-economic etiology, however, and especially on "traditions," also implicitly refer to Enrique's familial relationships. Enrique's aunts constitute his family; the aunts keep his mother confined to an upstairs room in the house, his father is dead, and Enrique has no recollection of him; his uncle Pepe dies before he can effectively benefit Enrique's development. In brief, Enrique's aunts dominate him and isolate him from society by rigidly imposing a traditional value system on his life. At one point Enrique painstakingly describes the various kinds of water heaters in order to contrast his desire for education and change with the "enfermiza mentalidad retrógrada" of his aunts. This backwardness

> . . . las hace vivir a contrapelo de la ciencia, ignorantes de los progresos de la humanidad, ajenas e indiferentes a nuevos conceptos higiénicos y morales instituidos sabiamente por la sociedad moderna para aliviar a sus miembros de la pesada carga de amarguras y desgracias con que cada criatura inocente es arrojada al mundo. (39)

In brief, Enrique proposes that his aunts mistreat him as vengeance on his mother whom they had to nurse during years of illness. As a result, Enrique deduces, they planned his marriage to Isabel "para tener a quién enloquecer depués de mi muerte" (130). Hence one might also conclude that Enrique's illness is motivated by the conflicts and complexes arising from his singular family environment.

The oppressive nature of Enrique's family situation is intimately related to the practices of traditional Catholicism. Indeed, Niño proposes that the fear of eternal damnation looms up as Enrique's principal concern.[15] The fear of condemnation emerges from a sexual obsession wherein he overheard a woman's confession of adultery and then denied having heard her during his own confession. He speaks of ". . . el pecado mortal que desde entonces cargo sobre mi conciencia junto con miles de comuniones sacrílegas cuya maldad llora Jesucristo nuestro señor clavado en una cruz por mi pecado. Llora y su sangre no cae, no llega hasta mí y no me limpia; permanece embarrada en el crucifijo de la iglesia" (62-63). The priest's complicity in all of the aunt's actions multiplies the weight of Enrique's guilt. Thus, Christianity represents only sexual repression and condemnation for Enrique. These oppressive religious practices later extend into his adult life by depriving him of any satisfactory or fulfilling sexual relationship. In the light of this oppression and condemnation, Enrique embodies all of his desire for redemption in the freedom of his son.

The "other discourses" elaborated on the basis of these three interpretations of the *histoire* (socio-economic, familial, and religious) all share the logical assumption of temporal and causal linkage. One event occurs before another, creates a pathological complex that manifests itself in the present symptom, Enrique's illness. Although these readings of the *histoire* provide three causal series that may explain the motivation for Enrique's illnes, in each one the psychological interpetation arises from the application of exterior patterns of normalcy onto Enrique's subnormal story. In other words, the source of causal linkage lies within the readers and their application of extratextual interpretive norms. Readers, nevertheless, have no basis for believing any of Enrique's story other than the fact the he tells it. Indeed, the verisimilitude of these causal interpretations of the *histoire* is problematic with regard to certain details: the purported confinement of Enrique's mother, the dubious fact of Raul's twice helping a known madman escape from mental institutions, and the alleged incarceration of Enrique's seven-year-old son in the basement. Given the difficulty of integrating these "facts" into a verisimilar *histoire*, a shift in focus to the language of

Enrique's *récit* and his choice of rhetorical strategies unmasks a different motivating source for his illness.

Observation of the manner in which Enrique speaks consists of analyzing his communicative strategies. In this perspective, Enrique's "faublatory behavior," his style of narrating, reveals a different motivation through his choice of language and organizational devices. Accepting the principle of psychic determinism, there can be no equivocations in what Enrique says; instead, false starts and slips of the tongue lead to the topics that Enrique refuses to recognize.

One example of a significant slip of the tongue arises in conjunction with the issue of Enrique's son. Readers have sufficient information to know that the aunts claim he died, and that Enrique's principal crises arise simultaneously with his denial of their claim. Through his *récit* Enrique strives to convince the interlocutor that the freedom of his son is vitally important. However, near the beginning of the text, Enrique mentions "nuestra casa de cuatro paredes donde nací, viví, y sufro encerrado" (13). In this series of verbs in past tense (*nací, viví*), temporal coherence demands that the last verb also appear in past tense: *sufrí*. Although Enrique no longer lives in the house in San Angel, he says that he is presently confined there. This grammatical slip suggests that Enrique's imploring for the liberation of his son is in reality a demand for his own freedom and that he figuratively uses the house in San Angel as an image embodying his repressed fears. Indeed, all references to the house in San Angel appear with contradictory qualifications: "la horrible querida casa de San Angel" (29).

All of Enrique's accounts contrast the oppression and sadness of the house in San Angel to the freedom and happiness found any place outside of or away from the house (20, 126). The basis for this dichotomy appears to reside in the absence of his parents, especially in the desire for a memory that he does not possess:

> Quisiera recordar ahora aquel instante transcurrido hace muchos, muchos años; quisiera cerrar los ojos para recordarlo, encerrarme en el cuarto, concentrar todos mis sentidos en un punto fijo del tiempo, explorar en mi memoria, penetrar en el pasado y encontrar a mi madre joven y feliz, inventando una canción, pronunciando una palabra como las palabras de Isabel cuando enlazó sus manos en las mías y me miró y dejó caer su corazón mientras su voz cantaba con la misma voz de mi madre capaz de transformar a la casa de San Angel en un palacio lleno de luz, de aire limpio, nuevo, lejos de los muebles antiguos y de los árboles genealógicos marchitos, rebanados por el rayo de la carretera que interrumpió mi viaje hacia la vida recobrada gracias a una fugaz sonrisa de Isabel. (131-132)

After an initial attempt to construct a memory of his mother, Enrique's attention shifts to a negative image that condenses many of the incidents of his narrative: the lightning that hit the tree during his childhood (21-22), the lightning that struck Raúl on the highway outside Mexico City (18), and the genealogy of Marías in his family (96) all become "los árboles genealógicos marchitos, rebanados por el rayo de la carretera." He also compares his appreciation for Isabel's voice to the fantasy version of his mother's voice. Yet all of this condensation serves to underscore the dichotomy between the negative connotations of the house in San Angel and his positive fantasy of "un palacio lleno de luz."

This passage also manifests one of the most characteristic aspects of Enrique's "fabulatory behavior": throughout the *récit* Enrique frames his account in the language of fairy tales. In the previous quotation the temporal frame for the desired memory begins as a child's fairy tale, "hace muchos, muchos años." The basic plot of this fantasy places Enrique under the negative power of the house in San Angel. The voice of his "madre joven y feliz" has the power to rescue him magically by transforming the house into a "palacio lleno de luz, de aire limpio, nuevo." Such use of fairy-tale language not only serves to express the present fantasy but also underlies the entire novel, producing a convoluted anti-fairy tale.

Enrique characterizes his childhood as if it were a horror story, openly acknowledging its similarities to English fairy tales:

> Llovía muy fuerte. La casa estaba a oscuras. Llovía muy fuerte y me espiaban desde la calle los robachicos, los ladrones disfrazados con el antifaz del Llanero Solitario, listos para raptarme porque sabían que yo estaba despierto, castigado, escribiendo cien veces No debo ser retobado, temblando de miedo por el ruido de las gotas de lluvia y por el ruido del viento que silbaba en la calle como en los cuentos de hadas ingleses ilustrados con el retrato de tía Ofelia montada en una escoba de varas, negra toda de vieja. . . . (19-20)

Throughout the *récit* his aunt Ofelia is always the evil witch who manipulates everyone else. His aunt Carmen often appears to "convertirse en buena, igual que ocurre en los cuentos de hadas alemanes cuando la bruja se transforma en princesa luego que un niño de mi tamaño le regala una flor cortada en la montaña mágica defendida por tres enormes dragones de tres cabezas cada uno" (21). Nevertheless, Enrique says that his aunt Ofelia "la obligó a transformarse en bruja como ella . . ." (114).

The story that Enrique narrates thus includes two witches who keep him in confinement. Their "diabólica colaboración" (127) exists in order to "tener a quién enloquecer después de mi muerte" (130). Thus, he characterizes his possible happiness with Isabel as "un instante detenido para siempre a pesar de lo que después ocurrió y que transformó nuevamente en fantasía aquellos meses demasiado felices para ser realidad" (126). It is noteworthy that

Enrique tells his story in the language of fairy tales while propounding its reality, and yet he relegates happiness to the unreality of "fantasía." The outcome of Enrique's anti-fairy tale consists of the witches' fulfilling their diabolical intention of sequestering his son; thereafter Enrique strives to escape from his banishment to a sanatorium in order to obtain the magical help that will triumph over the witches.

A shift in the analytical focus on motivation, from the causal sequences of a reconstructed *histoire* to the language of the *récit*, reveals a literary quality in Enrique's case history. Throughout the narrative he combines his need to convince with the effective narrative strategy of slowly revealing his goal as an enigma, after initially confirming its supreme importance. It is no surprise that Enrique deftly manipulates narrative strategies, for he repeatedly mentions his continually reading the "libros de la biblioteca llena de cuentos de puro espanto . . ." (20). Many of the incidents that he recalls occurred in or near the library. Moreover, as he recounts a conversation with Isabel, the implication arises that his solitary need to read is the source of his confinement. Isabel told him: "Eres joven, Enrique, y necesitas conocer el mundo. Vive. No permanezcas encerrado; porque no son ellas, eres tú el que se encierra en un cuarto. Vive, Enrique, vive" (125). Hence the question arises as to whether anything that Enrique has said bears any relation to reality or whether all of it is a fabrication that distorts the language and plots of fairy tales according to the needs of his maladjusted life.

In light of this conclusion, the deductions based on a reconstruction of the *histoire* cannot coexist with the inferences produced by a consideration of the *récit*. The *histoire* in *A fuerza de palabras* posits a bedrock of actual events, an empirically verifiable history; the *récit*, in contrast, reflects an active mind that exaggerates life in terms of books, much like don Quijote or Emma Bovary. In the speech situation, then, the conflict between empirically verifiable events and possibly invented episodes reveals the epistemological limits of the dialogue, the dilemma of establishing the truth of what Enrique says. Most importantly, however, in the case of both the reconstructed *histoire* and the explicated *récit* readers must come to grips with the fact that all of the cognitive operations involved in interpretation lie within their reading strategies: to understand the text is to apply the frames of knowledge acceptable in the readers' world--causal frames, psychological frames, or even literary frames--to the possible worlds evoked by Enrique's discourse.

The confrontation of Enrique's discourse with the interpretations of readers *qua* "analysts" arrives at an inevitable stalemate. Neither does Enrique truly master his discourse in a persuasive fashion nor do readers have the epistemological grounding to defend one interpretation over the other. Owing to the nature of language in the novelistic genre, however, the meanings of *A fuerza de palabras* do not halt with the aporias produced in the speech situation. M. M. Bakhtin points out: "Language in the novel not only represents, but itself serves as the object of representation."[16] At one level, then, Enrique's discourse is representing his life; the interpretive strategies invited by his style of representing include readers' identification with the role of *usted* and the formulation of inferences and deductions that will account for the disparity between thought and expression in order to unmask the "truer" motivating discourse for Enrique's verbal performance. Readers of the novel *A fuerza de palabras*, however, cannot simply interpret within the confines of the speech situation; rather, they must account for the text itself as a representation of Enrique's discourse. The generic context of the novel defines the interaction between text and readers and alters the terms of the interpretive impasse reached in the represented speech situation.

III

As a representation of language *A fuerza de palabras* lays bare its most profound asymmetry. The dialogue between Enrique and *usted* is a representation, framed by an opening dash that signals Enrique's narrative as direct discourse. Yet the source of this extended quotation neither offers editorial comments to guide readers nor includes the interlocutor's interpretation. Whether one speaks of a covert narrator, sender, implicit author, or authorial center of consciousness as the originating instance of Enrique's discourse or as a source of meaningfulness, these all result in vacant categories.[17] Likewise, in the absence of any objective characterization of a responsive interlocutor, readers have no reliable standard to guide their interpretation or to contrast against their possibly dissenting reactions.[18] In other words, whereas the literary critic usually believes that the text is the site of ultimate authority and meaning, *A fuerza de palabaras* radically disavows this belief by a "transference" of critical power and interpretive authority onto the readers.[19] This transference, moreover, is repeated on two levels, first as a snare set by Enrique's role in the represented speech situation, and then as the fundamental strategy of representation.

Within the dialogue, Enrique's verbal performance places *usted* in a position of power: Enrique presumes that *usted* possesses a certain knowledge and this presumed knowledge should enable *usted* to resolve Enrique's problems. Similarly, the power generated by belief and presumed knowledge extends beyond the represented speech situation to the interaction between text and readers. On the one hand, readers accept the initial transference of interpretive power to the degree that they identify with the role of *usted* as invited by Enrique's discourse. The text, on the other hand, equally positions readers to draw upon their presumed knowledge of novelistic conventions and narrative strategies to resolve the epistemological dilemma of the representation. Such a maneuver, however, in the represented speech situation and as the fundamental stragegy of representation, plays upon a contradiction. Whereas readers are enabled to interpret because of their presumed knowledge, it is, rather, Enrique's act of belief, on one level, and Leñero's strategy of representation, on another, that have the upper hand in *A fuerza de palabras*: the latter aspects have the power to place *usted* and readers in the illusory vantages of powerful and authoritative knowledge.

The contradictory shuffling of knowledge and interpretive power between text and readers ultimately defines the epistemological bind in *A fuerza de palabras*. Reading from within the illusion of authoritative knowledge leads interpretation to a referential impasse in the represented speech situation. The search for causal origins produces two psychological interpetations with opposing referents: first, an *histoire* that refers to empirically verifiable pathogenic events, and second, a *récit* that consists of distorted interpretations of fairy tales and solitary reading. An analysis of the representation itself, however, requires that readers not accept the transference of power that Enrique projects onto *usted* in the represented speech situation; rather, the text, in spite of its silences and apparent disavowal of knowledge, remains the authoritative site of meaning. In other words, the critical stance reverses the relationship and presumes the text "to know."

Readers of *A fuerza de palabras*, then, must examine the vulnerability of their interpretive conventions: they must become, as it were, the analysands under the scrutiny of an analyzing text.[20] As readers of a novel, in *A fuerza de palabras* we deal with a representation of language, a literary communication between author and readers whose expressive function is guaranteed. In spite of the subnormal status of Enrique's discourse within the novel, the interaction between text and readers rests on the "hyperprotected" convention that the literary work, as a whole, is meaningful.[21] These conventional expectations and interpretive strategies, nevertheless, trap readers in a double-bind: while the hyper-protected convention of meaningfulness is, in fact, the presumed knowledge transferred onto readers by the text, it is also the foundation that drives readers to attempt to understand, to presume that the text "knows." Moreover, the convention itself implicitly points toward such meaningfulness as a desire for mastery over the text and its knowledge. Seemingly, then, there is no outside to the snare that entangles readers of *A fuerza de palabras*, for to interpret the novel is, unavoidably, to operate within the illusion of presumed knowledge.

Although there is no outside to the interpretive dilemma, no meta-perspective that can resolve all contradictions and guarantee the absolute mastery of meaning, an exploration of the hyperprotected convention of meaningfulness will reveal how it both enables understanding, indeed drives readers toward it, as it also creates a blind spot for interpretation. At one point in the novel Enrique thematizes the problem of meaningfulness in communication as an inherent quality of language. In alluding to the difficulty, if not impossiblity, of intersubjective understanding, Enrique offers a parable:

> . . . para nada sirven los millones de libros que se han escrito y se siguen escribiendo en la infinita variedad de idiomas nacidos en el tiempo en que los hombres soberbios construían la torre de Babel donde Dios, precisamente para castigar esa soberbia, confundió sus lenguas de tal manera que de pronto los albañiles dejaron de entenderse, y cuando uno le decía a otro, pongamos por caso: Pásame un ladrillo para seguir construyendo esta magnífica torre que llegará hasta el cielo y destronará a Dios, ese pobre hombre recibía en lugar del ladrillo solicitado una viga, supongamos. Reclamaba: No te pedí una viga, te pedí un ladrillo. Pero entonces el hombre que había pasado la viga en lugar del ladrillo, contestaba en inglés, o en ruso o en el idioma que usted prefiera. Y venía la confusión, y todos comenzaron a enloquecer por eso, porque cada quien hablaba en un idioma distinto al idioma de sus compañeros; nadie con nadie se entendía; no podían continuar la torre

de Babel; enloquecieron como enloquecemos hoy al conversar con los amigos que no obstante compartir con nosotros un idioma aparentemente común, dan a una palabra pronunciada por A un sentido B ajeno o contrario o discorde al sentido de la palabra original pronunciada por A. ¿Se da cuenta? (118-119)

Enrique's parable portrays a shift from a world where meaning and communication both coincide in language, to a context in which the language of each subject remains unintelligible to others. In brief, the parable questions the effectiveness of dialogue; it underscores, rather, the impossibility of absolute knowledge and mastery of meaning. Although subjects may apparently share a common language, "eloquecemos hoy al conversar con los amigos" because they attribute to "una palabra pronunciada por A un sentido B ajeno o contrario o discorde al sentido de la palabra original pronunciada por A." Language bears a structure of alterity such that participants in a dialogue can never absolutely certify their interpretation of the words pronounced by the other. In this respect, it is the obsessive drive for the lost world of plenitude and for absolute mastery over meaning that gives structure to the madness in Enrique's discourse. With regard to the reading of *A fuerza de palabras*, the parable allegorizes the exile from meaningfulness as unity and coherence, an allegory that readers must accept in order to learn how meaning works in social and literary communication.

Enrique's parable and its allegorical interpetation, however, constitute yet another aspect of narrative contradiction. To interpret the parable, to understand it, is to ignore the meaning of the parable, that intersubjective communication is impossible. Conversely, to ignore the meaning of the parable confirms the law of communicative impossibility, thus forcefully performing its own efficacy. In this perspective, the convention of meaningfulness enables as it compels readers to ignore that which cannot be integrated into a coherent meaning. Meaningfulness and the desire to master meaning thus include a desire to ignore, a need to protect a certain ignorance. This insight radically determines and redefines the nature of knowledge and meaning to be found in *A fuerza de palabras*: it is not a positive knowledge that can be channeled or "transferred" *in toto* from one point to another--from Enrique to *usted*, from text to readers--but rather a condition for knowing that arises when one relinquishes the desire for absolute meaningfulness. As Shoshana Felman has written, ignorance is not "*opposed* to knowledge; it is itself a radical condition, an integral part of the very *structure* of knowledge." Ignorance "is not a passive state of absence--a simple lack of information: it is an active dynamic of negation, an active refusal of information."22

In *A fuerza de palabras* the active refusal of information occurs along lines of communication, in a relational context between speaker and listener, writer and readers. These lines of communication and their analogous pairings at different levels make more precise the location of the desire to ignore. The first analogy, which I have explored at length, relates Enrique to *usted* in the same terms as the text relates to readers: Enrique presumes *usted* to have knowledge as the text also presumes readers to possess knowledge. The second analogy, suggested as a strategy that does not accept the transference of the first one, relates Enrique to *usted* just as readers *qua* analysands relate to the text. Although the implicit comparison of a mentally disturbed character to the position of readers is discomforting, *A fuerza de palabras* challenges readers' capacity to master meaning in precisely these terms. Just as Enrique's narrative cannot generate the power necessary to create a persuasive plot for his life story, so readers cannot grasp the multiple perspectives sufficient to close or reduce textual meaning to a coherent and persuasive interpretation, in sum, to master the text. Indeed, the madness that underlies and distorts Enrique's discursive behavior--the obsessive desire for plenitude in meaning and communication-- suggests the frustrating and frustrated drive toward hyperprotected meaningfulness that motivates a critical understanding of the text. That is, like Enrique, critical understanding itself and the desire for meaning manifest aspects of subnormalcy, for they inevitably evidence a "disparity between thought and expression," between reading and interpretation. The remaining position for knowledge, then, is silence.

Silence, however, points toward other possible positions for understanding: the silence of *usted* and ultimately of Vicente Leñero. As the author, Vicente Leñero chooses to "hide" or to silence the narrating agency that represents Enrique's speech act. Similarly, the authorial decision to exclude *usted*'s response from the representation not only poses the question of what his response should be but also emphasizes the silence of the novel's authority figure. The silence of "the narrator" and *usted*, the authorial decision and the authority figure, points toward the unknown and the unknowable itself as ingredient in the production of meaning.

An inverse consideration of this silence reveals yet another set of analogous relations. Paradoxically, just as Enrique chooses to speak, so also Vicente Leñero and interpretation express meanings. Although this rapprochement brings madness, literature, and interpretation into dangerously close kinship, it also marks their difference. Whereas Enrique's journey into madness is determined by his obsessive desire for absolute meaningfulness, Vicente Leñero and circumspect interpretation occupy a curiously divided and seemingly contradictory position. Leñero, on the one hand, writes *A fuerza de palabras* yet also makes himself absent from the text by silencing *usted* and the agency of the representation. Similarly, persistent, critical readers, while unable to entertain dialogue with the text outside of the transference generated by the presumed knowledge of narrative conventions, can both admit the failure of meaningfulness and concurrently claim a triumph in relinquishing the obsessive desire for a mastery over meaningfulness that cannot exist. In other words, *A fuerza de palabras* does not communicate a single meaning nor a set of specifiable meanings; rather, and more profoundly, it creates a ground for a wisdom that strives to express itself, knowing that it cannot, and that also accepts the narrative knowledge it cannot control.

IV

In the final analysis, *A fuerza de palabras* instructs about the limits of dialogue, meaningfulness, and epistemological certainty. At every level of communication the novel mobilizes a structural asymmetry that enables readers to interpret and yet undermines the grounding for any validation of the interpretation. Within the represented speech situation, Enrique's "fabulatory behavior" invites readers to identify with *usted*, to uncover the other discourses that motivate his actions. In this perspective, a possible history of suffering confronts the rhetorical strategies that strive to shape the events into a convincing narrative. To put it another way, the relationship between the *histoire* of Enrique's biography as an empirical chronology of pathogenic causality and the highly literary organization of his *récit* as a convoluted, negative fairy tale, is "one of suspicion and conjecture, a structure of undecidability which can only offer a framework of narrative possibilities rather than a clearly specifiable plot."[23] In spite of this epistemological limit, Enrique's telling his life story manifests a desire, a drive toward meaningfulness, that attempts to narrate the significance of his biography to and for another. At the level of the represented speech situation, then, *A fuerza de palabras* explores the referential links that embed Enrique's experience in a social reality and, concurrently, it tests the narrative genres that give form to Enrique's experience and make it narratable.[24]

As a representation *A fuerza de palabras* extends the effects of the undecidability within the represented speech situation. Rather than resolve the epistemological limits of dialogue and meaningfulness, the novel recreates in readers the parameters of

Enrique's narrative dilemma as the difficulty in producing a meaningful interpretation. To strive to assert or verify the significance of Enrique's illness in the causality of the *histoire* or in the rhetorical constraints of the *récit* is to ally oneself with Enrique's obsessive nostalgia for meaningfulness as absolute unity and coherence. Moreover, the strategy of representation sets into play a transference of illusory interpretive power through the presumed knowledge of literary conventions. The illusion of authoritative knowledge catches readers up in an inescapable search for meaningfulness; simultaneously, it undermines the possibility of validating such meaningfulness in the structure of a dialogue between Enrique and *usted*, between text and readers. Instead, *A fuerza de palabras* can produce in persistent readers the tension between the need to know and the desire to ignore as concommitant forces ingredient in knowledge and understanding. In this perspective, the authorial decision to silence the agency of the representation and *usted* as an authority figure underscores the epistemological contradictions in narrative and interpretation, the paradoxical grounding of knowledge in the unknown and the unknowable.

Chapter Two:
Risk and Responsibility:
Detective, Readers, and the Postmodern in
Los albañiles

Leñero's first novel, *A fuerza de palabras*, lays bare the dual critical project that underlies his novels throughout the 1960s. In terms of Enrique's biography and the "truth" about society, *A fuerza de palabras* makes evident the vital need to construct meaningful and narratable stories about reality yet it also places in the foreground the inevitable undecidability that enters as words attempt to produce worlds and the self strives to communicate with the other. As a further exploration of this communicative difficulty, Leñero's second novel again sets into play the presumed knowledge of literary conventions and an extremely active participation for readers. In *Los albañiles* (1964), however, the communicative and epistemological difficulties are dramatized within the novel as a detective attempts to interpret social reality.[1]

Meaningfulness in *Los albañiles* at first appears to depend on an enigma and the discernment of truth: the identification of a murderer. Like *A fuerza de palabras*, however, *Los albañiles* questions the epistemological constraints that define truth in a social context. Although the novel earned Leñero his initial recognition when it was awarded the prestigious "Premio Bilbioteca Breve" in 1963 and it has generated the greatest amount of critical attention of all his novels, the difficulty of truth has continually baffled critical interpretations.

Much of the difficulty arises from the deceptive familiarity of the literary conventions associated with both the detective genre and its inversion, the anti-detective genre, as Leñero puts them into play in *Los albañiles*. Nevertheless, the novel does not easily fit into either of these categories and, in many ways, it is more a work of social criticism than detective or anti-detective fiction. *Los albañiles* considers the class structure of the *albañiles*, the hierarchichal organization of the police force, and the application of scientific methods to criminal investigation. In addition, a fragmentary structure, an array of literary styles, and a mixture of Catholic, archetypal, and psychoanalytic themes contribute to the complex texture of the novel, thus obscuring the familiarity of the readily recognizable elements. In the final analysis, however, the diverse aspects of *Los albañiles* come to bear on the question of knowledge, especially knowledge produced by scientific method and the epistemological dilemma of verifying that which is reported to be known. By attending to the ways in which *Los albañiles* works within and against the conventions of detective and anti-detective genres, and tests the limitations of criminal interrogation, it becomes evident that the text critically considers the mechanisms that produce knowledge, not simply in an abstract context but as an ethical dilemma with concrete political, social, and cultural implications for a specific historical moment.

I

> The first story, that of the crime, ends before the second story begins. But what happens in the second? Not much. The characters of this second story, the story of the investigation, do not act, they learn.

--Tzvetan Todorov, "The Typology of Detective Fiction"

The genres of detective and anti-detective fiction are fundamental in *Los albañiles* for the privileged position they give to knowledge: both predicate a teleological structure that continually moves toward the resolution of an enigma, the knowledge that solves the mystery of the crime. Although the status of the text itself, the narrating of the investigation and resolution of the crime, differs greatly in the two genres, the expectation of the ultimate return to the scene of the crime with the subsequent revelation (or frustration) of the "true" story that precedes the investigation is the driving force that sustains the plot and interest of both detective and anti-detective fiction. Turning to detective fiction first, this genre entails a series of literary conventions that, loosely construed, frame the overall structure of *Los albañiles*.

Tzvetan Todorov, in "The Typology of Detective Fiction," points out that detective fiction is based on a duality: the story of the crime and the story of the investigation. In their purest form, the stories have no point in common: "The first story, that of the crime, ends before the second begins."2 In addition, Todorov proposes that the story of the crime tells "what really happened," whereas the story of the investigation is excessive, it only tells "how the reader (or the narrator) has come to know about it."3

To a certain degree, *Los albañiles* manifests various traits that Todorov associates with the classic detective novel, the whodunit. The novel consists of eleven chapters. In the first chapter a crime is discovered, the brutal murder of the nightwatchman, don Jesús, at the construction site of a high-rise apartment complex in downtown Mexico City. In chapters two through ten a detective interrogates each of the principal suspects for the murder: Isidro, a fifteen-year-old *peón* for the construction workers and don Jesús's close "friend"; Jacinto, Patotas, Chapo, and the ex-seminarian Sergio, all *albañiles* at the construction site; and the son of the owner of the project, Federico Zamora, more commonly called "el Nene." As in the whodunit, the point of view of each suspect determines the tenor of the information that he gives, continually complicating and distorting the mysterious knot the detective must untie.

Throughout the investigation, the principal police detective stands out as the classic investigator. He plays the role of detective as defined by Michael Holquist in "Whodunit and Other Questions: Metaphysical Detective Stories in Post-War Fiction"; the detective is

> . . . the instrument of pure logic, able to triumph
> because he alone in a world of credulous men, holds
> to the Scholastic principle of *adequatio rei et
> intellectus*, the adequation of mind to things, the
> belief that the mind, given enough time, can
> understand everything. There are no mysteries,
> there is only incorrect reasoning.[4]

Indeed, by the last chapter of *Los albañiles*, the other policemen
have begun to call the detective Sherlock Holmes and Perry Mason.
He has justifiably impressed them by deducing from the
interrogations facts that empirical observation and research took
an entire week of work to produce. The detective in *Los albañiles*
tirelessly searches for truth and knowledge on the basis of pure
ratiocination, using scientific method to produce supposedly
objective and verifiable knowledge.

Nevertheless, such a loose construal of *Los albañiles* as
detective fiction can go no further. More often than not, the novel
violates the conventions of detective fiction. Whereas *Los albañiles*
is the story of how the detective comes to know about the crime, its
style cannot be made to appear "natural," as in the whodunit: the
complex narrative strategiees used to narrate the story of the
investigation call attention to the language of the novel, they make
the style opaque and cast a very perceptible shadow on the "real
story" of the crime. Moreoover, the *denouement* proposed in the
eleventh chapter is, in a certain perspective, an unacceptable
solution for the crime. It does not conform to the political protocols
of the police force nor can it be justified within the parameters
guaranteed by the detective's use of scientific methods. It is with
respect to the opaque style and the apparently inconclusive ending
of *Los albañiles* that the novel at first seems to be explainable as
anti-detective fiction.

Anti-detective fiction alters the conventions of the detective
genre with an inversion: whereas the latter elevates the status of
pure and abstract logic that will lead to the resolution of the

criminal enigma, in anti-detective fiction the opposite occurs as logic fails to mediate between the detective and the evidence of the crime. Knowledge, however, occupies a privileged position in anti-detective fiction, for the frustration produced by the detective's failure depends on the expectation that logic will suffice as a tool to arrive at the truth. As a consequence of such an inversion, the detective as hero becomes the detective as anti-hero. In addition, the imperceptible style of the whodunit, which appears to allow an unemcumbered transmission of knowledge through its stylistic transparency, becomes the evidently artificial style of the anti-detective novel, a style that foregrounds the detective's perceptions as an actively distorting force in reality, incapable of discerning knowledge of the truth. Also, in place of the syllogistic order of the detective genre, anti-detective fiction depends heavily on patterning or minute variations within repetitions. As one critic has noted, repetition in such texts may be one of the few factors that produce "patterns of coherence, and thus at least the incipience of meaning. . . ."[5] In brief, whereas the detective genre declares the supremacy of the mind and attempts to present pure logic in search of knowledge in a transparent literary style, the anti-detective genre frustrates the power of the mind, treats knowledge as an effect of textuality, and often draws attention to its own language as a literary style. In general, the anti-detective story "does not have the narcotizing effect of its progenitor; instead of familiarity, it gives strangeness. . . . Instead of reassuring, they disturb."[6]

Critics often mention the French *nouveau roman* in connection with the anti-detective novel, especially works by Alain Robbe-Grillet such as *Le voyeur* (1955). With reference to *Los albañiles* most critics allude to the possible influence of Robbe-Grillet's *Les gommes* (1953).[7] In many ways, comparison does bear out some of the resemblances between *Los albañiles* and anti-detective fiction, especially of the *nouveau roman* variety. Besides the detective's unacceptable solution, the closing passage of the novel returns to the scene of the crime where the detective finds another night watchman, a *velador* who remains unidentified yet enigmatically identical to the murdered don Jesús. In addition, since the temporal dislocations of the text impede any precise chronological reordering of the events leading up to the crime, the repetitions and patterning of the novel become increasingly important for the development of the story of the investigation. Moreover, the variety of narrative strategies and techniques that produce such temporal anachronies, combined with a series of literary stylizations, serve to make the text itself linguistically opaque. Knowledge of the crime is not transmitted through a natural or imperceptible style; rather, knowledge becomes an effect at play in the discursive organization of *Los albañiles*. In these very similarities, however, *Los albañiles* realizes its greatest differences from the anti-detective genre and the *nouveau roman*.

The patterning in *Los albañiles* is less a series of repetitions and variations on a theme than an alternation among temporal levels and enigmas. In *Reading for the Plot: Design and Intention in Narrative*, Peter Brooks comments that enigma "concerns the questions and answers that structure a story, their suspense, partial unveiling, temporary blockage, eventual resolution, with the resultant creation of a 'retarding structure' or 'dilatory space' which we work through toward what is felt, in classical narrative, to be meaning revealed."[8] In both detective and anti-detective fiction, as mentioned above, the drive toward meaning revealed-- the knowledge of the crime--works to propel the discourse forward. The conventions of detective fiction, the false clues, the confessions, the investigation, create the dilatory space between the discovery of the crime and the detective's solution. In anti-detective fiction, on the other hand, the opaque style and thematic patterning draw attention to the literary nature of the investigation, retarding the drive toward meaning revealed, and ultimately foregrounding such knowledge as an effect of textuality.

In *Los albañiles* the dilatory space between the discovery of the crime and the revelation of meaning serves to introduce a series of secondary enigmas that compete with the criminal

mystery for the principal interest of the narrative. The novel
begins:

> Lo encontró Isidro, el peón de quince años que
> cargando un bote de mezcla, arrastrando una
> carretilla, enrollando la manguera, corriendo a traer
> un refresco, recogiendo las palas, buscando el bote
> de clavos, regresando a la bodega, aparecía y
> desaparecía como un fantasma urgido por los gritos
> de Jacinto.   Apúrate-apúrate-apúrate-apúrate-
> apúrate.
>   Tropezaba en el andamio:
>   --Bruto.
>   Al tratar de conservar el equilibrio soltaba el bote de
> mezcla:
>   --Imbécil.
>   La mezcla se derramaba en las vigas y goteaba al
> suelo:
>   --Pendejo.
>   Reían los albañiles y reía don Jesús.
>   --Pero lo que pasa es que yo no me río de ti igual
> que ellos. . . . (7)

On the one hand, the discovery of the crime itself is enigmatic, for
the novel begins with the pronoun *lo*, which at first has no
identifiable referent.   The text continues, however, with a
characterization of Isidro's clumsiness, his relation to the *albañiles*
and don Jesús, and the story of the murder of don Jesús's father
and a death curse that has haunted the *velador* since adolescence.
Three pages later, the mysterious *lo* that opens the novel receives a
referent: "Isidro encontró el cadáver en el baño del departamento
201 y en cinco segundos de pánico recordó la historia que a él --
completa-- y a los albañiles --incompleta-- les contó don Jesús en
torno al fuego . . ." (10). The crime is discovered, yet the cadaver
remains unidentified; the text, with no clear connection, proceeds

with the *albañiles*'s reaction to the story don Jesús told Isidro. Finally, four pages later, the mystery of the cadaver becomes clear: "--¡Mataron a don Jesús! ¡Mataron a don Jesús!" (14) With the sensational news a crowd gathers round until the detective arrives at the scene of the crime, *el hombre de la corbata a rayas.*

In spite of the slowly unfolding criminal enigma, the first chapter of the novel establishes a pattern of alternation that sets the pace for the police investigation. In the first pages, when the enigma of the murder comes to surface in the time of the investigation, the text concurrently gives greater emphasis to two previous temporal levels.9 First, *Los albañiles* includes copious and detailed references to the relationships among the *albañiles*, Isidro, and don Jesús during the nine months preceding the murder, the period of time when the apartment building is under construction. Second, as in the case of don Jesús's childhood story, the text often refers back to the time before the group comes together at the construction site. The pattern of temporal alternation throughout the police investigation serves to introduce the social criticism of *Los albañiles*.

The text produces a corpus of facts about the *albañiles* as an uprooted and disinherited social class: where they come from, how they survive in an overpopulated and rapidly growing Mexico City, and the attendant problems incurred by their separation from family and home.10 Indeed, at one point in the investigation the apartment owner's son, "el Nene," attempts to draw suspicion away from himself by interpreting the *albañiles* as a social class. According to "el Nene," the *albañiles* suffer

> . . . ese complejo de desadaptación tan característico de quienes dejan su pueblo, su pedazo de tierra, y se vienen a la capital deslumbrados por lo que oyen decir o impelidos por la necesidad. La ambición que produce el deslumbramiento y la necesidad de ganar más dinero son los dos móviles de su éxodo. La realidad que encuentran en la capital es totalmente

opuesta a la que habían imaginado. Viene entonces
el desengaño y la frustración. Sería muy interesante
--¿no le parece?--que los especialistas abordaran el
problema. (72)

In other words, the (anti-)detective frame of *Los albañiles*, while
providing a structure that demands a search for meaning revealed,
prefers to dwell on the social backdrop against which the crime
occurs. Because of this use of the dilatory space created by a
criminal enigma, *Los albañiles*, in a certain perspective, becomes
more a work of social analysis as the collective story of the
albañiles usurps the interest of the criminal enigma.

In addition to the socio-critical thematics, *Los albañiles* also
depends on a specific style of reporting and representation of
speech. In the course of the investigation, the *albañiles* talk more
often than they act. Leñero, with his skillful ability to recreate
popular speech patterns, uses this aspect of a criminal
interrogation to his advantage and allows the *albañiles* to speak for
themselves. As a result, the speech pattern of the group, their
collective idiolect, becomes one of the principal techniques of
characterization, emphasizing their unity as a social class.[11]
Although the genre conventions of a novel and of a real-life first-
person narrative differ in the way that the truth status of the
discourse affects interpretation, in *Los albañiles* the act of
speaking serves to characterize the individual and the group, and
pretends to evoke an interpretation of reality not biased by the
viewpoint of the interviewer or narrator.[12] Nevertheless, in *Los
albañiles*, as each suspect struggles to defend himself and
implicate someone else in the murder, the reliability of all
information comes under considerable doubt. Moreover, Leñero's
deft manipulation of the language of the *albañiles* through many
levels of temporal distortion and varying degrees of direct and
indirect discourse serves to establish surprising connections and
repetitions that might not otherwise become evident, and
similarly, calls attention to the style and language of the novel.

In the end, however, *Los albañiles* cannot be read solely as novelized social criticism that attempts to expose inequities. Even in view of the competing interest of the socio-critical consideration of the *albañiles*, the play of (anti-)detective literary conventions drives the narrative forward, toward the extirpation of guilt and the novel's own textual death with the meaning revealed in the solution of the crime. Indeed, the fundamental importance of the last chapter, the place of meaning revealed--knowledge--, together with the role of the dectective, the anonymous, bureaucratic *hombre de la corbata a rayas*, constitute the principal unifying factors for the various facets of *Los albañiles*.

II

If one retraces the role of the *hombre de la corbata a rayas*, a different story emerges from *Los albañiles*, the story of a dedicated detective who, in frustrating circumstances, searches for a scientifically objective and verifiable truth. Moreover, he believes that a scientifically established truth will be necessarily the most just and ethical truth. In part, this story arises as a consequence of the structural organization of (anti-)detective fiction: as the principal interrogator, the detective is also the interlocutor of all the speakers of the text; he occupies the intersection of all the narrative threads that produce the criminal web of *Los albañiles*. As Iris Josefina Ludmer notes in her article "Vicente Leñero, *Los albañiles*. Lector y actor," *el hombre de la corbata a rayas* "no puede narrar su propia historia pero agrupa y dirige las de los demás. . . ." The detective is "el que posibilita que exista un grupo: es el peligro del grupo, el objeto por el cual se constituye y se defiende; es el perseguidor, la meta común que determina la praxis común." In other words, *el hombre de la corbata a rayas* does not do much, he is a *trabajador intelectual*, a "receptor que escucha, organiza, piensa, lee": his function "es ordenar, dar forma, interpretar el material dado y recrear imaginariamente los hechos. . . ."[13] Although the *hombre de la corbata a rayas* cannot tell his own story, throughout the course of the investigation he undergoes a very noticeable metamorphosis as he reads and learns. Ultimately, in the eleventh chapter, *Los albañiles* becomes the detective's story.

The detective is known as *el hombre de la corbata a rayas* throughout the first ten chapters. In part, the synechdochic name underscores the asymmetric power relation between the detective and the suspects: in their desire to escape the gaze of the law, the suspects are all guiltily unable to look upon the face that represents the institutional power of the police force. In contrast, the synechdoche also foregrounds the detective in his bureaucratic position: he functions principally as the producer of a knowledge-- of guilt and innocence--that will legitimate the power wielded by the police force, the law, and the state. Whereas the asymmetric power relation derives from the structural and institutional necessity of the detective as the suspects' interlocutor, it is the bureaucratic perspective wherein *el hombre de la corbata a rayas* changes most dramatically. As the detective confronts the contradictions between the pressures of his position and his individual desire to arrive at an objective, and supposedly ethical, truth, *el hombre de la corbata a rayas* loses faith in scientific method and its application to social reality.

From his first appearance in the novel, *el hombre de la corbata a rayas* stands as much apart from the other police detectives as he does from the suspects he interrogates. The other detectives have faster means of obtaining a confession for the crime: the terror of brute force, regardless of the suspect's guilt or innocence. *El hombre de la corbata a rayas*, however, as the detective in charge of the case, repeatedly prohibits recourse to physical violence. Ostensibly, scientific theory insures him a method for obtaining a true confession, for solving the mystery with cold, objective logic. Nevertheless, as the days and interrogations go by, the pressure to identify the murderer mounts. Throughout the course of the investigation, *el hombre de la corbata a rayas* fights a losing battle: the other detectives

continually insist that they can make one of the suspects *cantar*;
the press is already pointing its finger at the inefficiency of the
police force; and with the passing of time, it becomes statistically
less probable that the murderer will confess.

Although the interrogations do not appear in chronological
order in *Los albañiles*, nor can one establish such an order, the
frustration experienced by *el hombre de la corbata a rayas*
increases in a steady, linear fashion from chapter to chapter. By
chapter eight, *el hombre de la corbata a rayas* loses his self-control
and breaks his own prohibition against physical violence.

> El hombre de la corbata a rayas puso sus manos
> sobre los hombros del muchacho y acercó el rostro
> hasta casi tocarlo con la
> nariz. . . .
> --¡Habla!
> El tirón de cabellos: los ojos de Jacinto. La
> cachetada.
> --¡Habla!
> Jacinto avanzó:
> --¡Déjelo! (153)

After this outburst, and concurrent with the increasing
frustration of *el hombre de la corbata a rayas*, chapter eight
intercalates extensive passages of scientific theory about the
methodology of criminal interrogation. The first intercalated
fragment makes evident the methodological crisis *el hombre de la
corbata a rayas* is suffering: "Se tiende cada vez más a utilizar
medios científicos que absuelvan a la policía de la eterna sospecha
de tercer grado y garanticen una mayor credibilidad de las
confesiones. ¿Puede la ciencia moderna, singularmente la
psicología, ayudar a resolver efectivamente este problema?" (161).
The interjection of the technical discourse serves to classify the so-
called scientific presuppositions underlying the methods of *el
hombre de la corbata a rayas*, and simultaneously, by means of a

rhetorical question, skeptically undermines the theoretical goal of producing objective and verifiable truth.

Nevertheless, it is in the concluding chapter where the doubts, conflicts, and crises of *el hombre de la corbata a rayas* surface in their most dramatic form. Chapter eleven begins:

> Entró Dávila.
> --¿No juegas un dominó?
> Munguía se aflojó el nudo de su corbata a rayas y miró a Dávila, pero no contestó. (225)

As *el hombre de la corbata a rayas* loosens his tie, he receives the name Munguía. He also initiates a process that removes him from his bureaucratic position as a producer of knowledge, a state technician who applies scientific theory. This action both brings him down to the position of all the other characters with his loss of power and sets him forth as the center of interest in the last chapter.[14] The crime was discovered on Tuesday and it is now Friday. As the other detectives chidingly call Munguía "Sherlock Holmes," he reprimands them for having physically abused one of the suspects.

In a last defense of his method, Munguía shows off his deductive logic by correcting the facts that the other detectives have gathered after days of searching for and interrogating everyone who knew don Jesús. In reaction to such deductions, one of the detectives, Suárez, inquires:

> . . . ¿cómo lo sabes?
> Munguía sonrió. Se puso de pie y palmeó el hombro de Suárez.
> --Sé otras cosas.
> --Ya lo estoy viendo --Suárez se rascó el bigote y miró fijamente a Munguía--. ¿A poco ya resolviste el caso?
> --En cierta forma, sí.

--¿Ya confesó?

Munguía se volvió de espaldas. Suárez preguntó nuevamente:

--¿Ya confesó? (227)

In response to the question, Munguía affirms: "Está muy claro: usted tenía muchas razones . . ." (227). The next thirteen pages of *Los albañiles* consists of a single, direct quotation of Munguía's accusation, addressed to a mutating *usted/tú* that includes all of the six interrogated suspects: Isidro, Jacinto, Chapo, Patotas, Sergio, and "el Nene." With every accusation Munguía explains the motive and the moment in which each individual murdered don Jesús. Nevertheless, the solution proposed by Munguía is one that cannot, and never could, be uttered. On the one hand, Munguía's bureaucratic responsibility requires that he produce one murderer upon whose body society may mark the guilt and punishment for the crime: hence his solution is excessive. On the other hand, Munguía proposes that the guilt for the crime is collective: each suspect had motive to avenge that in don Jesús which reflected their own worst qualities; don Jesús is their scapegoat, a *pharmakos* that will supposedly insure the continuity of society by embodying the evil that it must expel from within.[15] Yet the remedy fails, for in a sense it produces an absence marked by the death of don Jesús, an absence that contemporary society judges to mark the presence of the poison of criminal passion, which is capable of destroying all social unity.

Munguía's investigation, then, the story of his listening, organizing, thinking, and reading, leads to a moment of critical decision: his methods of examination have produced information, but the information exceeds the limitations of appropriateness defined by legal institutions and scientific theory. Moreover, it is here that *Los albañiles* confronts the issues of the postmodern, for Munguía begins to learn that scientific method does not produce competence, the knowledge necessary for evaluating the supposedly truthful and objective information.

Jean-François Lyotard's study, *The Postmodern Condition: A Report on Knowledge*, outlines the relation of postmodernity to science. Briefly, according to Lyotard the postmodern "designates the state of our culture following the transformations which, since the end of the nineteenth century, have altered the game rules for science, literature, and the arts."[16] Throughout the study Lyotard characterizes the modern as the age of the rise of modern science, an epoch that places great belief in the the positivistic notion of the life of the spirit in speculative apparatuses, and in the emancipation of society through science, two beliefs that Lyotard calls "grand narratives." In the modern, however, "to the extent that science does not restrict itself to stating useful regularities and seeks the truth, it is obliged to legitmate the rules of its own game. It then produces a discourse of legitimation with respect to its own status, a discourse called philosophy." Lyotard qualifies as modern "any science that legitimates itself with reference to a metadiscourse of this kind making explicit appeal to some grand narrative. . . . Simplifying to the extreme," Lyotard defines the "*postmodern* as incredulity toward metanarratives."[17]

Incredulity is precisely the problem that Munguía must confront. Whereas *el hombre de la corbata a rayas* of chapter eight presupposes the grand emancipatory narrative of scientific method absolving the police of the eternal suspicion of third degree and guaranteeing more credible results (161), the Munguía of chapter eleven is learning that the logic of scientific method will not suffice. Munguía's accusation/solution includes fragments of scientific discourse. The fragments, however, all refer to the problem of the interpretation of evidence, for the truth of a crime often exceeds the workings of logic.

> En el curso de la investigación, por ello, el criminalista deberá desconfiar de la evidencia que a veces es muy engañosa; debe desconfiarse de la lógica corriente: el malhechor, actuando en el estado precipitado que supone todo acto criminal, se

> preocupa poco de la lógica y realiza, a lo mejor, actos absurdos. Pero ha de tenerse en cuenta que el valor de las pruebas no es jamás ni matemático ni absoluto. Siempre se encontrará en ellas un porcentaje de error. La certidumbre, dice el doctor Locard, se halla en función del rigor técnico que se emplee, de la abundancia de los elementos que se utilicen y de la concordancia de las pruebas que se recojan. Se llega a la conclusión negativa con más rapidez y seguridad que a la positiva. El indicio no prueba necesariamente la culpabilidad, dice Leon Lerich. (235)

Munguía has followed to the extreme all of the guidelines dictated by scientific theory: he has an abundance of *pruebas*, laboratory examinations, and interrogations. Yet, when he must evaluate the evidence, he finds that science does not provide him with the necessary competence, and he learns about the very game of criminology as a scientific discipline and its bureaucratic relation to the state.

As Lyotard's essay contends, science is a process of debate, a "language game" as he defines it, with its own rules or pragmatics for establishing the truth. The problem of science, however, is that as a discipline it views itself as an autonomy, theoretically separate from the problems of ethical, social, and political praxis. Nevertheless, scientific debate determines truth on the basis of the consensus of the scientific community, which is always immersed in ethical, social, and political praxis. Whereas science pretends to establish "good" denotative statements about reality, "there is nothing to prove that if a statement describing a real situation is true, it follows that a prescriptive statement based upon it (the effect of which will necessarily be a modification of that reality) will be just."[18] There arises, then, "the conflict between a language game made of denotations answerable only to the criterion of truth, and a language game governing ethical, social, and political practice that necessarily involves decisions and obligations, in other words, utterances expected to be just rather than true and which in the final analysis lie outside the realm of scientific knowledge."19

In *Los albañiles* Munguía must deal with the conflict between the use of scientific method in a social context, and the ethical question of the justice of the information he produces. According to his method, every member of the social group involved is guilty: guilt is a social characteristic. Nevertheless, such a solution does not correspond to the rules of the game played by the police force. As a result, Munguía learns about a power that operates by means of terror. As Lyotard points out: "Whenever efficiency (that is, obtaining the desired effect) is derived from a 'Say or do this, or else you'll never speak again,' then we are in the realm of terror. . . ."20 Immediately following Munguía's accusation in the last chapter, he is removed from the case for his inefficiency: whereas Munguía searches for truth, the policemen, as a group, play a game of efficiency, a game whose rules Munguía has violated for he has not produced the desired effect, the identity of the murderer.

Munguía's metamorphosis, however, is not yet complete. He still asks for more time and does not fully realize all that he is learning. After his being dismissed, Munguía goes to a bar with Pérez Gómez, a fellow detective who tries to comfort Munguía. Although Pérez Gómez praises Munguía's dedication, "Tú nos pusiste una muestra. Con veinte tipos como tú ningún mugre periodista se atreve a volver a escribir sus mamadas . . . ¿No me crees?" (244), Munguía bitterly recriminates the so-called efficiency of the policemen as a group.

> --Para ustedes todos son culpables. ¡Aunque sean inocentes, son culpables! ¿No es eso lo que quieres decir? . . . No estoy exagerando. ¡Mátenlos, qué esperan! Denles en los güevos, rómpanles la cara, son animales. (243-4)

Munguía has, in a certain sense, solved the mystery, but he still cannot accept his own discovery of guilt as a social, rather than individual, attribute. He wants more time on the case, he still speaks of *inocentes* and *culpables*, and he holds his method to be above the violence of the other detectives.

When Pérez Gómez responds to Munguía's outburst, however, the final realization begins to occur to Munguía:

> Pérez Gómez apretó los puños y gritó:
> -- ¡¿Y crees que no es lo mismo fregártelos a preguntas y más preguntas?! No me vengas ahora a decir que porque no los tocas ya eres un santo. ¡Cómo dejaste al plomero! Qué necesidad tenías de tenérmelo tantas horas dale y dale con lo mismo: qué hizo el lunes; cuéntame qué hizo el lunes en la mañana, qué hizo el lunes en la tarde, qué hizo el lunes en la noche. Ahora otra vez: todo el día. Cómo se llama, en dónde vive, en qué trabaja . . . El pobre ya no sabía ni su nombre. ¿Eso cómo se llama? ¿No es todavía peor? -- Mientras Pérez Gómez gritaba, agitando las manos, el rostro de Munguía palideció. Bajó la cabeza y se restregó las sienes. Pérez Gómez se detuvo en seco--. No me hagas caso.
> Durante largo rato permanecieron en silencio.
> (244)

Munguía's method may produce "good" denotative statements, that is, truthful pieces of information. But such a method in no way frees Munguía from the ethical recriminations he heaps upon the other detectives for their violent brand of efficiency. It all comes back to him: "¿Eso cómo se llama? ¿No es todavía peor?"

Munguía spends the rest of the day insisting that he will give up detective work and trying to get away from Pérez Gómez. When the latter goes off with a prostitute in a local brothel, Munguía finally has the chance to escape. After Munguía spends the night wandering the streets of Mexico City, *Los albañiles* ends at sunrise with the most enigmatic scene of the novel: Munguía returns to the scene of the crime.

> Caminó toda la noche y a las siete de la mañana llegó a la esquina de Cuauhtémoc y Concepción Béistegui. Largo rato contempló el edificio desde la acera oriente. Cruzó la calle. Empujó la puerta de fierro: tras ella, a no más de cinco pasos de distancia, estaba un hombre envuelto hasta la cabeza con un sarape. Se frotaba las manos sobre las brasas donde se calentaba un pequeño jarro de cafe. El ruido de la puerta lo hizo enderezar la cabeza. El sarape resbaló por su espalda, hasta caer al suelo.
>
> --¿Buscaba a alguien?
>
> Munguía avanzó tres pasos. El hombre se levantó.
>
> --¿Buscaba a alguien?
>
> --¿Es usted el velador?
>
> --Sí--dijo el hombre--. ¿Qué se le ofrece?
>
> Munguía lo miró de arriba abajo.
>
> --Nada --Avanzó un paso más. Sonrió--. Nada . . . --
>
> Y le puso una mano en el hombro. (249-50)

The paradox of this passage arises from the ambiguity of the *velador*'s identity. The description blatantly corresponds to that of the murdered don Jesús. Yet, given the high degree of verisimilitude and the referential reality of copious social details maintained throughout the novel, it seems contradictory to accept the *velador* as don Jesús. Although the episode functions as a repetition, its meaning remains, to a certain degree, indeterminate.

Rather than the identity of the *velador*, perhaps the most significant aspect of the final sequence results from the description of Munguía's nonverbal behavior. From the representation of the meeting, it seems apparent that Munguía and the *velador* do not know each other. Munguía's physical movements, however, violate the socially appropriate protocol for behavior between strangers. At first, the *velador* appears at "no más de cinco pasos de distancia." After a question, Munguía "avanzó tres pasos." Munguía then carefully looks at the *velador* "de arriba abajo," takes another step forward, smiles, and then "le puso una mano en el hombro." Their physical proximity, face to face, scarcely a step apart, and Munguía's placing his hand on the man's shoulder constitute kinesthetic signals, nonverbal signs described in the language of the novel. In the context of all that has happened in *Los albañiles*--a murder, deceits, interrogations, all actions bordering on violence and brute force in attempts to maintain social order--, this is the first moment in which Munguía, no longer a bureaucrat or scientific detective but another human being, reaches out in a gesture of simple human solidarity. Whereas the murder of don Jesús as a scapegoat pretends to restore social unity by the ritualistic expulsion of evil from within, and the investigation and the law attempt to maintain social unity through prescribed social order, every detail in *Los albañiles* has pointed toward a society in dispersion. Indeed, the preferred means of insuring social unity has been violence: the brutality of murder, the physical violence of efficient police investigations, and Munguía's bureaucratically inefficient psychological/scientific torture. In contrast, the closing scene of *Los albañiles* affirms the social bond, for the first time, in non-violent, although enigmatic, terms.

In summary, in addition to the (anti-)detective and socio-critical stories in *Los albañiles*, there is also Munguía's story, the transition to the postmodern where the detective must confront his contradictory and risky position in the web of society. *Los albañiles* is the story of the anonymous, bureaucratic technician of modern scientific theory, *el hombre de la corbata a rayas* who becomes the powerless and resisting postmodern individual, Munguía. In the course of this metamorphosis, Munguía confronts the inherent dilemma of modern science, that truthful information does not necessarily lead to ethical practice. In addition, Munguía learns that as a producer of knowledge, he is bought by the state for a very restrictive, bureaucratic form of efficiency--an efficiency that wears a mask of justice but does not know ethics. In the end, it seems, it is Munguía alone who has learned about the risk and the responsibility of the social bond for postmodern humankind. Nevertheless, the stories of *Los albañiles* do not end here: besides Munguía there is one other group that cannot "narrar su propia historia," the readers.

III

The fiction of a reader is absolutely central to the reading of fiction. What we discover when we try to explain fiction by reference to the reader is the central role of fictions of reading. There is a certain circularity here that seems to me central to the theory of fiction.

--Jonathan Culler, "Problems in the Theory of Fiction"

The readers of *Los albañiles* go through a metamorphosis no less dramatic than that of Munguía: readers must learn to interpret the text. Indeed, the structural organization of *Los albañiles* works to apprentice readers, to place them in a position analogous to that of Mungía in the last chapter in order to understand the novel as a critical consideration of knowledge, to comprehend that knowledge, more than a universal metaphysical construct, it is an ethical dilemma with concrete political, social, and cultural implications. *Los albañiles* has the ability to place readers in such a position because of its textual power, an asymmetric power relation similar to that established between Munguía, in his bureaucratic position as *el hombre de la corbata a rayas*, and those suspected of the murder.

Peter Brooks has written that "a given narrative weaves its individual pattern from pre-existent codes, which derive, most immediately at least, from the 'already written.' The reading of a narrative then tends to decipher, to organize, to rationalize, to *name* in terms of codes derived from the 'already read.'"21 The deceptively familiar contours of *Los albañiles* as (anti-)detective fiction or novelized social criticism attest both to Leñero's use of the "already written" and to readers' recognition of the "already read." Moreover, the overall dynamics of the novel derive from the familiar working of the enigma, the play of enigma and solution that "acts as a large, shaping force, allowing us to sort out, to group, to see the significance of actions, to rename their sequences in terms of their significance for the narrative as a whole."22 On the one hand, Leñero's use and transgression of identifiable literary genres sets into motion such a play of enigma and solution, driving the narrative forward toward the moment of meaning revealed.

On the other hand, *Los albañiles* also constrains readers, exerts power over them through the role of Munguía and the privileged position of knowledge in (anti-)detective fiction. Munguía does not act much, he listens, organizes, conjectures, and learns. In his role as the receiver of all information, he also functions as a surrogate reader in chapters one through ten. Readers of *Los albañiles* always receive information filtered through Munguía, already in the act of being interpreted. Parallel to the mounting frustrations of *el hombre de la corbata a rayas* in the course of the investigation, readers encounter increasing difficulties in the process of reading the text. Just as the detective's method eventually betrays him, so also readers must come to terms with the ways in which *Los albañiles* diverges from the "already read," implicitly violating the genre conventions associated with (anti-)detective fiction and social criticism and hence, betraying readers' expectations and cognitive models for understanding. Finally, as *el hombre de la corbata a rayas* becomes Munguía, as the detective loosens his tie and is displaced from the power invested in his bureaucratic position, so also does *Los albañiles* unshackle readers from Munguía's constraints and role as surrogate reader. Indeed, as Lucía Garavito has written, "puede advertirse en *Los albañiles* una progresión del interior hacia el exterior . . . ." In terms of Garavito's description, the novel moves from a group of narrator-characters who tell their versions of the events in their own words, to a narrator outside the events who observes Munguía externally. "La obra ha concluido y observamos lo exterior desde el exterior."[23] The manipulation of genres and narrative techniques produce, then, a move outward, yet it is a movement that forces readers into a specific pragmatic relationship with respect to the text.

Through the asymmetric power relation of chapters one through ten, Los albañiles disarms readers of the "already read." As a result, there is less overt guidance for the interpretation of chapter eleven. Just as Munguía has moved out of his official bureaucratic position, and, in a postmodern gesture, discovers the insufficiency of the grand narratives, the metanarratives that pretended to legitimate his scientific detective work, so also readers occupy a discursive position with no recourse to the cognitive frames and genre models that would help to realign expectations and interpret Munguía's emergence as a character, his internal conflicts and realizations, or the significance of the enigmatic encounter with the velador.

It is with respect to readers' lack of cognitive models for understanding Munguía's final encounter that the greatest interpretive difficulties arise. On the one hand, even as the text works to subvert the explanatory power of metanarratives, archetypal patterns, and religious symbols, most critics, even when recognizing a degree of incompatibility in these models, invoke their presence as the symbolic interpretation necessary for a complete "reading" of Los albañiles.[24] On the other hand, critics have often invoked a metaphysical construct that place in doubt the occurrences of the entire (anti-)detective story: "todo lo acontecido no fue más que un ejercicio mental o clínico de parte del hombre de la corbata a rayas."[25] One critic accepts the entire novel as indeterminate and ambiguous, an epistemological fable demonstrating that "all proposed solutions for the identity search may also be valid" and that the novel exposes "the futility of the search, and of all similar searches for absolute knowledge in the midst of epistemological chaos and competing possibilities. . . ."[26] Although all of these attempts to interpret *Los albañiles* -- archetypally and metaphysically-- are necessary, interpretation cannot stop here. Moreover, the so-called "universal" pretense of such interpretive models and metaphysical arguments are reductivistic in that they ignore the copious details pointing to the worldliness of *Los albañiles*. The specific power of *Los albañiles* works to destroy the explanatory power of such models and to force readers to learn the incredulity of the postmodern in a precise cultural and historical context.

In a certain perspective, *Los albañiles* minutely investigates a finite series of cultural institutions. Against the backdrop of a growing metroplex, the novel foregrounds a matrix of contradictions among the changing class structures, the practices of the police force, and the role of bureaucracy in the maintenance of social order and state power. Munguía, as a meticulous detective, observes and studies the ways various individuals, social classes, and institutions are positioned at the often conflictive and contradictory intersections of the cultural matrix. In addition, he also learns that neither he nor his scientific method are exempt from the conflicts and contradictions of the socio-historical context. Indeed, Munguía must finally confront the contradictions among his institutional power position, his scientific method, the bureaucratic imperative for efficiency, and the nature of social justice. Thus it is that Munguía learns of incredulity; he also learns that postmodern humankind bears the risks of and the responsibility for justice and the social bond in the world in which we live.

Similarly, *Los albañiles* produces an incredulity in readers. Although such incredulity may appear nihilistic,[27] it is also the movement by which *Los albañiles*, as a literary text, reinforces Munguía's last action: the affirmation of the social bond. Underlying *Los albañiles*, and many other Spanish American novels grouped under the aegis of the New Novel, or later the

Boom, is a desire to draw readers closer into the problematics of the production of the text and meaning. Indeed, as Morelli proposes in *Rayuela*, Julio Cortázar's influential novel published in 1963, the year in which *Los albañiles* won the "Premio Biblioteca Breve," there exists a very special possiblity for readers: "la de hacer del lector un cómplice, una camarada de camino. Simultaneizarlo. . . . Así el lector podría llegar a ser copartícipe y copadeciente de la experiencia por la que pasa el novelista, *en el mismo momento y en la misma forma.*"[28] Moreover, according to Morelli, a novel that achieves such a unity of experience in the writer and the readers

> . . . no engaña al lector, no lo monta a caballo sobre cualquier emoción o cualquier intención, sino que le da algo así como una arcilla significativa, un comienzo de modelado, con huellas de algo que quiza sea colectivo, humano y no individual. Mejor, le da como una fachada, con puertas y ventanas detrás de las cuales se está operando un misterio que el lector cómplice deberá buscar (de ahí la complicidad) y quizá no encontrará (de ahí el copadecimiento). Lo que el autor de esa novela haya logrado para sí mismo, se repetirá (agigantándose, quizá, y eso sería maravilloso) en el lector cómplice.[29]

In brief, *Los albañiles* practices a propaedeutics of the *lector cómplice, copartícipe* and *copadeciente* of the textual process of the postmodern: a writing/reading structure that serves to reaffirm the social bond, "con huellas de algo que quizá sea colectivo, humano y no individual." In this perspective, *Los albañiles* also produces the story of readers' learning, the story of a drive toward meaning revealed that, in the end, is not a revelation at all but the working of knowledge.

In conclusion, *Los albañiles* is a novel of many stories. On the one hand, there emerges the worldly story of the *albañiles* and the problems of certain sectors of Mexico City in the late 1950s and early 1960s. On the other hand, *Los albañiles* weaves the social and quasi-anthropological material into an (anti-)detective story, one that in the end is the story of Munguía's metamorphosis from a modern technician of scientific theory and state bureaucrat into an incredulous postmodern social being. And finally, there is the story of readers. With respect to what happens to readers when they read, Jonathan Culler has written:

> The outcome of reading, it seems, is always knowledge. Readers may be manipulated and misled, but when they finish the book their experience turns to knowledge--perhaps an understanding of the limitations imposed by familiar interpretive conventions--as though finishing the book took them outside the experience of reading and gave them mastery of it.[30]

Indeed, attentive readers of *Los albañiles* do learn, and experience turns to knowledge. Contrary to Culler's conclusion, however, such knowledge in *Los albañiles* does not place readers outside their experience nor lead them to believe they can have mastery of it.

In every perspective, *Los albañiles* deals with the problems of limitations, of being inside the workings of institutional, social, and metaphysical values. First, the social matrix of *Los albañiles* permeates the reality of the the characters involved: there is no "outside" of social reality for them. Second, the workings of the plot, together with the drive toward meaning revealed in the (anti-) detective genres, keep the novel within the play of conventions associated with these literary genres. On the one hand, detective fiction presupposes a hierarchy between the world and logic: logic holds a superior position relative to the world--reality--, it believes itself to be invested with an unassailable mastery over the ways of the world. Anti-detective fiction, on the other hand, is a reaction against the privileged position of logic. Nevertheless, the anti-detective genre is still determined by the same hierarchical opposition, for it merely inverts the play of values, privileging the power of reality over the fall of logic. In contrast, *Los albañiles* displaces the hierarchy, it marks the interval between logic and reality.[31] In this perspective, *Los albañiles* does not lead to an "outside" of the conventions of (anti-)detective fiction; rather it works within the space of the conventions, testing their limitations in order to demonstrate the ethical risks and responsibilities such boundaries and conventions entail.

Similarly, *Los albañiles* exerts a power that places readers in a specific interpretive position. In the end, readers must come to terms with their own precarious position relative to that discursive structure as *lectores cómplices*. Readers cannot move "outside" their position, master the meanings of the text, nor control the social bond as it is at work in and through *Los albañiles*. Indeed, we read in specific circumstances and with a specific relation to the text and to the world, no different than Munguía's position in *Los albañiles*. Even in the end of the novel, as Munguía reaffirms the social, "Y le puso la mano en el hombro" (250), both the detective and readers must recall that the same action began the transgression of Munguía's proscription of violence during the interrogations: "El hombre de la corbata a rayas puso sus manos sobre los hombros del muchacho . . ." (153). In the final analysis, *Los albañiles* is a consideration of knowledge, of a detective and readers who learn; but it is a critical consideration, for even in the reaffirmation of the social bond and the apprenticeship of the *lectores cómplices*, the lesson of the postmodern is that we never move "outside" our experience, beyond the conflicts and contradictions of knowledge and reality that determine our position in the world. Rather, we are all, always already, involved in a practice that involves risk and responsibility for justice and meaning in our world.

Chapter Three:
The Boundaries of Metafiction:
Estudio Q and *El garabato*

Leñero's *Estudio Q* (1965) and *El garabato* (1967) continue to explore the risk and responsibility of social conventions, knowledge, and readers' involvement in the text.[1] Rather than further elaborating the crucial hierarchy between scientific logic and the ethical constraints of social truth, however, these novels consider the opposition of reality to fiction and the nature of the boundary that divides the two terms. In a sense, then, *Estudio Q* and *El garabato* investigate the limits of the novelistic genre, that is, the boundaries that contain fiction as a separate and almost material object within the continuity of everyday social reality.

Written in a metafictional mode, these two texts fold inward on themselves. The folds constitute sites where the texts incorporate the external practice of critical commentary, attempting to contain the ordinarily extratextual function of criticism within the textual boundary. This movement toward the self-containment of narrative and its commentary draws attention to the novel genre as a boundaried space, both erasing and highlighting the boundary necessary for demarcating the opposition between the inside of the text and the outside, and by extension, between fiction and reality. Moreover, this double gesture of the texts, both undoing and preserving the boundary between fiction and reality, has profound implications for the slave-master relation thematically expressed in each novel and allegorically re-enacted in the moment of critical intervention, the relation between reader and text.

In recent years many theoretical endeavors have proposed divers characterizations of metafiction. Yet no one has so clearly and cogently confronted the problem of definition as Robert C. Spires in his recent study *Beyond the Metafictional Mode: Directions in the Modern Spanish Novel*. After an insightful revision of the numerous proposed explanations of the metafictional phenomenon, Spires concludes: "The failure to make the basic distinctions between genre as a diachronic concept and mode as a synchronic concept helps to explain the problems critics have been creating in defining metafiction."[2] Hence, as a mode, metafiction is a narrative possibility, a synchronic capacity that writers have exploited ever since Cervantes inaugurated the modern novel with *Don Quijote de la Mancha*. That the number of novels written in a metafictional mode becomes more pervasive in certain historical periods is thus a diachronic question of genre development.

The nature of the metafictional mode cannot be separated from that of the fictional mode in general. Fiction depends on the boundary that inscribes it as a world separate from reality. Indeed, the many narratological formulations by theoreticians such as Gérard Genette, Mieke Bal, Seymour Chatman, and Shlomith Rimmon-Kenan all demonstrate the necessity of the boundary for the definition of fiction.[3] Within a given text the boundary is in principle inviolable and hence the necessity of rigorously differentiating the discrete unity of each narrative level or world. Spires, following Genette, defines this boundary within the text as a function of the act of narrating, pointing out the separation between "the world *from* which one speaks and the world *of* which one speaks . . . ."[4] Genette has observed that any transition between these worlds or narrative levels must be overtly narrated in order to respect the inviolability of the dividing boundary. The most common thrust of metafiction, however, is either a nonnarrated or covert transition between narrative levels, resulting in a transgression of the boundary. Commenting on the effect of such transgressions Genette states:

> All these games, by the intensity of their effects, demonstrated the importance of the boundary they tax their ingenuity to overstep, in defiance of verisimilitude--a boundary *that is precisely the*

narrating (or the performance) itself: a shifting but sacred frontier between two worlds, the world in which one tells, the world of which one tells.[5] (Genette's emphasis)

Although Genette implies that the "sacred frontier" also separates the world of the text from that of the author and readers of the text, Spires explicitly states that this boundary may also be violated in order to create metafictional effects. Hence Spires characterizes the metafictional mode in the most rigorous and general fashion as resulting "when the member of one world violates the world of another," including the world of the author and the readers of the text.[6]

Although the metafictional mode may be most distinguishable in cases where transitions between worlds are either nonnarrated or covertly narrated, other ruptures in the conventional respect for the boundary will result in the same effect, confusing the inside and the outside of the text through the erasing and concurrent highlighting of the boundary. In *Estudio Q* each transition between a narrative level is overtly indicated, yet the nature of the indications and their ordering within the text serve to inscribe the novel within the metafictional mode.

From the outset *Estudio Q* announces the intention of presenting a soap opera based on the biography of a famous soap opera actor named Alejandro Jiménez Brunetiere. Such a formulation leads readers to deduce a dichotomy between two worlds within the text, the world of the soap opera itself and the world in which the actors cooperate in order to produce the soap opera. In this second world the principal actor, Alex, enters into a series of arguments with the *director escénico* and the script writer, Gladys Monroy. As the novel progresses, however, another level complicates the simple dichotomy between the world of the soap opera and that of the actors: an overt shift in narrative level places both of the previous levels within a soap opera about the making of a soap opera where the leading actor Alex does not agree with the *director escénico* and the script writer as to the logic of the opening scene of the soap opera. Alex comments: "--Las cosas no se han planteado bien y ahí está el problema. Ha faltado lógica" (136).

The true twist to the novel, however, derives from this posterior engulfing of the previously dichotomized worlds into a larger world, a movement that occurs in a continual and infinitely regressive pattern. Each time readers have sufficient reason to believe that a new and definitive boundary has been established between the fiction and the fictive reality, an additional novelized world emerges in order to subsume all previous levels. The engulfing emergence of the superior world is always perceivable, either overtly narrated, or signaled by typographical indications, or inferred from posterior comments. Nevertheless, thematically the various worlds all form a single and infinitely reflected mirror image in which the principal actor Alex disagrees with the *director escénico* and the script writer as to the inner logic of the soap opera that they are producing.

The infinite regression of subsuming narrative levels creates a confusion between the inside of the story--the soap opera proper --, and the outside--the world of the actors making the soap opera. When the text presents a synopsis of the soap opera that is in process, it includes a description of Alex's confusion of the interior fiction and his exterior reality as he falls in love with the leading female character/actress of the soap opera. Speaking of Alex, the synopsis states:

> Pero un día, los productores de la serie le proponen hacer una obra basada en su vida aprovechando la popularidad y la bien ganada fama de Alex. El acepta. Se comienza a preparar la historia cuya trama se inicia en el momento en que Alex conoce, en circunstancias por demás azarosas, a una singular mujer. El actor traba intempestiva relación con ella, al grado de que la misma noche en que la conoce

tienen contacto carnal. La aventura parece comenzar y terminar allí, pero sucede que cuando Alex se pone a ensayar los capítulos de la obra descubre que el personaje femenino no es otro que la misma mujer con la que ha pernoctado. Esto lo confunde. Por un momento creyó haber encontrado el amor de su vida y ahora se da cuenta que la mujer pertenece a la ficción. Se atormenta. Lucha consigo mismo. Se interroga, vacila, cree volverse loco y huye. Corre a tirar su dinero en el juego. No quiere pensar en nada. Y cuando parece que va a hundirse en el pozo de la angustia toma conciencia de su situación. Decide afrontar su destino. Ha conocido el verdadero amor y está dispuesto a no perderlo. Ella no es un fantasma, un simple personaje de la historia; es una mujer de carne y hueso que lo ama y lo está esperando. (181-182)

In this passage the basic confusion of the inside and the outside of the fiction becomes patent, not only for Alex but also for the author of the synopsis.

The last sentence of this passage equates a series of substantive constructions that violate the logic of fiction as determined by boundaries: the woman is not a *fantasma* or a *personaje*, she is a *mujer de carne y hueso*. However, that which is real (*mujer de carne y hueso*) is identified with that which is fictional (*pertenece a la ficción*)--the female protagonist both is a *fantasma* to the degree that she is only a character in a soap opera, and she is not a *fantasma*. Hence the boundary between fiction and reality does not serve to distinguish the character from the real person yet it is necessary in order to name her as if she were both inside and outside of the story.

The folding of the textual surface in *Estudio Q*, however, continues with a centrifugal impetus, extending outward to enfold the readers within the text. Allegorically, passages of the novel dramatize this situation. In chapter four, the penultimate of five chapters, readers discover a mother and daughter watching the proposed soap opera. The newly introduced television viewers form a part of the world of the actors that produced the soap opera. The subject matter of the program scandalizes the mother because of its sexually explicit nature. As she moves to turn off the television in protest, the scene breaks and the following comments lead readers to infer that reality has once again receded into another textual fold, subsuming the previous "reality" into fiction while positing another level that *mutatis mutandis* assumes the label of reality.

> Aunque el cuerpo de la madre cubre la pantalla, ella se encuentra a una distancia suficiente para que la diagonal de su mirada--simultáneamente a la mirada con que el director escénico observa en el monitor cinco a la madre de pie frente al televisor--le permita percibir el momento en que el abrazo parece fijarse en la pantalla. (197)

This continual movement within the text, enclosing the soap opera viewers, inverting the outside and inside of the text, carries the novel to a melodramatic ending that also serves to violate the sacred boundary between the text and readers, and thus suggestively creates a fold that includes the readers of *Estudio Q* within the fiction while leaving the category of reality in a void.

The final episode of the soap opera consists of a scene wherein Alex, who insists on using real bullets in a scene of Russian roulette, commits suicide. According to rehearsals, he will aim at a chandelier in the moment of pulling the trigger, thus creating a dramatic joke for those present at the party. However, in the supposed outside reality another actor suggests to Alex that his only escape from the control of the *director escénico* and the script writer is truly to commit suicide. Hence during the filming of the final scene, Alex "cayó fulminado, instantáneamente muerto ante el azoro de sus compañeros y de los técnicos incrédulos de lo que veían, pero convencidos a poco de que era inútil ya tratar de devolver a Alex la vida que él mismo se quitó" (300).

The following dialogue, nevertheless, once again leads readers to infer that the suicide is merely another episode in this soap opera about a soap opera about a soap opera *ad infinitum.*

> --Absurdo.
> --Inverosímil, diría yo.
> Había pues una oportunidad de morir, pensó Alex.
> --De vencer--rectificó Gladys.
> Sonrió el director escénico. Se miraron entre sí los miembros del staff. Todos cuchicheaban mientras en el monitor cinco se veía el actor en el momento de llevarse el cañón del revólver a la sien. (300)

Whereas readers have just observed Alex's suicide, and expect the following comments to be remarks about his death, the implication is that all of this has just been one more surprising turn in a staged episode. The comments also repeat the thematics of the disagreement over the logic of the soap opera events, although in this case the participants in the disagreement are not identified by dialogue tags. In addition, the presentation of the statement that Alex *pensó,* followed by the rectification of Gladys Monroy, serves to suggest that Alex still lives. However, the circular sequence of presenting the scene and then watching it on the monitor remits emphasis to Alex's suicide.

The final paragraph of the novel portrays in detail all of the thoughts that Alex would think as he put the revolver to his head. The closing phrases of the novel evoke the double frame of the television screen and of those watching it:

> . . . pero siempre con la figura de Alex en el centro de la pantalla, de manera que todas las miradas

> convergen necesariamente en él, polo magnético al
> que se dirigen los aplausos de un público entregado
> al actor cuyo genio conmovió a las multitudes frente
> a las que ahora se yergue como si en lugar de un
> simple personaje fuese un hombre vic/ (301)

The complicated representation of the sources of the perceptions in this passage will neither confirm nor disavow the ficticious or real nature of the scene in *Estudio Q*. All of the paragraph, subordinated to a series of verbs in conditional tense, suggests a future of probability framed within a past moment. Hence, this summary passage retrospectively represents Alex's anticipatory thoughts as to the outcome of his actions and the subsequent reactions to them. Nevertheless, in the final analysis this apparent suicide constitutes a circle of probability, offering no firm grounding for erecting a boundary between the fiction (the soap opera) and reality (the world of the actors).[7]

The closing typographical mark, " / ," in addition, serves to highlight the arbitrary closure of the novel. It either suggests the moment in which Alex dies, truncating his retrospectively anticipatory judgment, *vic* (to be read "victorioso" or an ironic recognition of "víctima"?), or signifies the gratuitous moment of turning off the television set. The very ambiguity of the truncated ending leaves the typographical notation open to a multitude of possible interpretations. The ultimate implication of these interpretations, however, bifurcates in contradictory effects. On the one hand, the entire text of *Estudio Q* is the script of a soap opera. The title pages of each chapter become more integral in this perspective as they provide a list of blank categories to be filled in for the filming of the soap opera. There has been no reality or true event, only the virtual project of a self-consuming soap opera plot.

On the other hand, the impetus of the centrifugal folds of the text implies another, all-inclusive fold, again undermining the boundary between fiction and reality. This ultimate fold, however, threatens to consume the very readers of *Estudio Q*. As Jorge Luis

Borges has noted, "tales inversiones sugieren que si los caracteres de una ficción pueden ser lectores o espectadores, nosotros, sus lectores o espectadores, podemos ser ficticios."[8] Evidently *Estudio Q* has repeatedly suggested this fact as the spectators and producers of the soap opera become regressively embedded within the soap opera itself. In the end, this all implies that the readers of *Estudio Q* may be part of a fiction also.

In comparison to the layers upon layers of folds that confuse the inside of *Estudio Q* with the outside, the pockets of commentary enclosed within *El garabato* deceptively depend upon emphasizing the boundary between fiction and reality, a frontier that the text eventually erases, reconstructs, and displaces. In its most schematic reduction *El garabato* consists of a series of three embedded novels. Beginning at the most exterior and all-encompassing border of the text, the title page announces the novel *El garabato* by Vicente Leñero. The following three pages consist of a letter addressed to Vicente Leñero, signed by Pablo Mejía H. In the letter Mejía expresses his excitement over the fact that Leñero has managed to find a publisher for his novel so quickly. Mejía discusses various aspects of his novel, questions the influence of Borges in his writing, and includes both a biographical sketch and a brief review for the jacket. The page following the letter is also a title page, *El garabato* by Pablo Mejía H. Mejía's novel consists of a narrative written by Fernando J. Moreno, a famous Mexican literary critic who is suffering from writer's block, impeding him from writing the great Mexican novel.

Moreno's narrative deals with two issues: his abandonment of Lucy, his mistress of five years, because of a deep religious conflict produced by the illicit affair; and the incomplete reading and critique of a novel presented to him by Fabián Mendizábal. As one might expect, Mendizábal's novel also bears the title *El garabato*. In juxtaposition to Moreno's narrative combining a religious/ existential debate with literary criticism, Mendizábal's novel is based on the genre of detective fiction and develops the only true suspense of the entire text. In the innermost *El garabato*,

Mendizábal has written the story of Rodolfo, a young Mexican law student who becomes accidentally involved in an enigmatic plot that threatens his life. Moreno does not complete his reading of Mendizábal's novel and thus leaves Rodolfo's destiny frustratingly concealed from readers.

The presentation of each embedded novel, preceded by an appropriate introduction, serves to emphasize the finished nature of a series of texts. Hence, the narrated passage from one novel into another strengthens the boundary dividing the worlds of fiction and reality. In another perspective, however, these narrated transitions are each contained in the exterior text *El garabato*, by Vicente Leñero. Thus each narrated penetration into a subordinate narrative level creates a fold that integrates a theoretically exterior individual into the interior of the text. This integration occurs at each level in which a novel is embedded within another: Vicente Leñero's *El garabato* contains Pablo Mejía's *El garabato*, and Fernando Moreno's narrative contains Fabián Mendizábal's *El garabato*.

In addition, throughout the entire text various forms of citation serve to fold reality into the fiction. Luciana Figuerola's excellent study, "Los códigos de veridicción en *El garabato* de Vicente Leñero," examines at great length the disproportionate inclusion of elements of recognizable reality within the fiction of the text. According to Figuerola, readers at one level posit the existence of a real Vicente Leñero who wrote *El garabato*.[9] The opening letter by Pablo Mejía H. places him as a fictional construct on the same level of reality as the real author Vicente Leñero. Moreover, the abundant references to contemporary reality in Mejía's letter underline his equality with Leñero. Everything about Mejía's letter is verisimilar except that he is a fictional construct addressing a real person on the other side of the boundary between fiction and reality.

In addition, in Mejía's novel the fictional narrator Fernando J. Moreno repeatedly cites existing journals and books (*Diorama de la Cultura*, *La palabra y el hombre*, J. Middleton Murry, Erich

Fromm, etc.) alongside quotations from his own articles published in the same magazines. In part, the citation of various aspects of reality within the text contributes to the mimetic effect that Roland Barthes would call *l'éffet de réel*.[10] Yet the abundance of such citations combined with the overtly invented citations of Moreno's own articles, just as in various texts of Jorge Luis Borges, foreground the fictional nature of the text, raising the dividing wall between fiction and reality even higher while simultaneously transgressing it.

Although the narrated transitions between narrative worlds and the citation of reality within *códigos de veridicción* contribute to the solidification of the boundary between fiction and reality, even in the very moment of transgressing the frontier, a more subtle and conceptual game begins in the innermost *El garabato*, unfolding the text and eventually folding it back on itself, thus erasing the boundary between fiction and reality. The conceptual play begins as a fusion of identities, bending outward from the center of the novel and consuming all of the so-called authors of the various texts. At the most central point Fernando Moreno's comments and Fabián Mendizábal's *El garabato* fuse into a single voice, variously disguising and dividing itself. The first clue to this confusion appears in a comment made by Moreno before beginning to read Mendizábal's text: "Me llamó la atención que el original de Mendizábal estuviese escrito con un tipo de letra idéntico al de mi máquina" (30). Although such a comment may at first sight appear to underline a coincidence, several errors in Mendizábal's text cannot be attributed to mere typographical carelessness.

At three points in Mendizábal's novel, the name *Lucy* appears in the place of another word.

> (1) "Pero rechazó de inmediato la suposición porque
> a todas lucy Frida no parecía una mujer a la que le
> preocuparan los convencionalismos de esa clase."
> (53)

(2) "El muchacho decidió hacerlo así en el momento en que Lucy le entregaba el vaso con whisky, pero antes de que él tuviera" (55)

(3) "Sólo pensaba en Lucy, anhelante por escuchar su voz, cuando sintió a sus espaldas, muy cerca, la presencia de alguien." (166)

In the first case, the appropriate phrase would read "a todas luces," not "a todas lucy." In the other two examples, Mendizábal's narrative should use the names of two female characters in his novel, Frida in (2) and María Luisa in (3). The misplacing of the name Lucy in these three sentences parallels the distracted concerns of Fernando Moreno in his conflict over whether or not to return to his estranged mistress Lucy.

Moreover, several critical commentaries made by Moreno on the psychological nature of a character in a novel, the parallel conflicts in Moreno's life and Rodolfo's adventure, and Moreno's deductions about the autobiographical nature of Mendizábal's *El garabato* break down the barrier between Moreno and the text he reads. Whereas Moreno complains of the "problemática psicología del escritor" (104) when pointing out the autobiographical faults in Mendizábal's novel, the confusion of Mendizábal and Moreno turns the statement inside out, the text enfolds exterior criticism into its interior. The autobiographical failure to create true psychological projections is the result of Moreno's inability to resolve his own sexual, psychological, and religious conflicts. Hence the reading of Mendizábal's novel serves to extend outward past the textual boundary to where Moreno resides, offering a more penetrating vision of Moreno's own conflicts.

The confusion of Moreno and Mendizábal thus erases the innermost boundary between fiction and reality, projecting the division between text and world to the next outermost level, the presentation of Pablo Mejía H.'s *El garabato*. The cover "blurb" advanced by Mejía confirms the fusion of Moreno and Mendizábal. Mejía states that *El garabato* presents the story of the "enfrentamiento de dos individuos" who in the "unitario" text "se convierten en una sola persona" in order to reveal a "drama de impresionante verosimilitud" (8). In this perspective, the most telling details come from the intratextual echoes between Mejía's commentary and Mendizábal's reaction to Moreno's unfavorable criticism.

In the final pages of the novel Mendizábal returns to hear Moreno's opinion on his manuscript. Moreno, who never finishes reading the text, judges it as a second-rate novel. Mendizábal passionately responds that Moreno is mistaken. Later he elaborates his refusal to accept Moreno's judgement:

> --Pero usted no puede decirme eso --clamó--. Quiere decir entonces que no ha entendido.
> --He entendido perfectamente.
> --No.
> --¿Qué había que entender, a su juicio? --sonreí.
> --Todo, la novela, el sentido de la novela. Y lo sabe muy bien, mejor que yo. (182)

According to explicitly stated literary criteria, Moreno has rejected Mendizábal's text as a superficial detective novel, without even discovering Rodolfo's outcome or the meaning of the mysterious *garabato* that is supposedly the key to all of Rodolfo's misfortune. Yet both Mendizábal, on the inside, and Mejía, on the outside, encourage a search for a meaning that exceeds standard literary criteria.

Mejía's review proposes the same quest for such a special meaning in the novel by stating: ". . . el autor de esta obra intenta conformar una novela cuyo sentido y valor literario deben buscarse al margen de los simples atributos estilísticos" (8). Mejía further elaborates the criteria that would guide the reading of his novel, *El garabato*:

> De un caos aparente, el autor ha conseguido extraer la problemática individual, el rostro de quien se esconde, se satiriza y se desdobla mediante la palabra escrita. Y al hacerlo, sabe el autor que es él mismo quien se desenmascara y desdobla en sus personajes para buscar y mostrar --más allá del problema específico de la creación literaria, en lo profundo de la historia contenida en el doble relato-- el haz de problemas humanos con los que todos podemos conmocionarnos. (9)

Whereas Moreno rejects Mendizábal's *El garabato* on the basis of an autobiographico-literary standard, and Mendizábal denies the value of Moreno's judgments, Mejía opens his text to an evaluation based on a combination of these criteria. He specifically invites an autobiographical reading of his *El garabato*, speaking of the author (himself) who cognizantly "se esconde, se satiriza y se desdobla mediante la palabra escrita" (8). Once again the text invites readers to unfold the fiction outwards, applying to Mejía's reality the standards of his own creation, erasing the boundary between Mejía and his novel.[11]

Although the folds of the novel might appear to lie intact at this point, the impetus of the text continues to unfold further outward toward the page where Vicente Leñero presents his novel *El garabato*. At this outermost level the accumulation of details in a text whose meaning and value reside "al margen de los simples atributos estilísticos" (8), the margin between fiction and reality again begins to fade. As stated above, Pablo Mejía's letter to Vicente Leñero transgresses the boundary of the text and concurrently foregrounds it by virtue of the violation of a sacred frontier. The progression of the text, however, unfolds in reverse from the center and demolishes the wall between fiction and reality as the autobiographical criterion of the text and its enigmatic *garabato* carry back to Leñero. Vicente Leñero, just as Moreno, has not proposed the "creación de una novela, sino la creación de un autor," (113), Pablo Mejía.

Nevertheless, just as Mejía's promotional blurb for *El garabato* is a fold where the inside of the text consumes the outside function of critical commentary, the fictional autobiographical criterion of the innermost text can be extended outward to Leñero, suggesting that he also can be engulfed within the critique of a fiction. The issue then becomes an intimation that there is no boundary at all and that everything exists on the level of fiction; that is, the *mise-en-abyme* installs the text itself as reality and places the supposed author Vicente Leñero on the other side of a frontier, within the realm of fiction.[12]

The mirroring structure between the possible worlds of the texts also suggests an extension outward to the physical boundaries of the material object of the book *El garabato*. The promotional information on the back of the book that readers hold in their hands contributes to the melting of reality into fiction. Parallel to Mejía's blurb, the back cover of *El garabato* informs readers:

> En un mundo donde la ficción rige a la realidad tantas veces como ésta a la ficción, donde todo parece girar dentro de un vertiginoso laberinto, un novelista inventa a un novelista que inventó a un novelista que escribe o lee --con nosotros-- la novela de otro autor probablemente inventado. La lectura, así, se convierte en un engima que acelera a cada página nuestra curiosidad y nos enfrenta a las ambiciones y frustraciones de un grupo de personajes reductibles, tal vez, a uno solo.

The basic propositions of the passage are evident in the reading of *El garabato*. Fiction rules over reality as often as reality influences fiction. In appearance, the chain of a "novelist who invents a novelist who invents a novelist who either writes or reads" is a verisimilar description with an origin firmly embedded in the reality of the first author. The last sentence, however, when reducing these authors into one, posits them as a *personaje*, the character of a fiction. Thus, the entrance into the "vertiginoso laberinto," the *garabato*, makes the text "girar," and upon exiting, it is implied that readers return not to reality but to fiction. In this manner the unfolding of *El garabato* becomes totalizing, turning the book inside out, placing readers in fiction with the hope that reality continues to exist behind its sacred and inviolable frontier.

In this final reversal *El garabato* manifests its resemblance to *Estudio Q* in the use of the metafictional mode. Both novels manifest the manner in which the textual surface, discretely divided into possible worlds bordered by the discontinuity of an act of narrating, may also fold and unfold itself, providing the illusion of both reversing and erasing the boundary between fiction and reality. In the final outcome the boundary is reestablished but displaced. Spires comments on the displacement of the border of texts in terms of a necessary communicative situation for the linguistic construct:

> . . . there is a certain contradiction in this whole process. When the world of, say, the fictive author is violated and he is thereby made an explicit part of the fiction, standing beyond him is always another implied or fictive author. The same is true with the text-act reader, for once he is dramatized into the fiction there has to be another text-act reader to whom that dramatizing process is addressed. In the final analysis, therefore, metafiction violates one set of modes merely to replace it with another. Metafiction cannot escape its own prison-house of fiction.[13]

Spires's last comment marks the reinscription of the boundary between fiction and reality. Either as a necessity of the communicative presupposition, or for whatever reason at all, the coherence of readers' reality depends on the newly erected wall that delimits fiction. The subsequent wall, however, bears the traces of displacement, revealed in its necessary yet artificial nature as a textual convention: the boundary not only defines the previously subordinate nature of fiction to reality but also reveals the necessity of this subordination for the concept of reality, whence results an unsettling characterization of reality as arbitrary.

The use of the metafictional mode, producing the reversal of the hierarchy between fiction and reality, and in a double gesture reinscribing the hierarchy as a displacement, also reveals the nature of fiction as based on an arbitrary convention of exclusion. Whereas the fictional mode privileges the hierarchy, going to great lengths to dissimulate its arbitrariness, metafictions exploit the generative nature of writing through the foregrounding of the boundary. In this light, metafiction is perhaps much more than simply a synchronic capacity that literary texts may exploit. In fiction the boundary is the aspect of writing that one must attempt to master; yet metafiction gives it free rein.[14]

Estudio Q and *El garabato* also thematically explore the problematics involved in the mastery of textual borders.[15] In *Estudio Q*, Alex's suicide is a supreme attempt at controlling the boundary between the world in which he cooperates to produce a soap opera and the world in which he is a soap opera character. From the beginning the *director escénico* and Gladys Monroy are planning something secret that no one can disclose to Alex. In the various levels of the story, as Alex rebels against the *director escénico* and Gladys Monroy, the latter reconnoiter and subsequently make explicit the battle for control over Alex's autonomy. A section of the text simulating a draft of the script formulates the plan to dominate Alex in the following manner:

> Pero un oportuno telefonazo xxxxxxxxxxx
> telefonema de Actorfracasado pone sobreaviso al

> director escénico quien rápidamente llama a la escritora y le dice que aporovecharán (sic) lo hecho por Alex para impedir que éste salga con la suya; es decir, incluirán en la historia esa nueva situación que Alex considera xxx se está efectuando en l avida (sic) real y que de este modo pertenecerá también a la novela. (184)

Hence Alex has no control in any level of the story. Each successive fold in his reality includes the options that he is an actor following directions or that his actions will become part of the soap opera, also subject to the control of others.

In effect, Alex's sense of loss of autonomy begins to threaten his sanity as he can no longer distinguish reality from fiction. At one point Alex seduces the leading actress and then enters the bathroom, repeating a scene from the soap opera. Upon recognizing the repetition that he has just enacted, he looks at his reflection in the bathroom mirror. In a lapse of inability to know "quién soy, quién soy, qué hago aquí, de dónde vengo" (173), he begins to recite uncontrollably lines from Ayn Rand's *The Fountainhead*, Calderón's *La vida es sueño*, and Shakespeare's *Hamlet*. In these soliloquies Alex directly confronts the issue of slavery:

> Si la esclavitud es físicamente repulsiva, ¿cuánto más repulsivo no será el concepto de la esclavitud del espíritu? El esclavo conquistado tiene un vestigio de honor; tiene el mérito de haber resistido y el de considerar que su condición es mala. Pero el hombre que voluntariamente se esclaviza es la más baja de las criaturas. (176-177)

Within the story Alex's dilemma resides precisely in his being a victim of the worst kind of slavery, having freely chosen to participate in a soap opera about his life. Even in the final analysis, there is doubt as to whether or not Alex himself actually chooses to commit suicide. Gladys Monroy corrects Alex's thinking that it is an opportunity to die; she says that it is an opportunity "de vencer" (300). Therefore, even the concept of death itself does not serve to reestablish the boundary between fiction and reality. Death, the ultimate experience of reality, can be written into the script, totally denying the mastery of fiction by reality, marking defeat instead of triumph. Moreover, as the creators of the script become characters within it, they too cannot claim the autonomy necessary for making the originating decision. No one in the novel has the ability to govern the generative process of an unleashed metafictional mode.

The struggle against domination in *El garabato* also leads characters to sense a loss of control over their lives. Rodolfo, absurdly involved in a secret plot, recognizes the artificial nature of his plight: "--Porque estas cosas no ocurren más que en las películas. Son tan absurdas . . ." (138). Doubting the reality of the events and arguing against the causality that he imputes to them, Rodolfo concludes: "'Demasiada imaginación'--pensó. Aquélla era la ciudad de México. No estaba participando en una película ni era el personaje de una novela. Había ocurrido un crimen y nada más. Frida Campbell y su accidente eran cuestión aparte" (88). Throughout the adventure Rodolfo maintains a disbelief of everything yet yearns for freedom, "como él lo fue hasta esa tarde" (91).

The fusion of the narrator Moreno with Mendizábal is adduced not only from the unfolding effect of Mendizábal's/Moreno's text, but also from the resemblance between Moreno and Rodolfo in the loss of freedom. Moreno's dilemma, however, arises from the labyrinth of his religious convictions. He goes back and forth between the church and the psychoanalyst hoping that one or the other will give him an absolute answer: either his affair is a sin, or religion is a myth, hence he should feel no guilt. Nevertheless, given that Moreno cannot accept any absolute resolution, his final decision parallels the arbitrariness of the incomplete reading of Mendizábal's *El garabato*. In the closing paragraph of the novel Moreno writes:

> El jet despegó de la pista y yo sentí, al ascender en vuelo, que el aparato me raptaba para siempre inventando, anticipándome una muerte ante la cual yo podía escribir con su sentido absoluto (puesto que es muy probable que Cristo no sea Dios) la palabra fin. (187)

Although Moreno's decision is an irrevocable step, and he still posits death as an absolute, the criterion must carry the qualifer "muy probable," totally negating the possibility of an absolute. Thus, *El garabato* dramatizes the arbitrary nature of man's decisions. Although this treatment of the search for freedom does not follow the pattern of *Estudio Q*, in both cases the question of mastery is related to the issue of arbitariness: the arbitrary nature of the conventional boundary between fiction and reality in *Estudio Q*, and the uncertain, arbitrary nature of all decisions in *El garabato*.[16]

In addition, the labyrinths and the *garabato* of the novel serve to produce a struggle for the readers who accept the game of the text. Progressively penetrating the various novelized worlds, readers wander through a maze. At each turn of the path a mirror reflects the multiple yet single image of the guide, the narrator(s) of the text(s). In the end, the various challenges to discover the meaning of the novel at the "margen de los simples atributos estilísticos" (8) becomes another all-consuming labyrinth, a *garabato* that can only be deciphered within the *garabato* itself. In this sense, both *Estudio Q* and *El garabato* are novels that place readers in the precarious position of enslavement to a text. And even when readers escape the labyrinths, exerting mastery through reinscription of a conventional boundary between fiction and reality, their freedom is ungrounded, erected on unfirm, arbitrary, and yet necessary constructs. Reading itself becomes a question of masters and slaves.

In summary, *Estudio Q* and *El garabato* both inscribe themselves within the metafictional mode. Through various means the texts fold the outside practice of critical commentary into the inside of the text. Such inclusion, however, results in an unfolding that moves with such impetus as to undermine the boundary between fiction and reality, suggesting the integration of the author and the readers into the text. A posterior move then erects the conventional boundary, always already in place yet now perceived in its arbitrary and necessary function. The question of the boundary, functional in both the metafictional mode and the various fictional ones, is also an issue of the mastery of writing and reading. Although the texts dramatize the thematics of a master-slave relation, its most threatening implication resides in the moment when the last unfolding of the text intimates that readers and writers also live out a similar relationship to the socially defined fiction we call reality. Thus readers may reenact the struggle, self-consciously and arbitrarily erecting the boundary between reality and fiction, attempting to master the generative power of language and writing to insure the security of reality outside the text.[17]

Chapter Four:
Redil de ovejas:
The Novel as Cultural Criticism

The early novels of Vicente Leñero, as I have been demonstrating, evidence a gradually increasing emphasis on narrative strategies. Whereas social concerns clearly accompany this emphasis on technique in *A fuerza de palabras* and *Los albañiles*, the complexity of *Estudio Q* and *El garabato* may at first appear to have elevated even further the interest in the flexibilities of the genre and eliminated the critical relation between text and cultural context. Although the cerebral qualities of these metafictions place narrative technique in the foreground, they also lay bare the artifice of strategies that more traditionally provide a "natural" image of reality. This metafictional effect--the open demonstration of the artifice involved in novelistic representation --also suggests, by extension, that any "natural appearance" is ultimately a fabricated image and that the social definition of reality also relies on broadly accepted or unquestioned fictions of representation. The latter novels, published in the 1970s and 1980s, direct increasing attention to this fabricated image of reality and, more specifically, they address the fictions of representation involved in the historical process and in religious interpretations.

Redil de ovejas (1973) exemplifies both of these tendencies.[1] It serves as a transitional novel in which the structural and technical characteristics of the novels of the 1960s, "el primer ciclo" according to Lois Sherry Grossman, converge with the interest in fictions of representation found in the latter novels.[2] In *Redil de ovejas*, the demands for reader participation and the use of complex narrative strategies remain consistent with the earlier novels; yet the text underscores religious thematics, the historical process of social formation, and the lingering effects of Mexico's cultural representations, its collective fictions. In light of these emphases, attention to the worldliness of the text demonstrates how Leñero exploits the potentials of the novelistic genre in order to embed *Redil de ovejas* in its socio-historical context as a critical portrayal of the cultural contradictions of Mexican Catholicism.

I

In *The World, the Text, and the Critic*, Edward W. Said explores the notion of worldliness in relation to the literary text. In the perspective of worldliness, the critic strives to substantiate the circumstantial reality of the text. As Said writes: "The point is that texts have ways of existing that even in their most rarefied form are always enmeshed in circumstance, time, place, and society--in short, they are in the world, and hence worldly."[3] Although Said contends that worldliness is a quality of all texts, even those like the novels of Leñero's "primer ciclo" that go to great lengths to explore the formal and technical capabilities of the genre, in *Redil de ovejas* worldliness becomes an overtly dominant quality of the text. The novel evidences this dominance both thematically and structurally through its investigation of the historical and cultural dynamics of Mexican Catholicism in the 1960s. In order to comprehend the worldliness of a text, Said proposes that one "view the text as a dynamic field, rather than as a static block, of words. This field has a certain range of reference, a system of tentacles . . . partly potential, partly actual: to the author, to the reader, to a historical situation, to other texts, to the past and present."[4] In accounting for this series of tentacles in *Redil de ovejas*, the following pages will consider the thematic ambivalence of the text, its complex narrative situation and the subsequent tension between the *récit* and the tentative *histoires*. In the final analysis, however, consideration of these facets of the text will draw attention to the historical nature of the heterogeneous discourse of *Redil de ovejas* and the manner in which the text engages readers in a critical reevaluation of the role of the Church in Mexico and its difficult move toward liberalization in the 1960s.

Redil de ovejas regularly alternates between two thematic zones: one zone presents the historical dynamics of the evolution of institutionalized Mexican Catholicism in the 1960s while the other zone recounts the dubious conversion and religious education of a young boy by an aging religious fanatic. Throughout the text, the alternation between these zones follows a rigid pattern. On the one hand, the odd-numbered chapters form a panoramic mural of the practice of Catholicism in Mexico. In these chapters readers encounter diverse embodiments of varying attitudes toward Christianity and divers interpretations of Catholic doctrine. In brief, these chapters serve to present the various contradictory positions that produce the conflicts and dynamics of the historical period under consideration in *Redil de ovejas*. They constitute, among other things, a typology of the Mexican Catholic.[5]

The even-numbered chapters, on the other hand, tell the story of an orphan, Bernardo, who lives with his older siblings, Rubén and "la Güera." The ten-year-old Bernardo accidentally breaks a window pane in the apartment of the elderly *beata* Rosita. As punishment, Rubén orders that the boy assist Rosita in her daily chores. Whereas Bernardo and all of his delinquent friends speak of Rosita as if she were a witch, in actuality she is a fanatic, a *mocha* who attends mass at least once a day and lives in abject poverty with her mysterious black cat Angel and in a room full of religious articles. Rosita catechizes Bernardo and convinces him to become a priest in order to intercede for the spiritual redemption of his wayward brother and of his sexually promiscuous sister.

Chapter two of the novel accomplishes the crucial function of suggesting the tentative nexus between the two thematic zones. One of the longest chapters, it consists of a panoramic portrayal of Mexican Catholics attending an anticommunist demonstration at the Basilica of Guadalupe. A journalist, apparently assigned to report on the demonstration for the press, wanders through the crowd and comments on various individuals as he plans his news release. The characters introduced here, all bearing the names

Bernardo and Rosamaría, constitute the typology of Catholics that reappears throughout the subsequent odd-numbered chapters. Combining possible newspaper write-ups of the event, several anticommunist speeches, crowd reactions, and intimate background details of the lives of the various Bernardos and Rosamarías, the journalist also comments on his relation with the *beata* Rosita, whom he believes to be present at the demonstration. In response to the question of an unidentified voice, "--¿Quién es Rosita?" (42), the journalist proceeds to give a brief yet tender characterization of her solitude and religious fervor. The references to Rosita, the journalist's appreciation for her, and the coincidence of descriptive details all serve to establish an identification between the journalist and the ten-year-old Bernardo of the later even-numbered chapters.

In addition, chapter two sets into play the overt historicization of the text. As the chapter heading indicates, the demonstration occurred on May 15, 1961. It celebrated the seventieth anniversary of the 1891 encyclical *Rerum Novarum* endorsed by Pope Leo XIII, the "Carta Magna del Trabajo." Whereas constitutional law officially bars Mexican clergy from the political forum, the rally serves to foment the anticommunist sentiments of groups such as the *Acción Católica* and the *Movimiento Familiar Cristiano*. References to student violence in the cities of Puebla, Chihuahua, and Morelia evoke the confrontation between more conservative factions and the incipient pro-Fidel Castro group, the *Movimiento de Liberación Nacional*. Hence arises the expansive historical context of *Redil de ovejas*, beginning with the Church/State conflicts of Mexico in the wake of Castro's 1959 triumph in the Cuban Revolution, and extending back to nineteenth-century papal opposition to Marxism. Although *Redil de ovejas* does not politically analyze the interaction among these groups, the heterogeneous discourse includes simulated journalistic pieces and historical documentation as functional elements in the narrative structure. Also, whereas chapter two initiates the process of historical reflection in the novel, this referential tendency is generally confined to the panoramic survey of the odd-numbered chapters and culminates in the historical documents of chapter eleven.

The thematic ambivalence of *Redil de ovejas*, however, arises from the tensive relationship between the zone of historical referentiality and the story line of young Bernardo's conversion under the tutelage of *beata* Rosita. The obvious narrative technique of confusing characters under identical names and the patterned alternation of thematic zones serve both to suggest unity and yet impede any reductive correspondence between the panoramic vision and the individualized plot. The historical references of chapter two not only evidence the historical consciousness of the text but also appear to anchor the story of young Bernardo and *beata* Rosita in the bedrock of a specific temporal context. In addition, the narrative events and subsequent enigmas of the even-numbered chapters provide a cohesive and forward-moving impulse to the otherwise nonnarrative succession of stereotypes in the odd-numbered chapters. Nevertheless, at first appearance the connection between the two thematic zones is based on their temporal simultaneity in chapter two.

Moreover, whereas the panoramic succession of vignettes in the odd-numbered chapters depends on the young Bernardo-*beata* Rosita plot for cohesion and momentum, this plot further complicates and obscures the problematic unity because of its highly anachronic order. Generally, the pertinent chapters between four and twelve progress from Bernardo's initial relation to Rosita to his hearing of Rosita's death second-hand after his return to Mexico City as a priest. The movement between these two temporal points includes several analepses (or "flashbacks") and one very important prolepsis (or "flashforward") in chapter six. This chapter portrays a much older Bernardo who recalls the arguments he has had with his sister. Bernardo, upholding Catholic doctrine and the sacrament of matrimony, condemns "la Güera" for having left her impotent first husband Saúl, and for "living in sin" with her lover Manuel. Given the temporal anachronies of the plot, the connection between the two thematic zones rests on the logical fallacy of *post hoc, ergo propter hoc* reasoning. The text, however, ultimately resists this erroneous reasoning since identification of correspondences between the two thematic zones consistently leads to irreconcilable temporal and factual contradictions.

Although many critics have considered the fragmentation of *Redil de ovejas*, the contingent cohesion of the entire text, and the technique of similarly named characters to be major technical and structural flaws in the novel, these aspects constitute strategic moves in the production of critical cultural commentary.[6] While avoiding facile external critiques of the multiple ideological positions, juxtaposition of the various doctrinal interpretations produces an image of Mexican Catholicism as a cultural institution wielding considerable political power. The superficial or stereotypical portrayal in the typology of Catholics serves to underscore the contradictions between the external social roles and the internal frustration of individual needs. Indeed, Lucía Garavito has established a technical parallel between the use of external focalization in order to emphasize the stereotypical roles as a function of the collectivity of the institutional Church, and the use of internal focalization in order to manifest the personal conflicts of individuals forced to conform to the impersonal power of the social institution.[7]

Besides the careful manipulation of focalization, the text also exploits the strategic use of narrative voice in order to represent the ambivalence and contradictions that constitute the texture of the cultural drama under consideration in *Redil de ovejas*. Ana María Amar Sánchez, comparing several of Leñero's novels, points out in reference to *Redil de ovejas*: "En esta novela, a diferencia de en las otras, el sujeto de la enunciación se escinde en dos: el Padre Bernardo y otro narrador muy cercano a aquél y con el que suele confundirse: se identifican en su visión de Rosita, usan las mismas comparaciones y un mismo punto de vista para narrarla."[8] Or in more technical terms, the narrative voice of *Redil de ovejas* manifests a polar division between a third-person omniscient narrating voice and a first-person narrator. The separation between these two positions, however, dialectically fluctuates and from time to time produces a synthesis.

For example, the panoramic typology of Mexican Catholics proceeds exclusively from the third-person omniscient voice. In contrast, the presentation of the story of young Bernardo and *beata* Rosita oscillates between the third-person and first-person narrating positions. In chapter two, however, the establishment of the typology and the introduction of the principal plot coincide with a synthetic transition between the two narrative voices. Whereas the journalist speaks in first person, he also manifests the omniscient power of the third-person narrating voice when describing the various Bernardos and Rosamarías. The narrator describes the first man singled out as an "ejemplo del auténtico obrero mexicano padre de familia católico cumplido . . ." (18). After the journalist notes that the worker's wife, Rosamaría, has stepped in a mud puddle, a narrative ellipsis signals a shift in the time and place of the events.

> Sentada en la cama, a las diez de la noche, Rosamaría piensa en Acapulco mientras dirige la vista hacia sus pies delgados y largos. Bernardo entra en la habitación, se desprende del saco, lo cuelga en el clóset, se desnuda de cara a las cortinas y de espaldas a su mujer. (19)

The omniscient capacity of the journalist continues as he presents Rosamaría's confession to an unnamed priest. She complains about the frustrations of being a "good" Catholic wife:

> . . . no oír hablar de Dios. Me lo encuentro hasta en la sopa, padre; lo tengo atorado aquí como una espina de pescado. . . . Todo se gasta. La costumbre gasta al amor. Se vuelve rutina. La rutina, padre,

> es horrible, ¿A usted no le pasa lo mismo? ¿De
> veras no le gustaría tomar de cuando en cuando
> unas vacaciones y olvidarse por un tiempo de que
> es sacerdote? A que sí. Le haría mucho bien. Pero
> lo que se dice olvidarse: de todo: de la misa, de las
> confesiones, hasta de la castidad. Que en esas
> vacaciones usted pudiera hacer cualquier cosa.
> (21)

Throughout this passage the knowledge of the journalist exceeds the cognitive limits of a first-person narrator. Thus, within the context of the historical references of the second chapter, the journalist-narrator breaks all verisimilitude and factual veracity by conjecturing the intimate episodes occurring beyond his scope of possible knowledge. In the case of the Bernardo and Rosamaría cited above, he concludes by describing their making love after the demonstration, leaving Rosamaría empty and dissatisfied (23-24). In this manner the fluctuating origin of the narrative voice and the possible synthesis of the two dominant positions give rise to a peculiar combination of apparent objectivity and subjectivity that undermines, or at least stands in contrast to, the primarily referential nature of the text. The manipulation of narrative voice, then, also contributes to the fundamental ambivalence of the text.

Furthermore, the ambivalence related to the narrative voice, especially as a function of the identity of the journalist-narrator, becomes more problematic when considered in the light of the tentative *histoires* readers can reconstruct on the basis of the *récit*. As stated earlier, the fact that the journalist of chapter two openly infers his close connection to the *beata* Rosita suggests that he is the young Bernardo of the later even-numbered chapters. Especially pertinent for such identification are the details of Rosita's correcting the journalist as a child during mass (43). In addition, the style employed by the journalist to characterize Rosita in chapter two converges with the third-person omniscient and the first-person voices of the young Bernardo-*beata* Rosita story-line.[9]

Up until the conclusion, the cohesion of the text rests principally on the reconstruction of a logical *histoire* for the young Bernardo-*beata* Rosita plot. On the basis of the even-numbered chapters from four to twelve, one may infer the relationship between two groups: the three siblings, Rubén, "la Güera," and young Bernardo, and the *beata* Rosita who faithfully attends masses officiated by Padre Bernardo. Although the two Bernardos of this plot maintain potentially confusing roles, especially since the younger Bernardo eventually becomes a priest, their age difference and relation to either "la Güera" or to Rosita serve to differentiate them. In addition, the Padre Bernardo of Rosita's masses has a rather extensive characterization, occupying all of chapters one, three, and the beginning of chapter twelve, which contributes to his individualization in contrast to the younger Bernardo. These chapters characterize him as a clergyman, brilliantly educated abroad, who constantly wrestles with the question of his religious vocation.

Beyond the complexity of separating these two Bernardos on the basis of their actions rather than the use of an individualizing name, the prolepsis in chapter six sets into play a series of parallels that culminates in chapter thirteen. The extensive prolepsis of chapter six presents the young Bernardo, brother of "la Güera," many years later as an experienced priest. The first page of the chapter, however, includes a detail that confuses the two Bernardos. Chapters one and three present the unnamed yet doubtful priest who projects his worries into the interpretation of a stained-glass window in the church: "el enorme vitral donde se relataba, estampa por estampa, la vida milagrosa de Jesús . . . . En la porción herida por los rayos de luz, Jesús adolescente discutía con los sabios del templo" (14-15). In chapters one and three the priest who contemplates the window appears in conjunction with the sacristan Gonzalo. Later references to Gonzalo and the elder Padre Bernardo lead to the retrospective inference that the priest of chapters one and three is also the Padre Bernardo often praised by *beata* Rosita.

In the proleptic sixth chapter, readers first encounter references to Rubén, "la Güera," and Rosita. Next follows a reference to a Padre Bernardo and the stained-glass window:

> El padre Bernardo terminó de un sorbo el vaso de agua y se levantó para dar vuelta a la mesa y quedar más próximo a la mirada del muchacho que absorto escuchaba a su discurso, como los sabios del vitral escuchaban a Jesús adolescente. (67)

Although the identity of the priest and the proleptic nature of the passage remain unperceived for the first few pages, details enter that identify the priest as the young Bernardo catechized by Rosita.

While lecturing a young boy on the exemplary life of Christ, the priest comments:

> Y no pienses que yo era un muchacho piadoso, ¡ni soñarlo! Yo tuve una infancia muy difícil. Era huérfano, imagínate, y mi hermano y mi hermana no se preocupaban de que yo fuera a la iglesia ni me hablaban jamás de Dios. Todo lo contrario. Crecí en la calle con malas compañías, haciendo diabluras y aprendiendo todos los pecados que se aprenden por ahí. A los diez años era la piel de judas, y a los doce o trece un verdadero delincuente. No te imaginas qué clase de muchacho perverso era yo. Sin embargo, gracias a la intervención que yo considero milagrosa, de un alma beatífica, y a mil circunstancias que se encadenaron providencialmente, floreció en mi espíritu la semilla de una vocación sacerdotal. (69)

Besides the opposition between the attitudes of the Padre Bernardo of chapters one, three, and twelve and this Padre Bernardo concerning religious vocation, the past related by the priest corresponds to young Bernardo's life story. Information throughout the rest of chapter six indeed confirms the proleptic nature of the passage.

Nevertheless, the major part of the chapter consists of the analeptic memories of Bernardo as he recalls his last meeting with his sister "la Güera." Through Bernardo's recollections, readers learn that "la Güera" abandoned her husband to live with her lover. The husband later dies, leaving her free to marry the lover. During this time Bernardo has tried repeatedly to turn his sister back to the "redil de ovejas" just as Rosita brought him back into the "redil." Whereas the recalled past and the name "la Güera" convincingly differentiate the young Bernardo as priest from Rosita's favorite Padre Bernardo, the attitude toward the "ovejas descarriadas y el pecador arrepentido frente a noventa y nueve justos que no tienen necesidad de pentitencia . . ." (12) is identical in the two priests, serving to underscore similarities and de-differentiate them.

Equally important, the end of chapter twelve contributes to solidifying the separation between the two Bernardos. The passage appears in a fragmented typographical arrangement, and in it the young Bernardo acknowledges his ordination and return to Mexico City.

> Recibí la ordenación sacerdotal a los veintiséis. Me
> mandaron a muchas partes.   Estuve en Puebla.
> En Oaxaca.
> Regresé y un día supe de Rosita. (158)

She had died and "el padre Bernardo cubrió los gastos del entierro de Rosita al que sólo asistieron la portera del edificio y un par de vecinos que la visitaban de cuando en cuando . . ." (158). In this manner the young Bernardo, as a priest, confirms the existence of the older Padre Bernardo associated with Rosita. The pertinent details for separating the two Bernardos include their similar yet different relationships with Rosita, their age difference, and the family relationships of young Bernardo, principally with his sister, "la Güera."

At one point, however, the differences between Rosita and "la Güera" begin to fade as subtle indications reveal similarities. Even though *beata* Rosita's characterization insists on her religiosity, chapter ten refers to a younger Rosita.

> Rosita ya no recuerda el vestido, ni la fiesta, ni la estatura de su padre; ni se recuerda Rosamaría adolescente, soltera, novia, y otra vez soltera que esconde su risa tras un chal verde, cuando de pronto, en el espejo, al darse la vuelta, así nada más, de pronto, se le aparece el Sagrado Corazón. (129)

Although this passage negatively characterizes that which Rosita does not remember, it evokes a past history, even mentioning the possible young loves of the elderly fanatic. It is also the first moment when Rosita is equated with the other female characters of the novel by using her full name, Rosamaría.

Her fanaticism grows out of her vision of the Sacred Heart. The text includes the scene of Rosita's telling her confessor about the experience.

> ¿Estás loca?
> No, padre, lo vi en el espejo de mi cuarto.
> No has visto nada.
> Lo vi en el espejo.
> ¿Piensas que el Sagrado Corazón se aparece así como así a cualquier gente?
> Yo no sé, padre, pero lo vi en el espejo así como lo estoy viendo a usted.
> Lárgate.

> No, padre.
> Vete y cuida de tus animales. Ya te he dicho mil veces que no se puede comulgar dos veces el mismo día.
> Sí padre.
> Pide perdón a Dios, reza a María santísima una estación del rosario y a partir de hoy procura ser más recatada porque te haces directamente responsable de todos los malos pensamientos que provoque tu manera escandalosa de vestir. (130)

Although this passage serves to confirm the image of mental imbalance associated with Rosita's voodoo-like Catholicism (stealing holy water to baptize dogs, using talismans, seeing apparitions, etc.), it also portrays specific details about the younger Rosita of the past.

Similar to the characterization of "la Güera," Rosita too had her loves (although the text only vaguely suggests this aspect), and she dressed scandalously, drawing attention to her sexuality. Chapter thirteen, however, the last chapter of the novel, transforms these details, the similarities between Rosita and "la Güera," and between the young Bernardo and the Padre Bernardo, and thus offers a totally new perspective of the *histoire* that readers tentatively construct on the basis of the *récit.*

Chapter thirteen, the concluding chapter of the novel, sheds new light on the laboriously reconstructed *histoires*, either confirming or complicating such identification, depending upon the protocol of interpretation employed by readers. The problematic nature of *Redil de ovejas* ensues as a dynamic function of the signifying structures formed by the various narrative techniques. The use of similarly named characters, ambiguous temporal associations, and tenuous relations between the two thematic zones all appear in a new perspective with the revelation of withheld knowledge in the final lines of the novel.

Chapter thirteen, like chapter two, serves the function of connecting the two thematic zones. In this instance, the closure of *Redil de ovejas* arises when the panoramic thematic zone turns back onto the plot of young Bernardo-*beata* Rosita. The entire chapter consists of a series of responses to the question: "--La Güera, la Güera, la Güera . . . ¿Vas a creer que no me acuerdo?" (160). In each response the speaker offers a characterization of "la Güera," attempting to stimulate a recognition of her in the first speaker of the chapter. All of the speakers begin with "--Aquella . . . ," and proceed to render various interpretations of the lives of Rubén, Bernardo, and "la Güera," each vaguely similar and yet different from the plot developed in the even-numbered chapters of the novel. The characterizations insinuate everything from the virtues of "la Güera" for having reared her orphaned brother Bernardo, her virtually having been a prostitute, her being the mother of Bernardo, to her having seduced Padre Bernardo.

The final characterization, however, does not coincide with any previous references to "la Güera." To the contrary, the image of *beata* Rosita emerges. The speaker mentions all of the principal traits of Rosita. Finally, the speaker justifies the source of information as "la Güera" herself. Urged by a Padre Bernardo, the speaker had gone to visit the *beata* who told her life story.

> Yo estaba con la boca abierta porque no me
> imaginaba; bueno, porque no me ponía a pensar
> que ella también había sido joven. Una se
> acostumbra a verla como una anciana y no piensa
> que tuvo que ser una mujer como cualquiera.
> Estuvo casada dos veces, me dijo. Y tuvo una bola
> de pretendientes y de aventuras que ni se podían
> creer. Tal vez era pura cosa de su imaginación, pero
> sí me acuerdo que me enseñó fotografías ya
> viejísimas y cartas. Le caí bien. Pero su vida sí que
> era de película. De no creerse, te digo, conociéndola

así como yo la conocía: de beata loca que siempre
está en la iglesia rece y rece, o predicando en la calle
al primero que se encuentra. Pero no. Pobre mujer.
De joven había sido otra cosa. Según las fotos: muy
guapa, bien formada, rubia. Le decían la Güera.
--Pobre mujer, que en paz descanse.
--Sí, ya dejó de sufrir. (165)

Hence the conclusion extends the characterization of both "la
Güera" and Rosita. A strong suggestion of identification between
the two implies either that they are one and the same or that there
is a phenomenon of identical repetition between the two women.

In this perspective readers may reconstruct two possible
histoires. John S. Brushwood proposes that in *Redil de ovejas* "se
refiere a dos generaciones y un narrador, al final, nos da
información, relativa a sus identidades, que cambia la perspectiva
en la cual vemos la realidad del *récit.*"[10] Thus, on the basis of the
Bernardo-Rosita chapters, an *histoire* arises in which the
relationship Bernardo-"la Güera" reappears as a mirror image of
the relationship Padre Bernardo-Rosita. The text anachronically
follows the prior relation Padre Bernardo-Rosita from the time in
which young Bernardo enters it up to the death of Rosita and the
later death of "la Güera." In the case of both Rosita and "la Güera,"
a Padre Bernardo serves to bring the "oveja descarriada" back to the
"redil de ovejas."

On the other hand, John M. Lipski discerns a cyclical
temporal structure in *Redil de ovejas.* Lipski believes "it is clear
that the personages are intended to represent a sole narrative
unit, in various metamorphoses."[11] On the basis of this
presupposition he recognizes the impossibility of logically
reconciling the various subplots. He accepts this as a structural
paradox. In this perspective, there is only one Padre Bernardo and
"old Rosita is the Güera of earlier times."[12] The question of what or
who comes first in the chain of events evolves into a circular
question, leading to a cyclical repetition of the same story:

Bernardo returns "la Güera"/Rosita to the fold who returns Bernardo to the fold, etc.

Although Lipski's interpretation presupposes a cyclical temporal progression, in contrast to Brushwood's linear historical explanation, both of them are justifiable on the basis of textual data. The question of verisimilitude will not serve to validate either of these *histoires*, for in the final analysis both *histoires* lead to a concept of historical repetition, be it cyclical or linear. In the most encompassing perspective, then, it is the question of historical repetition that links the two thematic zones of *Redil de ovejas*.

II

The phenomenon of repetition saturates all aspects of the text and constitutes a semantic bedrock of signifying structures that move far beyond the precarious *post hoc, ergo propter hoc* association of the various represented events. In this light, the overt worldliness of the panoramic section of the novel acquires a greater suggestivity by virtue of the dynamics of the repetition in the Bernardo-Rosita plot; and concurrently, the historical tentacles of referentiality established in the panoramic view of Mexican Catholicism serve to imbue the Bernardo-Rosita plot with a productive polysemia that escapes the confines of a logically contained signification.

Commenting on the complexity of the "plot," Miguel Angel Niño deduces that Leñero

> . . . ha intentado plantear el problema del catolicismo en la sociedad mexicana. En *Redil de ovejas* como en sus obras anteriores le corresponde al lector reconstruir el crucigrama que el autor ha fabricado. Aquí no se trata de localizar a un criminal como en *Los albañiles*, sino de adivinar entre la maraña de datos a veces contradictorios las relaciones entre los diferentes personajes.[13]

Although the process of reading *Redil de ovejas* may not correspond to "guessing" (*adivinar*) such relations, the relations established extend far beyond the individual characters of the novel. The entire matter of repetition manifests the multiform dynamics of Catholicism as a fundamental aspect of Mexican culture. Indeed, the conflict between conservatives and liberals, between the Church and the State, evokes a series of historical confrontations throughout Mexico's past. Although the text openly refers to the Cristero Rebellion of 1926-1929, one could point out similar conflicts at the time of the Reform, the war for Independence, or even the process of proselytizing the indigenous population at the time of the Conquest. In short, since the formation of the Roman Catholic Church, western history has repeatedly witnessed Church/State conflicts between the political institution of the Vatican and various emergent, developing, or even established nation states.

Redil de ovejas, however, couches the issue in particularly Mexican terms. The text refers only to twentieth-century Mexican conflicts, such as the Cristero Rebellion and the move toward ecclesiastical liberalization after the Cuban Revolution. Rather than evoke the political dynamics of these confrontations, however, the text presents the cultural process of an unfolding and repetitive social drama. Moreover, the nature of the social drama bears intimate relation to a Mexican national symbol, the Virgin of Guadalupe.

Unlike the heterogeneous mixture of various registers of discourse in the other chapters, chapter eleven consists of purely historical discourse that underscores three specific moments. The first fragment of chapter eleven begins with the battle cry, "¡Viva Cristo Rey!: 1926" (142). The passage following this title simulates a political harangue designed to foment conservative religious opposition to the State on the basis of a religious analogy: the State is to the Church as Satan is to Christ. The battle cry of the May 15, 1961 demonstration of chapter two introduces the second fragment: "¡Cristianismo sí, comunismo no!: 1947-1961" (143).

The passage under this title consists of a moral refutation of historical materialism on the basis of several papal encyclicals dating back to the nineteenth century.

The final fragment, however, appears in two columns that divide almost four pages of text. On the left side of the page the title "A la derecha de Dios: 1967" (144) introduces an anticommunist diatribe, founded principally on the same arguments as the 1947-1961 passage, which even criticizes Pope John XXIII for the contemporary crisis in the Church. To a certain degree this diatribe constitutes an aggressive and yet paranoid defense of traditional Catholicism.

On the other hand, the right side of the page bears the heading, "A la izquierda de Dios: 1967" (144). This fragment issues a plea to Catholics to open a sincere dialogue for possible changes within the institutional organization of the Church. Arguing that self-correction from within the Church does not constitute an impiety, the speaker "a la izquierda de Dios" contends that the Church must assume greater social responsibility. Each of these fragments, however, in one sense or another, pleads for social change and the use of the Church as a social institution for obtaining the power necessary for effective cultural domination. The headings for the 1967 fragments obviously suggest the political "rightist"-versus-"leftist" nature of the conflict. The end of the "leftist" side, however, points to a different perspective in which to evaluate the conflict: "¡Pobre Iglesia! ¡Pobre catolicismo a la mexicana: tan lejos de Cristo y tan cerca de la Virgen de Guadalupe!" (148).

The phenomenon of *guadalupismo* permeates *Redil de ovejas*. Perhaps grasped as simply a function of the recognizable cultural codes, it more importantly acts as a fundamental element of the social drama under consideration in the text. Notably, the 1961 anticommunist demonstration of the initial historical reference takes place at the Basilica of Guadalupe. Whereas the 1961 conflict mediated under the aegis of Guadalupe concerned a perceived Catholicism-versus-communism opposition, throughout Mexican history the Virgin of Guadalupe has appeared repeatedly, each time intimately tied to revolutions and social dramas. For example, during the Mexican Revolution Emiliano Zapata exploits the power of this cultural symbol when he leads his toops into battle under the banner of the Virgin of Guadalupe. Indeed, the anthropologist Victor Turner, in his study "Hidalgo: History as Social Drama," analyzes the semantics of the Virgin of Guadalupe as an integral function of the movement for Mexican independence in the the nineteenth century.[14] The anthropologist Eric R. Wolf even traces the importance of the Virgin of Guadalupe back to the time of her discovery.

According to Wolf, the Virgin of Guadalupe, miraculously appearing to the Christianized Indian Juan Diego on the Hill of Tepeyac in 1531 and addressing him in Nahuatl, explains the phenomenon of religious syncretism in Mexico. The Hill of Tepeyac housed the temple of the earth and fertility goddess, Tonantzín, in pre-Hispanic times. Tonantzín, Our Lady Mother, was easily identified with the Virgin, Our Lady of Guadalupe. The ardent following that Guadalupe had among the Christianized Indians served to confuse the differences between the religions. Wolf contends that the process of syncretism, continuing throughout Mexico's history, elevated the Virgin of Guadalupe to a Mexican master symbol.[15]

In *Redil de ovejas*, the vestiges of syncretism determine the Catholicism practiced by *beata* Rosita. Lois Grossman describes Rosita's faith by pointing out:

> . . . Leñero's portrayal of Rosita's inner world gives a fascinating insight into the way in which the basic tenets of the Catholic faith can be twisted and deformed, all unknowingly, into a sanctified mumbo-jumbo as primitive and appalling as the cult of Voodoo appears to a "civilized" western Christian.[16]

In this perspective, the worldliness of *Redil de ovejas* becomes more palpable. On the one hand, the politico-religious demonstration in the Basilica of Guadalupe repeats a pattern familiar to Mexican culture. On the other hand, the seemingly invented story of Rosita manifests the same level of worldliness to the degree that Mexican cultural symbolism saturates its plot. Moreover, the choice of the names Rosamaría and Bernardo is not totally gratuitous. First, Rosamaría combines two recognizable names, Rosa and María. The prevalence of María as a name in Hispanic cultures is largely attributable to the historical dominance of Catholicism and the adoration of the Virgin Mary. The notion of Virgin associated with María echoes of Guadalupe when combined with Rosa, for the apparition of Guadalupe was confirmed when she performed the miracle of making roses appear on the sterile hill of Tepeyac. Hence the name Rosamaría also reverberates with implications of the Virgin of Guadalupe.

On the other hand, the text itself comments on the symbolism of the name Bernardo. In a hagiography that appears twice, the story of Saint Bernard is explicated. The hagiography concludes with the following prayer:

> San Bernardo, melifluo doctor, modelo de la vida activa de Marta y de la contemplativa de María, acuérdate de todos nosotros ante Dios, a quien ves cara a cara, y ante tu bendita madre a quien contemplas ensalzada y coronada. Acuérdate especialmente de tantos hijos e hijas espirituales que profesan la misma regla benedictina que tú profesaste y se empeñan en copiar tus rasgos mediante la oración, el trabajo y la mortificación, de que son vivo y continuo ejemplo en medio de una sociedad sensual y materializada, que no ve en la cruz y en el divino crucificado sino a una locura y a un loco. (116-117; 119)

The fundamental dynamic of Saint Bernard arises from the rejection of a "sociedad sensual y materializada" (as the "leftist" faction of the Church implores) and the request for his help in a reevaluation of Christ. According to the prayer, society sees in Christ only "a una locura y a un loco." To the degree that *guadalupismo* is a preference of the indigenous apparition of the Virgin over the symbol of Christ, the invocation of Saint Bernard strategically intervenes as a possible corrective.

During the years between 1961 and 1967, Roman Catholicism underwent a dramatic process of liberalization. The Second Vatican Council, begun under Pope John XXIII, especially characterizes the liberal position of "Poner al día la Iglesia" (146). The corresponding process in Mexican Catholicism, in the wake of the Cuban Revolution, gave rise to serious social disturbances as portrayed in *Redil de ovejas*. In this perspective, the opposition between the Virgin of Guadalupe and Christ, between the symbolic value of Rosamaría and Bernardo, constitutes a schematic representation of the realignment of social and political values underway in Mexican culture. On the one hand, the liberal faction attempts to establish a greater social conscience. Historically they have accomplished this through the dramatic reinterpretations of the life of Christ associated with the Latin American development of liberation theology.[17] On the other hand, given Mexico's history of revolutions and their anti-Catholic results, the conservative faction lashes out against the social change encouraged by the liberals and the "bad" example of the Cuban Revolution in order to protect its perceived religious and social freedom. As a master symbol of traditional Mexican culture, the Virgin of Guadalupe offers the most convenient banner for uniting the conservative Catholics of Mexico.

Although I have highly dichotomized the exposition of the opposition between Guadalupe and Christ for the sake of clarity, the worldliness of *Redil de ovejas* resists such facile categorization. Indeed, an exact ideological center for the cultural criticism of the text is characterizable only in general terms. The irreducible nature of the critical cultural commentary is evident first of all in the names Bernardo and Rosamaría. Although these two names achieve a fairly definite semantization through the interpretation of their cultural symbolism as based on the relations to Christ (through Saint Bernard) and the Virgin of Guadalupe, the names also undergo a kind of desemantization throughout the text. The use of identical names makes reading *Redil de ovejas* a process of identifying qualities, actions, and moral values associated in specific contexts. This reading structure, the inverse of the usual function of a name in narratives, serves to attribute multiple and contradictory values to the signifiers Bernardo and Rosamaría. Just as the narrative phenomenon of repetition in the Bernardo-Rosita plot interacts with the historical panorama of the text in order to stimulate and expand the suggestivity of the two thematic zones, so the desemantization of the names Bernardo and Rosamaría acts reciprocally with the symbols of Christ and Guadalupe, not eliminating the signifying power of the names, nor even reducing it, but exploding the semantic horizon and thus producing a surplus of meaning not yet containable or organizable within the standard protocols of coherence. Amar Sánchez recognizes this aspect of the novel in commenting, "El juego ambiguo del texto, determinado por la pluralidad de personajes diferentes con el mismo nombre que desdibuja toda posible identidad definida, contradice cualquier pretensión de optar por significados precisos."[18]

In general, the ideological center of *Redil de ovejas* functions by providing surplus meaning. Although the conservative faction of the Church does accumulate certain negative associations, the portrayal of the liberalization of the Church by no means rises as the perspective in which everything must be interpreted. The ambivalence between the thematic zones, the fluctuation in narrative voice, and the dynamic use of cultural symbols all participate in the representation of a period of history in emergence. *Redil de ovejas* portrays the historical process of the social drama in multiple and dynamic perspectives, avoiding any teleology of events and yet emphasizing the phenomenon of repetition.

In several instances the text allegorically plays on the difficulty in describing its own ideological center. There is a fundamental ambiguity in *Redil de ovejas* as to the perspective in which one views something. The first chapter of the novel introduces the issue of perspective when the priest, later assumed to be Padre Bernardo, interprets the meaning of the stained-glass window.

> Era blanco el sayo de Jesús adolescente, y desfigurada y monstruosa la pequeña cabeza de uno de los tres doctores del templo que el artífice del vitral no había sabido dimensionar o que quizás, adrede, deformó para dar con ello una interpretación satírica de todo aquél que se consagra al cultivo de la inteligencia e ignora en su tarea que de nada vale desentrañar misterios, porque los únicos que ameritan el esfuerzo resultan inapresables para la mente humana. Así lo comprendían los doctores del templo. Para aquel adolescente casi niño no había misterios. Era una sola persona con su Padre creador de todo lo que ha sido hecho en el cielo y en la tierra. Hijo del Padre en el Espíritu Santo levantando su índice amarillo.
>
> Me sentí de pronto representado en el sabio deforme del vitral, cuya cabeza parecía desplazarse excéntrica al eje de ese cuerpo envuelto en una túnica morada y surcado por líneas de plomo en todas inclinaciones. Era mi retrato, pensé, mi propia caricatura. Yo mismo. (15)

The question of artifice failing to represent properly corresponds to the major category on which critics have dismissed *Redil de*

122

ovejas. Yet the text instantly adopts the attitude that it was purposive (*adrede*), presenting deformations and caricatures in order to criticize.

Whereas the stereotypes in chapter two correspond to the concept of purposive deformations and caricatures in the formation of a typology of the Mexican Catholic, chapter three reconsiders the window.

> El artífice del vitral tenía razón. Tiene razón.
>
> Pero levantó la vista, y al observar con más atención la colorida estampa se dio cuenta de que la cabeza del sabio no era en realidad excéntrica a su cuerpo. Si así lo parecía era tan sólo porque su actitutd de asombro ante lo que Jesús adolescente parecía indicarles con su índice en alto, lo obligaba a adoptar una postura en la que necesariamente la cabeza se inclinaba dejando atrás el tronco, pero sin separarse de él. Los pliegues de la túnica daban perfecta continuidad anatómica a la figura del sabio. El artífice no había cometido un error ni había querido expresar un sarcasmo. El único estúpido era él. (48)

Here Padre Bernardo learns the lesson of perspective. The meaning of the window was a function of his own perspective and the presuppositions necessary for validating it. On the one hand, the window does not deform the figure because of poor artifice. On the other hand, neither does it manifest a purposive caricature. The artifice is adequate, and the caricature was a function of the perceiver, not of the perceived object. The consciousness of easily deceived perception keeps the ideological center of *Redil de ovejas* in constant play. Moreover, it encourages readers to participate actively in the signifying structure of the novel. At every level ambivalence over a definite truth creates a tendency toward dispersion, the appearance of diversity within unity, while searching for unity within diversity.

The plurivocity of *Redil de ovejas* makes the worldliness of the text function in an active manner. The constant shifting of perspective combined with the insistent referentiality of the text further problematizes the concept of history. Primarily, the factor of perspective has already made evident the subjective nature of interpretation. In a later instance, however, the text again questions the notion of a definite truth lying behind reality. Describing Rosita's senility, the narrator writes:

> No conseguía reordenar escenas, diferenciar épocas, remodelar rostros y devolver nombres a los fantasmas que barajaba desordenadamente haciéndolos adoptar actitudes y desempeñar papeles que tal vez nunca les correspondieron en la realidad. (129)

In every case, the interpretation of reality functions as a quality attributed by the perception of the subjective conscience. Yet memory often "shuffles" the past, confusing the remembrance with the reality of the past. Given the importance of historical and narrative repetition in *Redil de ovejas*, the question of reality and its interpretation is vitally important. The text, however, maintains a constant skepticism toward the establishment of any absolute interpretations accepted as or believed to correspond to a true, definite, and unchanging reality.

The most constant ideological quality of the text is movement, the constant shift in perspective with a certain skepticism toward any static vision. The issue of repetition, however, implies a certain static model that time and again imposes itself on events and situations. In terms of the conflict between movement and stasis, then, the worldliness of *Redil de ovejas* manifests a great urgency for understanding and yet a mistrust of the capacity for understanding. Just as Padre Bernardo demeans himself before the stained-glass window, with either a correct or an incorrect interpretation, so also the memory of Rosita suffers a disease: "Probablemente un geriatra, luego de un cuidadoso examen, diagnosticara la existencia de un tumor cerebral que al obstruir las funciones evocativas la anclaba en un presente de situaciones sin historia, de efectos sin causas: amnesia senil. Probablemente" (131).

On the whole, *Redil de ovejas* evidences an overt consciousness of its worldly nature. The issue of historical and narrative repetition stands out as a major signifying structure of the text. Yet, to the degree that the social drama portrayed in the novel occurs in "un presente de situaciones sin historia, de efectos sin causa," so also the specific worldliness of *Redil de ovejas* gives rise to the criticism that the historical memory of culture is ineffective, it suffers a "tumor cerebral" or "amnesia senil." With regard to memory, *Redil de ovejas* formulates a critical cultural commentary: the repetition of unresolved conflicts arises from the inability to remember. Memory, however, is subject to the distortions and deformations of subjective perspectives. Hence arise the ironic desire to correct the errors of the past and thus escape the tyranny of repetition, and a skeptical attitude toward the possible attainment of such a desire.

III

Throughout this chapter I have attempted to demonstrate the worldliness of the text, the manner in which Leñero exploits the flexibility of the novel genre in order to embed *Redil de ovejas* in its socio-historical context as a critical portrayal of the cultural contradictions in Mexican Catholicism. In such a perspective, the text reveals a dynamic system of real and potential references to Mexican culture and history that are drawn out and made explicit in the act of reading and interepreting. Principally concerned with the issue of repetition, *Redil de ovejas* employs fragmentary and alternating patterns, both thematically and structurally, in order to represent the emergent nature of the narrative and historical processes under consideration. On the one hand, Leñero focuses on the conflicts between individual needs and the social roles imposed on the individual by the impersonal power of the institutional Church. On the other hand, the individual and social conflicts reflect broader confrontations at the cultural and historical level. The Church/State opposition and the liberalization of Catholicism in the 1960s repeat a pattern common to Mexican history. Contradictions and social dramas repeatedly emerge as traditional structures of cultural meaning and social organization fail to adapt to evolving historical circumstances.

The final formation of critical cultural commentary in *Redil de ovejas*, however, in no way asserts a dogma. While representing the inadequacy of cultural memory to resolve and escape from a repetitive pattern of contradictions and conflicts, the constant shift in interpretive perspectives avoids facile judgments. Moreover, the techniques of using stereotypical and similarly named characters eventually serve to expand the significations of the text past the boundaries of understanding contained by logical knowledge and categorization. Perhaps in this sense *Redil de ovejas* achieves its most profound effect, for it encourages readers to participate actively in the novel, almost rewriting the text in order to understand it, and hence directly confronting its worldliness. Yet the rewriting enacted by attentive readers produces both a recognizable critical cultural commentary and an irreducible knowledge of Leñero's Mexico, a worldliness that saturates the text but cannot be contained within its textuality.

Chapter Five:

Effective Translation, Effective Intervention:

Demystification as Textual Process

in *El evangelio de Lucas Gavilán*

Understanding liberation theology requires a certain act of imagination, a willingness to look at familiar happenings and figures in a different light, a readiness to recognize that those who are heroes for some will be villains to others. Liberation theology is part of a larger history of protest.

--Harvey Cox, *Religion in the Secular City: Toward a Postmodern Theology*

Now the critic's task is obviously first to understand (in this case understanding is an imaginative act) how the text was and is made. No details are too trivial, provided that one's study is directed carefully toward the text as a vital aesthetic and cultural whole. The critic therefore mimes or repeats the text in its extension from beginning to whole, not unlike Pierre Menard. . . . Only by reproducing can we know what was produced and what the meaning is of verbal production for a human being. . . .

--Edward W. Said, *The World, the Text, and the Critic*

El evangelio de Lucas Gavilán (1979) continues to address the fictions of representation that emerge in *Redil de ovejas*.[1] In this case, however, the novel focuses specifically upon the artifices involved in religious interpretation. Joint with this sharply focused thematic scope, *El evangelio de Lucas Gavilán* avoids the structural enigmas and complexities characteristic of the earlier novels; rather, at the level of technique it exploits an extreme simplicity. Such subtle use of narrative strategies produces an easily read text offering no major obstacles to understanding. Nevertheless, the simplicity is only apparent. John M. Lipski points out that in *El evangelio de Lucas Gavilán* "Leñero does not abandon his fondness for structural deviations and paradoxes; he has merely shifted the manipulation to a higher semiotic level. . . ."[2] The "shift" in *El evangelio de Lucas Gavilán* sets into play a process of demystification whereby the text lays bare its grounding *qua* text.

As a rewriting of the Gospel of St. Luke, the biographer Lucas Gavilán narrates the life of Jesucristo Gómez and demystifies modern Christologies according to the propositions of Latin American liberation theology. In this perspective, *El evangelio de Lucas Gavilán* constitutes a reading; that is, the writing of the text presupposes an act of imaginative reading, reinterpreting the biblical text and translating it to a contemporary setting. The events narrated by Lucas Gavilán follow the biography of Christ rendered in the Gospel of St. Luke. In contrast to the other Gospels, St. Luke's places greater emphasis on the poor, the sick, the oppressed and the individuals marginalized by society. Although the events and the focus of Jesucristo Gómez's social concerns make this parallel clear and justify the selection of St. Luke's Gospel over the others, the novel constantly evokes the prior version by following its subdivisions and by citing the eloquent, archaically phrased section headings found in the Jerusalem translation of the Bible. Readers of the translation confront a heterogeneous and multilayered text, reading not only the novel itself, but also the novel as a counter-text evoking the Gospel of St. Luke and its divers interpretations.

The multiple layers of reading produced by *El evangelio de Lucas Gavilán* demonstrate Leñero's abiding interest in the novel genre as an openly creative and innovative literary form. Rather than deriving from thematic or technical originality, however, in this novel creativity involves the act of translating. Translation sets into play the demystifying process of the text itself and of Christology, exposing the ideological nature of religious beliefs and practices. Indeed, the translation manifests that a text not only arises from an ideology but also generates one. Consonant with

Leñero's preoccupation with critical cultural commentary, then, the demystifying process of *El evangelio de Lucas Gavilán* proposes the possibility of Christianity as a socially responsible and critically conscious practice within the complexities of socio-political reality. In brief, *El evangelio de Lucas Gavilán* sets into play a dynamic process that demystifies its own textuality and, simultaneously, it reworks the tenets of Christology. Moreover, the process of demystification makes evident the affinities between Leñero's strategy of effective translation and the general strategies of deconstruction proposed by Jacques Derrida.

I

From the outset, the demystifying thrust of the novel emerges playing off against the underlying Christian Scripture and its surrounding tradition. The title evokes the biblical *Evangelio según San Lucas*, while modifying it in accordance with more contemporary usage (substitution of *de* for *según*). In addition, omitting the canonic title of San and adding the surname *Gavilán* opens the iconoclastic practice against Sacred Scripture. Indeed, the choice of *gavilán* as Lucas's surname goes against traditional Christian symbols and also refers to the act of writing. On the one hand, *gavilán* generally signifies "sparrow hawk," quite different from the preferred ornithological symbol of Christianity, the dove. On the other hand, a *gavilán* is a flourish of the pen in writing, or the point or sides of the nib of a pen, obliquely suggesting Lucas Gavilán's labor as a scribe or writer. Moreover, as if the iconoclasm of the humorous title were insufficient, a Gustave Doré engraving portraying a public book burning precedes the initial page of the novel.

The development of the text follows "con máximo rigor" (11) the Gospel of St. Luke, divided into seven chapters according to the major divisions of the Jerusalem Bible ("Nacimiento y vida oculta de Juan Bautista y de Jesús," "Preparación del ministerio de Jesús," "Ministerio de Jesús en Galilea," "Subida a Jerusalén,"

"Ministerio de Jesús en Jerusalén," "La pasión," and "Después de la resurrección"), and identifying each subsection with traditional headings, chapter, and verse references. As an introduction to the text, Lucas Gavilán includes a letter addressed to Teófilo, imitating the traditional prologue of St. Luke's text. As a part of the demystification process, Lucas Gavilán's "Prólogo" sets the tenor of the text and produces a series of forestructures that guide the interpretation of the novel.

In the "Prólogo" Lucas Gavilán acknowledges the worldliness of his effort, dating his letter "Mexico, D.F. Pascua de Resurrección de 1979" (13), and alluding to his present-day circumstances. In spite of the recognized proliferation of versions of the life of Christ in literature, cinema, and theater, he has decided to write his own version in accordance with the liberation theologians Jon Sobrino, Leonardo Boff, and Gustavo Gutiérrez, "las actuales corrientes de la teología latinoamericana" (11).[3] Most of all, however, Lucas Gavilán claims his greatest inspiration in the "trabajo práctico que realizan ya numerosos cristianos a contrapelo del catolicismo institucional . . ." (11). Thus, even from the first page, the text demystifies the reason for its own existence, and establishes an emergent oppositional, unorthodox stance in relation to the institutional Church that Lucas Gavilán portrays throughout the following pages.

Yet Lucas Gavilán not only relates to Teófilo his initial motivation; he also discloses his method and intention in writing his own *evangelio*. He proposes to

> . . . escribir esta paráfrasis del *Evangelio según San Lucas* buscando, con el máximo rigor, una traducción de cada enseñanza, de cada milagro y de cada pasaje al ambiente contemporáneo del México de hoy desde una óptica racional y con un propósito desmitificador. Mirado con criterios históricos, el intento resulta disparatado en su origen porque es imposible hallar equivalencias

lógicas de la época de Jesucristo a la concreta y muy compleja realidad nacional de los días en que vivimos. Sólo un alarde de cinismo literario podía forzar los hechos a tales extremos, pero no encontré una manera mejor de reescribir el evangelio de Lucas con estricta fidelidad a su estructura y a su espíritu. (11-12)

Hence Lucas Gavilán asserts both his "óptica racional" and "propósito desmitificador," overtly establishing ties with worldly circumstances ("ambiente contemporáneo del México de hoy," and "la concreta y muy compleja realidad nacional de los días que vivimos"). Although Lucas Gavilán points out the disparity between Palestine in the epoch of Jesus Christ and contemporary Mexico, the issue of translation must wrestle with the complexities of such temporal, geographical and cultural differences in a logical manner.

In reality, the problems of translation and logical equivalents are the dynamic force activating the demystifying impulse of the text. First, Lucas Gavilán openly states the relation of his text to the Biblical version of St. Luke. Much more than an oblique intertextuality or parody of the prior text, *El evangelio de Lucas Gavilán* stands as a reading of the Gospel of St. Luke, seeking the possible meanings that it might have for the present. In this regard, translation in *El evangelio de Lucas Gavilán* is an act of interpretation that recalls Edward W. Said's comments on the reader and critical understanding quoted at the beginning of this chapter: "Only by reproducing can we know what was produced and what the meaning is of verbal production for a human being. . . ."[4]

In this perspective, Leñero serves as a critic of the Gospel of St. Luke. In order to write his analysis of the biblical text, he invents a narrator-scribe, Lucas Gavilán. The text attributed to Lucas Gavilán reproduces St. Luke's version, carefully considering the Gospel as an aesthetic and cultural whole. The translation presupposes an imaginative understanding of the genesis of St. Luke's gospel, extending the range of reference of the prior text to contemporary Mexico and maintaining the relationship that Luke's text had with its contemporary circumstances. Whereas Pierre Menard eventually reproduces paragraphs from the *Quijote* word for word, Lucas Gavilán reproduces the worldliness of the biblical text, reducing the distance between contemporary Mexico and first-century Palestine through logical equivalents in their concrete and complex national realities. Leñero's novel begins the demystification of its textuality, then, by laying bare the criteria for the translation and by openly flaunting its preoccupation with the worldliness of texts, both itself and Sacred Scriptures.

In a different perspective, reading *El evangelio de Lucas Gavilán* also requires imaginative understanding as a process of repetition and mime. Just as Leñero's text stands beside the Gospel of St. Luke, repeating its worldliness, so readers of *El evangelio de Lucas Gavilán* follow the translation of Lucas Gavilán, miming how the text was and is made, extending its range of reference from beginning to whole, to the present of reading. In part, the simplicity of the text results from the manner in which Lucas Gavilán commences the hermeneutic act for readers. The *Prólogo* openly explains the manner in which the text was made, its coming-into-being as both a reading and a text. Hence interpretation of *El evangelio de Lucas Gavilán* must continue the hermeneutic processes begun by the text, not supplement it under the guise of demystifying that which the text itself demystifies.

On the other hand, understanding the way the text is made shifts the point of view to the nature of the translation. Given the radical results of such translation, it is useful to recall Harvey Cox's comments on liberation theology in *Religion in the Secular City: Toward a Postmodern Theology*, quoted above, which call for "a certain act of imagination, a willingness to look at familiar happenings and figures in a different light," an understanding that "liberation theology is part of a larger history of protest."[5]

Given that liberation theology casts a different light on *El evangelio de Lucas Gavilán*, the enigma of how Lucas Gavilán will translate each episode continues the demystifying process throughout the presentation of the life of Jesucristo Gómez. Indeed, as each section heading of the novel cites verbatim the polished, archaic style of the subtitles used in the Jerusalem Bible, readers face a constant uncertainty as to how the familiar happenings and figures will appear in their new setting. The unorthodox *imitatio Christi* represented by Jesucristo Gómez serves not only to demystify the text as text, constantly reminding readers of the text as translation, but also to demystify traditional Christologies.6

Before moving on to the topic of Christologies, however, it is important to note that at the level of textual demystification, the ideology of *El evangelio de Lucas Gavilán* begins to emerge. The constant allusion to the Gospel of St. Luke, the familiar beneath the unfamiliar, serves to foreground the question of translation. Moreover, the worldly circumstantiality of *El evangelio de Lucas Gavilán* adumbrates Leñero's text as part of a larger history of protest. It does not contradict the Gospel of St. Luke. Instead, as a critical search for valid meanings in the biblical text and significance in the life of Christ, *El evangelio de Lucas Gavilán* rises as a counter-text to other interpretations of Sacred Scripture.

First, the "Prólogo" speaks of Christian practices as "going against the grain of institutional Catholicism." The text illustrates this counter-textual aspect in two episodes wherein Jesucristo Gómez openly confronts the Church as institution. Parallel to Christ's ministry in his hometown of Nazareth, Jesucrito Gómez enters a church in his home village of San Martín el Grande, where:

> El padre Farías hablaba de la resignación cristiana:
> Dios vino al mundo, queridos hermanos, para enseñarnos a soportar las penas de la vida y para decirnos que allá en el cielo recibiremos la recompensa de su amor. Por eso, con una gran fe

en Dios y en su madre santísima debemos aceptar
las desgracias y tolerar nuestros sufrimientos
confiados siempre en la promesa divina de esa vida
perdurable que él nos vino a anunciar.

--¡Mentira! --Un trueno estalló en el sagrado
recinto. La voz potente de Jesucristo Gómez hizo
abrir de golpe los ojos de quienes dormitaban
aburridos y giró cabezas hacia la orilla izquierda del
presbiterio. El padre Farías respingó la espalda.
Los de las organizaciones piadosas se levantaron
de las bancas o se empinaron sobre los
reclinatorios. --¡Dios no vino a eso!--prolongó su
grito Jesucristo Gómez. . . . --Dios vino a proclamar
la libertad a los cautivos, a dar la vista a los ciegos y
la libertad a los oprimidos. Esto dice el Evangelio. . . .
--Vine a decir la verdad. . . . (65-67)

Throughout his life, Jesucristo Gómez continually combats the
fatalism that the priest proffered. In contrast to the resignation
typically endorsed by institutional Catholicism in Mexico,
Jesucrito proposes and lives a Christianity of action and liberation.

In a later episode Jesucristo Gómez formulates his objections
to institutional Catholicism in different terms. Recalling Christ's
statements against the pharisees and lawyers, Jesucristo Gómez
attends a dinner offered by the faculty of a seminary. Whereas the
various faculty members hope to entrap Jesucristo Gómez in his
own theology, he "turns the tables" on them. From the beginning
of the dinner everyone hurls insults at Jesucristo Gómez and he
refutes them point by point. Finally, the professor of "Doctrina
Social de la Iglesia" claims that Jesucristo Gómez has
misunderstood them. He believes that Jescristo Gómez's
complaints apply to the ecclesiastic hierarchy. "No somos
párrocos ni obispos, ni funcionarios de la Iglesia. Somos simple y
sencillamente estudiosos de la palabra de Dios, catedráticos,

intelectuales que no ambicionan más riqueza que la del espíritu" (166).

In response to the professor's defense, Jesucristo Gómez censures:

> --También culpo a los intelectuales. . . . De un mensaje clarísimo y directo han hecho un aparato ideológico aplastante. . . . Por defender dogmas absurdos y mantener su poder político, la Iglesia ha quemado santos y perseguido inocentes; ha combatido la ciencia, ha arrancado las alas al espíritu, ha empequeñecido a Dios. . . . Los intelectuales de la Iglesia se han robado las llaves de la verdad; no han entrado ustedes, pero tampoco han dejado entrar a los humildes. (166-167)

Through this episode with the intellectuals of the Church and the previous one with the local priest, Jesucristo Gómez evidences his objections to institutional Catholicism as an ideological manipulation designed to maintain the political power of the Church at the cost of oppressing the poor.

In this perspective *El evangelio de Lucas Gavilán* stands as a counter-text to other interpretations of Sacred Scripture. Whereas the text openly acknowledges its basis in an ideology and its generation of an ideology through the process of translation, it also imputes that other uses of Sacred Scripture both rise from and produce ideologies. And it is not that the ideological use of Sacred Scripture for gaining political control is wrong in and of itself; Jesucristo Gómez contends that other ideologies are wrong when they contribute to social and economic oppression, misusing Sacred Scriptures to maintain an unjust situation.

Furthermore, *El evangelio de Lucas Gavilán* also stands as a counter-text to the discourse of modern theology. Harvey Cox explains:

Modern theology was Christianity's answer to the modern age. It assumed a variety of expressions, from Friedrich Schleiermacher to Karl Barth, from Jacques Maritain to the Roman Catholic modernists, from Nicolai Berdyaev to Paul Tillich. In fact, some theologians would argue that the differences among these thinkers are so great, it is misleading to call them all "modern." However, these disparate modern theologians were all preoccupied with one common underlying question--how to make the Christian message credible to what they understood as the modern mind.[7]

In contrast to modern theologies that make Christianity intelligible to a modern, secular society, Jesucristo Gómez never minces words over doctrine. For him Christianity is not a matter of systematic doctrines coherently contained within a dogma of interpretation. Jesucristo Gómez argues:

Si yo hablo de Dios y su justicia, y por seguir a Dios y trabajar por la justicia la gente se aleja del Dios que ustedes predican, eso quiere decir, o al menos así lo entiendo, que ustedes y su sociedad y sus intereses han hecho de Dios una idea al servicio de las situaciones injustas. Han ensuciado su imagen. Han puesto las verdades de cabeza. . . . Pero ya es tiempo de enderezarlo todo y devolverle a Dios su verdadero sentido. (160-161)

Historically, the adjustment of Christianity to a secular society followed the division of labor typical of industrialization, relegating questions of the spirit to religion. Meanwhile, science assumed the task of explaining the physical world, and even the socio-political world through the rise of social sciences: economics, political economy, political science, sociology, etc.[8] As a counter-text to modern theology, *El evangelio de Lucas Gavilán* stands in opposition to such a division of labor. In this sense the "aparato ideológico aplastante" of modern theology is its rendering ineffective the potentially positive, formative role of religion in culture. As portrayed in *El evangelio de Lucas Gavilán*, modern theology errs not in doing something wrong, but in not doing anything socially useful.

Harvey Cox points out that the "'liberation method' is political from the outset. It rejects the notion that there can be any neutral theology or any detached understanding of who Jesus was and is."[9] Indeed, the principal demystification of *El evangelio de Lucas Gavilán* is that as a text it both presupposes and generates a political and oppositional ideology. Moreover, in laying bare its own textual grounding as ideology, it rises as a counter-text evoking other interpretations of the Gospel of St. Luke, protesting their ineffectiveness in accounting for the nature of their own worldliness. Hence the translations of *El evangelio de Lucas Gavilán* are effective to the degree that they successfully account for the worldliness and ideological nature of other texts and interpretations. In addition, the process of demystifying multiple texts, including itself, must maintain the effectiveness of the translations through a critical and self-aware production of an alternative ideological position.

Through the practice of effective translation, *El evangelio de Lucas Gavilán* opposes the isolation of religion from mainstream cultural and political life. Indeed, this opposition is not unique to Leñero's text or Latin American liberation theology. The spread of liberation theology to Asia and Africa has become a major form of social reorganization at a grass roots level. Moreover, the formation of Christian base communities has exerted considerable political force in Holland, East Germany, and Italy, especially with respect to labor and nuclear arms issues. On the other hand, the conservative, politically oriented religious revival in the United States beginning in the late 1970s attests to the return of religion to the secular city. Furthermore, the renewed interest in religion is not a specifically Christian phenomenon. The recent past has witnessed the political leverage wielded by resurgent Islam in Iran and the combative power of the Sikhs in northern India. Indeed, for years the Zionist movement of Israel and the protestant-Catholic conflicts of Ireland have given evidence that religion does not wither away with technological progress and modernization.

The common factor uniting these various religious movements is a desire to reconquer some part of a political power that such groups had at one time relinquished in the face of contemporary secularization. "Human societies," writes Harvey Cox, "will always have some 'religion.' The task of postmodern theology, therefore, is not to work out a 'religionless' interpretation of Christianity but to recover the real purpose of Christianity from its modern debasement into a conscious means of personal self-discipline and social control."[10]

In this light, Edward Said's move toward the development of a secular critical consciousness underestimates the role of religion in culture. Whereas the introduction to *The World, the Text, and the Critic* bears the title "Secular Criticism," proposing the interrelations of critical inquiry, culture, State, and secular society beyond the closure of religious beliefs, the concluding chapter, "Religious Criticism," manifests a hesitancy in regard to the resurgence of religion throughout the world. According to Said, the religious revival in contemporary society and in criticism "expresses an ultimate preference for the secure protection of systems of belief (however peculiar those may be) and not for critical activity or consciousness."[11]

Undoubtedly many contemporary religious movements do prefer security to critical activity or consciousness. Said's judgments, however, cannot be taken categorically. *El evangelio de Lucas Gavilán*, liberation theology in general, and much contemporary feminist theology all manifest an inquisitive compulsion toward the development of critical activity that is thoroughly compatible with the work of Said. However, in contrast with Said's compartmentalization of religion away from secular culture, these "new" theologies, or postmodern theology in the words of Harvey Cox, attempt to carry out Said's basic theorem of critical positioning, to stand between culture and system. Indeed, Said's explanation (in "Secular Criticism") of what such critical positioning means, applies equally to the Christianity of postmodern theology and *El evangelio de Lucas Gavilán.*

> To stand between culture and system is therefore to stand close to--a closeness itself having a particular value for me--a concrete reality about which political, moral, and social judgments have to be made and, if not made, then exposed and demystified. If, as we have recently been told by Stanley Fish, every act of interpretation is made possible and given force by an interpretive community, then we must go a great deal further in showing what situation, what historical and social configuration, what political interests are concretely entailed by the very existence of social communities.[12]

The effective translations of *El evangelio de Lucas Gavilán* are designed to develop a critical consciousness, to demystify the interests of its own textuality, Sacred Scripture, and other uses and interpretations of Sacred Scripture. For Jesucristo Gómez the practice of Christianity is political and compromisingly ideological at its base; yet this is not a closed and secure system of beliefs. It demands a great risk and self-awareness, risking even life itself in opposition to injustice. Moreover, as I will explain shortly, the general strategy of such Christianity, in its attempt to maintain oppositional force, closely resembles the general strategy of deconstruction.

In summary, one of the dominant mechanisms of signification in *El evangelio de Lucas Gavilán* is the textual process of demystification. The iconoclasm against the received traditions of Christianity and modern interpretations of Sacred Scripture exposes the worldly and ideological nature of all texts. Furthermore, the physical artifact of the book *El evangelio de Lucas Gavilán* manifests its opposition to a romanticized reading of the Bible. Exhibiting a polychromatic depiction of the "Leyenda de San Lucas del Evangelio" (1368) by Johannes von Troppau on the cover, the rest of the book mimics the nineteenth-century Bible illustrated by Gustave Doré. The public book burning of the frontispiece is an ironic emblem, however, as are the Doré engravings that introduce each chapter of the novel. In opposition to the filtered, romantic depiction of the Holy Birth by Doré, in the first chapter of the novel María Gómez gives birth to Jesucristo in the patio of a tenement in the red-light district of Mexico City. Lucas Gavilán spares no details when he describes the dirty mattress, the smells of filth that permeate the air, or the rats that scurry from the trash heaps where José Gómez places the bedding. Moreover, in contrast to the heroic pathos evoked by Doré's interpretation of the Crucifixion, Lucas Gavilán describes the abandonment of Jescristo Gómez, tortured like a political prisoner, eventually rendered unconscious with a *picana eléctrica*, and finally expiring in a puddle of blood and vomit on the floor on a police transport van. Throughout the novel Leñero practices demystification in a similar fashion, translating each episode of the Gospel of St. Luke into a contemporary setting so that the worldliness of the pre-text and its interpretations becomes more evident.

As the text itself begins the process of imaginative understanding for readers, it not only demystifies its own textuality, and that of Sacred Scripture and its interpretations, it also rises as a counter-text, standing in opposition to the ideologically repressive nature of both institutional Catholicism and modern theology. Yet, just as *El evangelio de Lucas Gavilán* exposes the interests of the various uses of Sacred Scripture, it in no manner pretends to hide its own ideological bias, its interest in combatting social injustice. In this perspective, the choice of the Gospel of St. Luke as a pre-text for Lucas Gavilán's narration is not gratuitous. Beyond the issues of literary style and structural integrity, Jorge von Ziegler writes that, compared with the other Synoptic Gospels, "la originalidad de Lucas consiste en subrayar que Jesucristo ha venido a liberar a los oprimidos de su época, y entiéndase que los oprimidos son los pobres, las mujeres, los enfermos, los extranjeros y los pecadores."[13]

In the final analysis, *El evangelio de Lucas Gavilán* demonstrates that texts and interpretations are worldly. Demystification underscores the manner in which such worldliness also presupposes an ideological interest, for texts and interpretations attempt to validate and authorize a specific position in the world. Nevertheless, beyond the demystificatory recognition of these facts, the effective translation of *El evangelio de Lucas Gavilán* also generates an ideological view of Christianity as a self-critical and socially responsible practice. In its attempts to avoid the enclosure of Christianity within blind dogma, it is at the level of Christology that *El evangelio de Lucas Gavilán* demystifies the social nature of religion.

II

The argument continues today. The centuries-long battle over how to answer the question "Who do you say I am?" is in part a debate between those who want to control the meaning of Jesus because they recognize his political significance all too well.

--Harvey Cox, *Religion in the Secular City: Toward a Postmodern Theology*

Christology is "that aspect of theology which deals with how one is to understand the significance of Christ. . . ."[14] Indeed, two of the liberation theologians cited by Lucas Gavilán in the Prólogo have written Christological studies: Leonardo Boff's *Jesus Cristo Libertador: Ensaio de Cristologia para o nosso Tempo* (1972), and Jon Sobrino's *Cristología desde América latina (esbozo a partir del seguimiento del Jesús histórico)* (1976). In reference to liberation theology (and pertinent to *El evangelio de Lucas Gavilán*), Harvey Cox writes:

> For liberation theology the principal objective of christological thought is not to make sure this or that formulation is conceptually aligned with one of the orthodox confessions. It is to determine how a given formulation actually contributes to the coming of the kingdom, and this is a question to which people other than Christians can contribute. Words mean different things at different times and in different settings. The same christological title that once clarified the meaning of Jesus and signaled the coming of the New Era can now distort the original meaning. Therefore theologians must always ask how, by whom, and for what purposes various christological images are used. The most difficult continuing critical task of Christology is to prevent the misuse of ideas about Jesus to thwart his purpose, stifle his emancipatory message, and control the people among whom he was and is opening God's reign.[15]

The life of Jesucristo Gómez exemplifies the issues to which Cox alludes in this passage. The question of "contributing to the coming of the kingdom" guides Jesucristo Gómez in his continual drive toward effective intervention in his society.

Although the level of textual demystification wrestles with "how, by whom, and for what purposes various christological images are used," the *imitatio Christi* of Jesucristo Gómez actually offers an image of a critical and self-aware Christian practice. Although Harvey Cox comments on the "original meaning" of Jesus, *El evangelio de Lucas Gavilán* manifests the multiplicity of *meanings* of the Gospel of St. Luke. Through the imaginative acts of reading, understanding and translating, Lucas Gavilán reveals in Jesucristo Gómez the potential significations of the life of Christ.[16]

In reference to *El evangelio de Lucas Gavilán*, John M. Lipski comments that "the paradox resides in the fact that the life of Jesus is being related at two different points in history, presumably as two separate events, and yet, strangely enough, the characters in the second 'incarnation' live in the Christian era in Mexico, and are aware of the life of the original Jesus Christ."[17] In contrast, however, I believe the text ultimately resolves this paradox.

The final chapter of the novel, "Después de la resurrección," patently deals with the question of Christ's being-in-the-world, even after his death. The following comments aim at formulating the manner of Christ's being-in-the-world as depicted through the life and death of Jesucristo Gómez. As I hope to demonstrate, the guiding principle for Jesucristo Goméz's actions and for Lucas Gavilán's translations is a deconstructive approach to injustice. Such a formulation will clarify how the prescriptive nature of theology arising from the ideology of *El evangelio de Lucas Gavilán* does not solidify into an orthodox dogma, but has the potential value of becoming a critical and self-aware social practice. Additionally, the recognition of such a practice resolves the paradox of Christ's presence at two distinct points in history.

First of all, beyond the ideological bias toward the Gospel of St. Luke because of its emphasis on the liberation of the poor, the pre-text of *El evangelio de Lucas Gavilán* possesses distinct formal qualities that allow for its artistic reelaboration by Leñero. St. Luke's version is structured around the nonredundant presentation of episodes of the life of Christ. In addition to the closure he gives to each episode, Luke establishes a mythic pattern for Christ's journeys: he travels throughout Israel and eventually arrives at the political center of the day, Jerusalem, where he dies and is resurrected. Such a heroic pattern is readily translatable to contemporary novel form.

In every detail Lucas Gavilán successfully translates the life of Christ into contemporary Mexico; and he does so in a manner that emphasizes the worldly situation of Jesucristo Gómez. Born in Mexico City in 1942, Jesucristo Gómez begins his activities in the late 1970, "los últimos años del sexenio presidencial del licenciado Luis Echeverría o en los primeros del licenciado José López Portillo . . ." (49). During the short time that Jesucristo Gómez performs his activities he travels throughout the Mexican republic and eventually arrives in Mexico City where he dies.

The activities of Jesucristo Gómez correspond to the miracles and teachings of Christ. Yet through the rational optic of liberation theology, readers see Jesucristo Gómez accomplish goals humanly feasible. The success of Jesucristo Gómez depends on his undying faith in humankind: "--La gente siempre responde cuando se lucha desinteresadamente por la justicia--. . ." (148). Nevertheless, the exact actions of Jesucristo Gómez and his results are always unpredictable in translation. Although readers face the multilayered effect of the familiar beneath the unfamiliar, no formula permits an exact foreknowledge of how the episode will be translated. As the counter-textual nature of the novel emerges, generating a worldly vision of Christian practice, readers will often have the experience of being off-balance, having to readjust expectations in order to understand what Jesucristo Gómez is doing and why he does so.

For example, the section "Resurrección del hijo de la viuda de Naím (7, 11-17)" deals with the widow Genoveva Galindo de Nares. After the death of everyone in her family, she mourns so much that her wailing becomes the principal entertainment of the village. "Vamos a ver llorar a Genoveva, se decía ya por el pueblo, y lo que en un principio había sido un sentimiento de compasión vecinal se transformó en un motivo para inventar chistes crueles" (100).

Finally, a certain Dr. Dorantes takes Jesucristo Gómez to visit the widow.

Given the important role of motherhood in Hispanic culture and the Mexican vision of death, one might expect Jesucristo Gómez to have the gift of finding the words of compassion that would soothe the sufferings of the widow. Instead, Jesucristo Gómez intervenes with a dramatic command: "--¡Trabajar!---interrumpió Jesucristo Gómez con un grito que cogió desprevenido al doctor Dorantes y lo hizo soltar su maletín--. ¡Trabajar!" (101). As the widow begins to sob, Jesucristo Gómez shakes her "como a una mula atascada" and continues: "--¡Tu hijo no está muerto, estúpida! La que ha estado muerta eres tú. Siempre atenida a tu esposo, a tu padre, a tu hijo. ¡Floja, inútil, miedosa, inservible, muerta!" (101). And finally, Jesucristo Gómez explains: "--¡Nadie va a vivir por ti!, ¡nadie va a perder su tiempo compadeciéndote! . . . ¡Tienes la fuerza de tu hijo, la sangre de tu hijo, el alma de tu hijo! Compréndelo, mujer. ¡Levántate, con un carajo! ¡Vive!" (102).

In this scene the text alludes to the stereotypes of compassion and kindness when Dr. Dorantes is taken aback by Jesucristo Gómez's words and actions. However, Jesucristo Gómez's anger effectively restores the widow to social life. In this perspective, the teaching is double. On the one hand, total dependency on others for meaning in life is wrong. On the other hand, kindness does not always appear in the expected form; whereas Dr. Dorantes sees Jesucristo Gómez as an "energúmeno capaz de cachetear a una mujer indefensa" (101), true compassion resides in his success in bringing the widow back into society, no longer "una mujer indefensa."

Throughout the novel, readers find the common virtues of Christianity translated into surprisingly unfamiliar terms. Each episode evokes the enigma of how the translation will work. Yet readers never learn the lesson well enough to predict Jesucristo Gómez's action. Furthermore, the disciples, the *pepenadores de hombres*, have an equally difficult time learning to imitate their *maestro*.[18]

In the episode of "El endemoniado epiléptico (9, 37-43)," Santiago el de Aguascalientes and Simón Vázquez arrive in Salvatierra ahead of Jesucristo Gómez. In the town, one of the families has a homosexual son.

> Fue la desgracia de la familia, la deshonra, el acabose. Su padre se dio a la bebida y empezó a desatender los negocios. Sus hermanos reprobaban en la escuela y a su hermana que tenía dos años menos no quisieron darle trabajo en la presidencia municipal porque en tu familia hay un puto: contó que le dijeron. Sólo las Ramírez y su madre Eloísa se compadecían de Marito y lo seguían tratando muy bien . . . . (137-138)

With the news of the arrival of the *pepenadores*, Marito's mother runs to see them, hoping they can "cure" her son. However, when the *pepenadores* go to visit Marito and to share with him their ideas about "las injusticias sociales" (138), their strategy proves useless: "el muchacho se burló de ellos apenas escuchó la palabra injusticia. Incluso exageró sus amaneramientos y se puso a chulear a Santiago el de Aguascalientes" (139). Only after Jesucristo Gómez arrives in Salvatierra does the situation take a significant turn.

Before meeting up with the disciples, Jesucristo Gómez finds Marito's drunken father who relates the entire story to him. In response, Jesucristo Gómez tells the father that Marito's homosexuality is not a punishment from God. Instead, he claims that it is the father's responsibility and, in order to remedy the situation, that the father should not make his homosexual son feel like "un anormal ni un vicioso" (140). The conversation closes when Jesucristo points out the only real problem is that "todos lo desprecian" (140).

Jesucristo Gómez later meets Marito; rather than "echándole un discurso," he asks Marito to play guitar and to sing for him. Marito does so and then explains that his problems would be solved if his father would give him six hundred *pesos*, allowing him to go to Guanajuato where he has been invited to join a rock group. The father, however, has not only refused him the money but also threatened to kill him if he goes.

Jesucristo Gómez convinces the father to give Marito the money and explains: "--El que necesita enderezarse es usted, compadre . . ." (141). The father then gives Marito the money so that he can leave for Guanajuato. Later the *pepenadores* comment on the episode with Jesucristo Gómez.

> --La regamos, ¿verdad?
> --Quisimos agarrar la cosa por el lado del compromiso. Por eso tratamos de hablarle de las injusticias sociales y de la marginación.
> Un camión de redilas se detuvo. Antes de subir a la zona de carga, Jesucristo dijo:
> --Sólo que aquí el marginado era él. (141)

Whereas the *pepenadores* believe that they were imitating the actions of Jesucristo Gómez, he teaches them that they had not learned to understand the nature of social injustice. On the one hand, the *pepenadores* start from the presupposition that homosexuality is wrong. In contrast, Jesucristo Gómez merely accepts Marito as he is, demanding that he receive the opportunities in life that anyone would have, regardless of sexual preference.

In the cases of both the widow and the homosexual, the motivation to action is both a desire to correct social injustice and a keen interpretation of the social situation in which Jesucrito Gómez must intervene. Whereas the *pepenadores* firmly believe that injustice is wrong and must be eliminated, they have not yet learned how to interpret effectively the social situation and to intervene responsibly. Contrary to Jesucristo Gómez, the *pepenadores* approach the concept of injustice as if it were a concrete entity, a fixed principle of social organization they must eradicate. For Jesucristo Gómez, on the other hand, injustice arises as a fluid and almost imperceptible play of social differences, at times demanding an acutely critical conscience in order to trace its workings.

In Jesucristo Gómez's attempts to live an authentic Christianity, his insight into the nature of Christ's example produces his critical conscience, allowing him to intervene effectively in situations of social injustice. Such insight, I contend, bears a close resemblance to deconstructive theory. In Derridean terms, the actions of Jesucristo Gómez demonstrate that injustice, rather than being a fixed, positive element in society, arises from a play of differences that suppresses the recognition of certain absences. In the cases of the widow and the homosexual, injustice implies a hierarchization of values, privileging one set of values at the expense of the other set.

When confronting the widow, Jesucristo Gómez effectively intervenes by recognizing the problem of social dependency. The accepted norms of a patriarchal society require the secondary positioning of women in relation to men. Thus, the loss of father, husband, and son separates the widow from society. Moreover, such dependency had left the widow unprepared to assume responsibility for her own life. In this light, Jesucristo Gómez must intervene in a situation of multiple injustices: the inequities of a patriarchal society, the burden of self-serving dependence on others, and the weakness of never having asserted one's rights as a social being. In each of these instances, the widow holds the undervalued position in the oppositional hierarchy. The solution proposed by Jesucristo Gómez overturns the hierarchy, "¡Trabajar!" (101). He accuses the widow of choosing dependency, daring her to accept responsibility for discovering meaning in her existence. In so doing, Jesucristo Gómez also combats the other injustices, urging her to enter a patriarchal society oppositionally, independent of men and searching for strength within her own being. It is to be noted that such an intervention does not merely reverse the hierarchy nor place the widow in a privileged position. It places her on a level of responsible equality which she must strive to maintain.

In the case of the homosexual, Jesucristo Gómez repeats the same general strategy. The issue of the propriety of homosexuality becomes a moot point. As a human being Marito has the right to the same opportunities that all members of society enjoy. Nevertheless, because of the importance society gives to sexual preference, Marito holds a secondary position in the dominant hierarchy. Whereas the father interprets Marito's homosexuality as a punishment from God or an inherent deviation, Jesucristo Gómez overturns the hierarchy by pointing out that the family is the source of Marito's homosexuality. The intervention, however, does not end by reassigning guilt within a closed system of balances. Successful correction of the injustice includes the father's giving Marito money and approval to leave town and work. In this perspective, Marito will stand on a socially equal grounding with others, now free to contribute to society and responsible for defending his freedom.

In each of these cases, Jesucristo Gómez's strategy of intervention parallels step by step Jacques Derrida's "general strategy of deconstruction" as outlined in *Positions*. Although Derrida principally deconstructs the tradition of Western metaphysics, he aslo underscores the political implications of such analyses. It is this politicized aspect of deconstruction that Jesucristo Gómez illustrates as he continually intervenes in situations of social injustice. The similarities in procedure between Derrida and Jesucristo Gómez are striking. Derrida points out that deconstruction must proceed by a double gesture. The first gesture is

> . . . a phase of overturning. To do justice to this
> necessity is to recognize that in a classical

> philosophical opposition we are not dealing with the peaceful coexistence of a vis-a-vis, but rather with a violent hierarchy. One of the two terms governs the other. . . . To deconstruct the hierarchy, first of all, is to overturn the hierarchy at a given moment. To overlook this phase of overturning is to forget the conflictual and subordinating structure of opposition. Therefore one might proceed too quickly to a *neutralization* that *in practice* would leave the previous field untouched, leaving no hold on the previous opposition, thereby preventing any means of intervening in the field effectively.[19]

With both the widow and Marito, Jesucristo Gómez first recognized the "violent hierarchy" that produced injustice. Overturning placed the widow in the position of responsibility (previously occupied by the men on whom she depended) and the parent's in the position of fault (for Marito's homosexuality). At this point in Jesucristo Gómez's intervention, and in a deconstruction, the hierarchy remains, but inverted.

The second gesture of a deconstruction must follow. As long as the inverted hierarchy stands, the analysis operates "on the terrain of and from within the deconstructed system. . . . We must also mark the interval between inversion, which brings low what was high, and the irruptive emergence of a new 'concept,' a concept that can no longer be, and never could be, included within the previous regime."[20] Jesucristo Gómez makes his intervention effective by "marking the interval" of the inversion. In the case of both the widow and the homosexual, after the initial inversion of the hierarchy, each is brought equal with society, enjoying the freedom of and responsibility for maintaining their "new" social status. It should be noted that, in a deconstruction, the gesture of overturning "is the necessity of an interminable analysis: the hierarchy of dual oppositions always reestablishes itself."[21] This

comment looms pessimistically over the ultimate goals of
Jesucristo Gómez, especially in light of the history of repression in
human society. Nevertheless, the perhaps temporary and finite
results of Jesucristo Gómez's "deconstruction" never appear
quixotic; such limitation constitutes the necessity for his
interminable social labor.

Jesucristo Gómez's principal preoccupation, however,
attempts the laborious deconstruction of the hierarchy of the rich
over the poor. Even as a child, Jesucristo Gómez plagued his
parents with the question, "--¿Por qué hay ricos y por qué hay
pobres?" (40). Indeed, even before his birth, María decided on the
name of Jesucristo for this reason:

> "--Jesucristo vino a defender a los pobres y a
> luchar contra las injusticias. Maldijo a los ricos.
> Combatió a los explotadores. Dio su vida para
> cambiar este mundo . . . Por eso quiero que mi hijo
> se llame Jesucristo . . ." (24).

In the case of the hierarchy of the rich over the poor, however, the
deconstructive practice of Jesucristo Gómez carries its most
profound implications. First, Jesucristo Gómez preaches an
overturning. Reinscription of the inverted hierarchy, however,
merely results in another unjust situation. The true dilemma
resides in how to "mark the interval between inversion," creating a
context of economic justice that "can no longer be, and could never
be, included within the previous regime." The only references to
this ultimate deconstruction underscore the difficult and still
distant time of its realization. Speaking to the *pepenadores*,
Jesucristo Gómez remarks:

> --La justicia va llegando sin dejarse sentir. No es
> que alguien diga: ya se ve por allá, o ya viene por
> acá. De hecho la justicia ya está entre ustedes. . . .
> Entonces aprendan a distinguir quién tiene la

razón y de qué cuero salen más correas. No
confundan a cualquier merolico con un líder de la
causa. Los líderes no se dan en maceta. Yo más
bien les garantizo que no volverán a ver otro hasta
el momento del cambio total. Y para ese cambio
todavía falta tiempo; antes van a sufrir muchos
desgracias, mucha represión. El cambio no se dará
pacíficamente. Costará muchas vidas. Habrá
guerras y se desatará la violencia contra todos los
que traten de conservar sus bienes y sus
privilegios. Pero abusados, óiganme bien: todo el
que trate de salvar su vida la perderá, y el que la
pierda la salvará. (209-210)

Although these comments point to Jesucristo Gómez's failing to
achieve a universal deconstruction of injustice in his own life, such
failure paradoxically leads to the understanding of the significance
of Christ's being-in-the-world and the *imitatio Christi* observed in
Jesucristo Gómez. Moreover, it also leads to the resolution of the
paradox of Christ's presence at two distinct points in history as
pointed out by John M. Lipski.

Immediately following the death of Jesucristo Gómez, the
pepenadores and his various followers lose their confidence, feeling
incompetent to continue their struggle wihout a leader. First,
María Magdalena, Juana Morales and María la de Santiago go to
the Panteón de Dolores to search for the common grave where the
authorities supposedly disposed of Jesucristo Gómez's body.
Having no success in locating the cadaver, they ask a gravedigger if
he knows where to find the body. He responds: "--Para mí esos
hombres no mueren nunca. . . . Pueden matarlos pero no se
mueren. Al contrario, siguen cada día con más vida, como quien
dice" (301). Although the phrase "como quien dice" openly qualifies
the preceding sentence as figurative, the women report it literally
to the *pepenadores*.

--Nos dijeron que el maestro estaba vivo.

--Que seguía caminando.

--¿Eso les dijeron?

Juana Morales buscó apoyo en María Magdalena y María la de Santiago:

--Eso mismo, ¿verdad?

--No puede ser. El señor Artime está muy enterado de todo.

--Pues eso nos dijeron.

--A lo mejor resucitó.

--¡No seas pendeja!--gritó Santiago el de Aguascalientes a su esposa.

Los discípulos no quisieron seguir discutiendo con las mujeres, pero esa misma tarde Pedro Simón fue al Panteón de Dolores.

No encontró a los sepultureros ni en las oficinas le supieron informar. Tristón, cariacontecido, se echó a caminar por las callecitas, entre las tumbas, y entonces comprendió. (301-302)

Whereas the three women had made the mistake of believing only in a literal Jesucristo Gómez of flesh and blood, Pedro Simón finally understands another significance in the life and death of Jesucristo Gómez.

The novel further elaborates this significance in the next episode. Santiago Zepeda and his brother Juancho leave town to avoid the police after the death of Jesucristo Gómez. A stranger on the bus overhears their conversation, and contrary to their despair, he explains: "El mismo les avisó que lo iban a agarrar y a convertir en un chivo expiatorio . . . Ahora es cuando su muerte coge sentido. Está clarísimo" (304). After the stranger disappears from their home in Yecapixtla, the Zepeda brothers decide to return to Iztapalapa immediately. Upon arriving they seek out Pedro Simón "y le explicaron su decisión de no echar todo a la basura, de seguir para adelante, de no permitir que el grupo se desmoronara . . ."

(305). Jesucristo Gómez lives after death to the degree that the various followers continue his activities.

Nevertheless, Pedro Simón and the Zepeda brothers cannot convince the other *pepenadores* of their understanding. The others still want a leader. During the private meeting where they discuss the issue, the stranger who earlier met the Zepeda brothers silently enters. Shocked by his sudden appearance, all but Pedro Simón and the Zepeda brothers suspect him of being a police spy. Nevertheless, the stranger tells them: "El único modo de hacer que Jesucristo no se muera es continuando su obra . . ." (306). Although the stranger refuses to become their leader, Tomás Carrillo insists on knowing who he is and what he does. His response stirs up a frenzy of insults and accusations.

> --Trabajo con la gente, en los pueblos, donde me necesitan-- respondió el hombre--. Soy sacerdote.
> --¿Sacerdote?
> La palabra cayó como una palada de tierra en las brasa de una fogata. El primero en gritar fue Tomás Carrillo, pero al rato ya casi todos estaban insultando al señor de las mandarinas.
> --Al maestro le fue como le fue por culpa de los curas.
> --Son unos desgraciados.
> --Infelices.
> --Bola de hipócritas.
> --No me juzguen por lo que soy sino por lo que hago--replicó el hombre, puesto en pie, cuando Pedro Simón llegó a su lado y lo encaminó hacia la puerta.
> La escandalera continuaba.
> --Perdone usted, pero es mejor que se vaya--dijo Pedro Simón empujándolo suavemente. Con la cabeza señaló a sus compañeros y agregó, en voz muy baja: --Ahorita los ve así porque no es para

menos, pero ya entendimos que el maestro no está
muerto. Y eso es lo importante.
--Sí--dijo el hombre, tranquilo.
Se dio la media vuelta y salió a la noche. (307-
308)

As Pedro Simón points out, the *pepenadores* finally realize that the
meaning of Jesucristo Gómez's life and death is that he lives
through the continuation of his work by others. Nevertheless, the
pepenadores do not fully comprehend that there is more than one
way to continue the life of Jesucristo Gómez. The *maestro* had
directed his anticlerical criticism against the abuses of
institutional Catholicism. The stranger, however, manifests that a
clergy can also practice the critical and socially responsible
Christianity of Jesucristo Gómez.

Furthermore, the priest explicitly directs judgment away
from the hierarchization of social roles and toward one's actions:
"No me juzguen por lo que soy sino por lo que hago . . ." (307).
Earlier Jesucristo Gómez had responded to the issue of the
manners in which one may be a Christian. When questioned about
the divisions within the Church, and about which interpretation of
the Gospel is correct, Jesucristo Gómez responded: "El Evangelio
se cumple o no se cumple, no hay otra" (179). After repeatedly
refuting his interlocutor, Jesucristo Gómez explains:

> --Cuando triunfe la justicia de Dios no se va a
> medir a nadie por su fe, sino por sus obras. Y tenga
> la seguridad de que habrá muchos creyentes que
> serán acusados de haber entorpecido la justicia, y
> muchos incrédulos que serán reconocidos como
> creyentes por haber favorecido la justicia de la que
> habla el Evangelio.
> --Ahí es donde está precisamente el problema,
> maestro. Una cosa es la justicia de Dios y otra cosa
> es la justicia a secas.

> --No hay más que una justicia. . . . Lo único que
> puedo decirle y hasta jurarle es que hay ateos más
> cristianos que los cristianos, y cristianos más
> ateos que los ateos.
> --Eso es pura semántica, maestro.
> --Tampoco sé mucho de esa cosa--sonrió
> Jesucristo Gómez, y dio por terminada la
> discusión. (179-180)

Beyond any doubt, Jesucristo Gómez affirms that men are judged not for what they are but for what they do. Given that Jesucristo Gómez has lead a life of "doing," the continuation of his activities must also be a life of doing.

Finally, the emphasis on action presents the meaning of the life of Jesucristo Gómez as a dynamic force. That is, understanding the nature of Jesucristo Gómez's being-in-the-world is a becoming. Indeed, the *imitatio Christi* of Jesucristo Gómez is a becoming-in-the-world of Christ, for if the action ever ceased, so would Christ's way of being-in-the-world. Likewise, the followers of Jesucristo Gómez will never achieve a perfected, static repetition of him; they can only continue his becoming. In this way, the Christological vision of *El evangelio de Lucas Gavilán* resolves the paradox that Lipski sees in the presence of Christ at two distinct moments in history. Christ is never present as a fixed Incarnation. The meaning of Christ is an active continuation of critical social intervention, a dynamic and changing "becoming."[22]

In summary, *El evangelio de Lucas Gavilán* makes a Christological commentary through the life of Jesucristo Gómez. First, Jesucristo Gómez exemplifies the critical and self-aware practice Lucas Gavilán translates into contemporary Mexico. The basic characteristic of such Christian practice lies in Jesucristo Gómez's deconstructive approach to reading and intervening in the text of social injustice. In addition, Lucas Gavilán's translation emphasizes the active quality of Christian practice, pointing out that "El Evangelio se cumple o no se cumple, no hay otra" (179).

Furthermore, underscoring Christianity as action, *El evangelio de Lucas Gavilán* shows that the critical and interventionary practices are the becoming-in-the-world of Christ, depicting Christ's existence not as a static Incarnation of God in the flesh, but as a constantly evolving movement at play in history.23

III

In conclusion, the process of demystification generates multiple meanings in *El evangelio de Lucas Gavilán*. Through Lucas Gavilán's translation of the Gospel of St. Luke, Vicente Leñero lays bare the worldliness of his own novel and the worldliness of Sacred Scripture. This translation becomes effective as it multiplies the layering effect of *El evangelio de Lucas Gavilán*, manifesting its nature as counter-text in contrast to other modern and institutional interpretations of Sacred Scripture. As counter-text, Lucas Gavilán's translation shows how texts and interpretations both presuppose and generate political ideologies.

Demystification also arises from the christological vision produced by the text. In the perspective of liberation theology, the Christology of *El evangelio de Lucas Gavilán* presents the significance of Christ's being-in-the-world as an active becoming, a quality that is reiterable throughout history. Furthermore, the practice of Christianity as a becoming of Christ avoids dogmatic ossification through a highly critical, deconstructive approach to social injustice and effective intervention.

In the final analysis, novelization and liberation Christianity in *El evangelio de Lucas Gavilán* emerge as kinds of critical activity. Moreover, they follow the notion of criticism proposed by Edward Said:

> Were I to use one word consistently alongside *criticism* (not as a modification but as an emphatic) it would be *oppositional*. If criticism is reducible neither to doctrine nor to a political

> position on a particular question, and if it is to be
> self-aware simultaneously, then its identity is its
> difference from other cultural activities and from
> systems of thought or method.[24]

In this perspective, then, *El evangelio de Lucas Gavilán* extends the dual critical project of Leñero's novels. First, it further explores the potentials of the novelistic genre, this time in terms of a critical translation. By reframing the recognizable structure, events, and characters of the Gospel of St. Luke in the language and cultural moment of contemporary Mexico, the novel interrogates and renews the dynamics of meaning in the interaction between text and context. And second, by revealing the aspects of meaning that are suppressed by Mexican Catholicism, *El evangelio de Lucas Gavilán* addresses the fictions of representation involved in religion; it opposes the worldly effects of textual interpretation that become institutionalized as practices obedient to tradition, doctrine and blind dogma. Through these two oppositional stances, then, *El evangelio de Lucas Gavilán* establishes its critical identity.

Chapter Six:

Narrative Transformations in *Los periodistas*, *La gota de agua*, and *Asesinato*: World, Text, and Nonfiction Novels

Leñero's three nonfiction novels, *Los periodistas* (1978), *La gota de agua* (1983), and *Asesinato: El doble crimen de los Flores Muñoz* (1985), continue the critical exploration of fictions of representation that emerged in *Redil de ovejas* and in *El evangelio de Lucas Gavilán*. In the case of these novels, however, the movement to nonfiction is not a mere change in thematic zones that places paramount importance on socio-historical context or referential value. Rather, through the effects of narrative strategies they extend the critique of "natural appearances" that became evident in the earlier metafictional novels *Estudio Q* and *El garabato*; and, in addition, they further expose the problematic relation between text and context, already operative in *Redil de ovejas* and *El evangelio de Lucas Gavilán*, as a site of struggle over the meaning and definition of social reality. In this respect, then, *Los periodistas*, *La gota de agua*, and *Asesinato* require a reading that is equally attentive to the problematics of the transformation of world into text and to the manner in which the texts exploit certain formal characteristics associated with the novel.

From the outset, the term used to categorize these works-- nonfiction novel--signals the need for a doubly focused reading. As opposed to the label "novel," the added qualifier "nonfiction" immediately marks a difference: the novel implies both fiction and a series of possible narrative forms; "nonfiction," in contrast, excludes fiction. Although roughly formulated, this dichotomy foregrounds a prevailing literary convention that regulates, to a certain degree, the signifying forces of the texts under consideration here. In addition, the post-Tlatelolco context in which these novels appear delimits the specific dialectics of the opposition between fiction and nonfiction.

In the Mexican novel, nonfiction has a long and complex tradition. Jorge Ruffinelli has pointed out that in the context of socio-political and economic crises throughout Latin America, the Mexican novel has been a "vehículo de conocimiento de la realidad." Throughout the nineteenth and twentieth centuries, and particularly after the Revolution, the Mexican novel has usefully responded to "la necesidad de comprender la historia al mismo tiempo que se ayudaba a crearla." Hence, Ruffinelli writes, "la novela raramente es 'entretenimiento,' al contrario, muchas veces resulta densa y tediosa exploración de lo real."[1]

To understand history, to create history, and to explore the real are phrases that make evident the deeply-rooted importance of the relationship between text and world in the Mexican novel. Whereas the world has been a consistent preoccupation in the novels of the nineteenth and twentieth centuries, its literary transformation has responded to immediate historical needs: Independence, solidification of the state, the Reform, the French Intervention, the Revolution, nationalism and the search for national identity. After the Tlatelolco incident in 1968, however, the usefulness of the novel as a means to understand and to create history takes on a new urgency as a chronicle of the present. Although the *novela-testimonio*, documentary narrative, and nonfiction are modes of narrating that are available throughout the trajectory of the Mexican novel, they perform a more specific function after 1968.[2] By the 1960s the "Mexican miracle" of economic growth guarantees the state a secure place in society and the political machinery moves toward reproducing the conditions that would insure its continued power and dominance. Although the thematics of the Revolution and questions of national identity persist, after 1968 nonfiction novels tend to contest directly both the repressive powers of the state and the general ideological apparatuses through which culture and society grant the state its power.[3] Given such a tendency, the rhetorical need to convince readers dominates the use of narrative strategies for transforming, representing, and interpreting the world in the contemporary Mexican nonfiction novel.

Moreover, the complexities involved in representing the world and simultaneously producing a persuasive, contestatory representation endow the nonfiction novel with its greatest literary interest as a genre. In a study of Latin American documentary narrative, David William Foster has written:

> What distinguishes these works is not their fundamentally documentary nature, which routinely prompts libraries to classify them as nonfiction. Rather, all have authors who are important novelists, all display a high degree of novelistic interest, and, most significant, all overtly involve the difficulties of narrating a segment of Latin American reality. . . . The foregrounded attention to the relation between writing and reality, between narrative and fact, between detached novelist and involved participant links the documentary narrative to the intricacies of fiction in Latin America.[4]

Although Foster does not include Leñero in his study, the comments are equally valid with respect to his nonfiction novels. And the intricacies to which Foster refers are most evident in the way that Leñero's nonfiction novels exploit generic forms. Therefore, the necessary double reading of *Los periodistas*, *La gota de agua*, and *Asesinato*: on the one hand, one must consider the problems involved in the transformation of world into text, and on the other hand, one must give parallel emphasis to the often surprising use of novelistic techniques in the production of a contestatory representation.

Three considerations will serve to unravel the interweaving of these two perspectives. First, an analysis of the agencies of mediation will permit an examination of the transformation of world into text. Here the principal focus will be the role of authority in the act of narrating. Parallel to this movement, the second critical focus dwells upon the structuring force of narrative strategies as novelistic techniques: how the textual organization, particularly the technique of emplotment, not only endows events with meaning but invests them with a *specific* pattern of significance. Finally, the third consideration returns to the importance of the *contestatory* nature of the text. The combined effects of authority, nonfictionality, and narrative strategies position readers ideologically, and claim the persuasive power to affirm that a certain view of the world, one that is often excluded from either official or popular versions of events, is a more proper interpretation of the significance of social reality.

I

As the works of the historiographer Hayden White demonstrate, the transformation between world and text, the movement from the "historical field" to the written text of the historical work, is an act of mediation.[5] Among the various narrative strategies that mediate any specific kind of historical work, the agency of the narrator, on the one hand, and that of references to the "truth" of the historical field, on the other, constitute points of departure that strive to establish the authority of the text. In these nonfiction novels this is no less the case. In each of the texts Leñero assumes a narrating role that represents him as a character inside the stories. The linguistic position of narrator is, however, an effect of the text, the representation of an enunciating or, in this case, a writing position. There is also an appeal to the "truth" of the events in the historical field. Although this reference to "truth" is overtly emphasized in *Los periodistas*, it eventually becomes problematic when *Asesinato* confronts the always already transformed nature of the historical field whenever it is perceived as meaningful. In sum, the self-representation of the author as narrator/mediator and the recognition of nonfictionality pretend to claim a "natural" authority for the novels while in part obscuring the artificial or at least constructed quality of the transformation of world into text.

Since its publication in 1978, *Los periodistas* has given rise to numerous and often quite personal polemics.[6] Although it has not received the extensive critical attention given to Leñero's earlier novel *Los albañiles*, the national resonance of the overtly political thematics of *Los periodistas* set off the sparks for a conflagration of exchanges that continue to circulate in any consideration of the *sexenio* of Luis Echeverría.[7] Whereas enigma and action are fundamental organizational devices that capture readers' interest and underscore the importance of events in the temporal unfolding of narrative, they immediately acquire a specific modality in nonfiction novels. With respect to *Los periodistas*, conflicting versions of the action and its outcomes were already common knowledge before the publication of the novel. The prologue overtly acknowledges the thematics of the text:

> El ocho de julio de 1976 el diario *Excélsior* de la ciudad de México sufrió lo que mereció calificarse como el más duro golpe de su historia y tal vez de la historia del periodismo nacional. El episodio, aislado pero elocuente ejemplo de los enfrentamientos entre el gobierno y la prensa en un régimen político como el mexicano, es el tema de esta novela. (9)

Beyond the interest that readers might have in the "morbid" details of the affair, the prologue turns attention to the specific version to be narrated in *Los periodistas*: the *golpe* that *Excélsior* suffered at the hands of the government.

Concurrently, the comments direct interest to the form in which the story will be told, a novel. The prologue proceeds to develop the concept of novel at work:

164

> Subrayo desde un principio el término novela.
> Amparado bajo tal género literario y ejercitando los
> recursos que le son o le pueden ser característicos
> he escrito este libro sin apartarme, pienso, de los
> imperativos de una narración novelística. Sin
> embargo, no he querido recurrir a lo que algunas
> corrientes tradicionales se empeñan en dictaminar
> cuando se trata de transladar a la "ficción" un
> episodio de lo que llamamos la vida real: disfrazar
> con nombres ficticios y con escenarios deformados
> los personajes y escenarios del incidente. Por el
> contrario, consideré forzoso sujetarme con rigor
> textual a los acontecimientos y apoyar con
> documentos las peripecias del asunto porque toda
> la argumentación testimonial y novelística
> depende en grado sumo de los hechos verdaderos,
> de los comportamientos individuales y grupales y
> de los documentos mismos. (9)

Although the term "novel" offers Leñero protection ("amparado") to
write his testimony, he immediately modifies the category to
eliminate the translation of events and persons into fiction
("disfrazar") and to underscore its formal characteristics, "los
imperativos de una narración novelística." Thus the prologue
incites readers to expect a novel while it also claims the authority of
history with references to "los hechos verdaderos." In brief, the
prologue acknowledges the transformation of world into text,
announces the author's privilege to use novelistic narrative
strategies to such an end, and rhetorically "apela a la complicidad
de sus lectores" (9) to accept the historical veracity of the
testimony.

The second chapter of part one continues the self-defining
function of the prologue. In addition to the traces of the time of
writing and complaints about the difficulty of narrating the story,
self-referential comments highlight the nonfictional status of *Los*

periodistas. The narrator first discusses the composition of a possible novel: "Todo ocurre en un periódico. . . . Digamos *Excélsior,* aunque no citaré a las personas por su nombre para no meterme en problemas" (58). After explaining the plot, however, the expressly stated intention for the narrative serves as a transition to statements obviously about *Los periodistas* and implicitly rejects the previously proposed "fiction":

> El tema me dará ocasión para describir por dentro la vida de un periódico, los problemas internos de una empresa editora de publicaciones en los momentos más críticos de su historia. Voy a contar desde mi punto de vista, en una crónica personalísima, el atentado a *Excélsior* y sus derivaciones, confieso a Miguel Angel porque de pronto voy caminando al lado de Miguel Angel Granados Chapa por Paseo de la Reforma a la una y media de la mañana. Estrictamente no voy a escribir una crónica ni un reportaje ni un documento histórico sino una simple novela enfocada a las anécdotas más que a los significados trascendentes que sólo tú podrás plantear y descifrar algún día porque sólo tú conoces a fondo el problema de fondo. Es tu tema, tu vida, digo a Julio, porque de pronto voy caminando al lado de Julio Scherer García por Paseo de la Reforma a la una y media de la mañana. (60)

All together, the prologue, the rejection of a "fiction" about *Excélsior,* and the constant insistence on novelistic form combined with historical events direct attention to the question of generic form ("simple novela"), delimit the nonfictional quality of the novel ("los hechos verdaderos," "crónica personalísima," "enfocada a las anécdotas más que a los significados trascendentes"), and guide readers' initial expectations toward the golpe and its enigmatic "problemas de fondo."[8]

In addition to the authority claimed by the prologue and the self-referential comments, the first part of *Los periodistas* shores up the authority of the narrator by implicitly representing his growth throughout and beyond the experience.[9] Following the interior monologue of the first chapter, which underscores a rival character's jealousy for Julio Scherer García's professional fame and position as director of *Excélsior*, the second chapter juxtaposes a series of temporal planes: a cocktail party in 1975, the previously mentioned references to *Los periodistas* as a projected novel, and evidence of the moment of writing. Like the latter two temporal planes, the third chapter occurs after the *golpe* and consists of an aggressive interrogation of the narrator that details his role in the internal problems at *Excélsior* and allows him to disavow any contribution, direct or indirect, to Scherer's downfall. The juxtaposition of multiple temporal planes throughout the first part implies an important historical change in the narrator: once a self-effacing journalist, unskilled in the internal politics of *Excélsior* and incredulous before the suggestion that Echeverría wants to do away with the newspaper, he has lived through the experience and gained the knowledge necessary to assume the authoritative voice of the novelist who "se siente obligado asumir con plenitud su relato . . ." (9). In sum, *Los periodistas* strategically begins with a prologue that claims the authority of true events, rejects the disguise of fictional transformation, and defends the use of novelistic techniques. Similarly, the first part of the novel extends the function of the prologue by further defining the nonfictional status of the novel and implicitly endowing the narrator with the knowledge and experience that will ratify his authority.

In contrast to the overt affirmation of authority in *Los periodistas*, *La gota de agua* depends more on an implicit recognition of its nonfictional status. *La gota de agua* deals with a social problem, Mexico City's recurring water shortages, in terms

of an isolated example: its effects on the Leñero household.10
More precisely, the narrator recounts in humorous, exaggerated
terms the domestic crisis provoked by a prolonged shortage in the
early months of 1982. Although the relationship between *La gota
de agua* and the world immediately emerges from the thematic
focus, references to the narrator's readings indirectly refer to the
nonfictional status of *La gota de agua* and inscribe the novel as an
example.

In the second chapter, unable to concentrate on a novel in
progress, the narrator reads three texts. First: "Recordé un
reportaje de Gabriel García Márquez, *Caracas sin agua*, que
apareció publicado en un pequeño libro. Busqué el libro y el texto.
Era un reportaje de once páginas y estaba escrito con la técnica de
un cuento . . ." (26). After a long quotation from the text, he
continues:

> Leí hasta el final el reportaje de García Márquez y
> salté a *La peste* de Camus y a *El año de la peste* de
> Daniel Defoe. Ya era muy noche cuando cerré los
> libros pero no me sentía cansado. La lectura de
> aquellas desgracias de la ficción y de la realidad
> habían tenido el poder de levantarme nuevamente
> el ánimo.
> Al fin de cuentas, nuestra catástrofe doméstica
> no era la única ni la mayor en la historia de la
> humanidad. (27)

Although the three texts obviously share the sentiment of crisis
felt by the narrator, they also suggest some of the parameters that
regulate the principle of example in *La gota de agua*. García
Márquez's text, "reportaje . . . escrito con la técnica de un cuento,"
parallels *La gota de agua* as a report written with the techniques of
a novel. Camus's *The Plague*, in contrast, invents a crisis, an
example that allegorically explores the plight of humankind's
existence. Finally, Defoe's *Journal of the Plague Year* personally

documents an historical tragedy in a manner similar to the diary-like chronology of *La gota de agua*.[11] The narrator's readings, then, suggest the parameters of signification in *La gota de agua*: a report written with the techniques of a novel; an allegorical example of one domestic crisis among many, "no era la única ni la mayor"; and moreover, a personal narration of an historical moment.

In addition to its indirect characterization as an allegorical report/journal of a real domestic drama, *La gota de agua* supports its relation to the world with the interweaving of a "nonfiction code," an extensive yet finely intercalated series of references to historical reality: allusions to specific dates, places, and persons, and the inclusion of newsclippings, propaganda from a water-conservation campaign, and even the diagrams, estimates and invoices for a new water-storage tank. The way such a nonfiction code embeds the text in the world notwithstanding, the code also contributes to the text's exploration of novelistic techniques. *La gota de agua* experiments with forms of novelistic representation associated with an earlier style of Realism. More precisely, the text relies heavily on a *costumbrismo* that portrays the daily frustrations of life in Mexico City: the cancellation of purchase orders because of a rumored devaluation of the *peso*, the stereotyped characterization of a gossipy Spanish shopkeeper, perennial conversations about government corruption or the quality of domestic manufacturing, the problems of bank bureaucracy, and even the poor service of a store clerk who attempts to resolve his love life over the telephone during business hours.

The combination of the references to the narrator's readings, the "nonfiction code," and the *costumbrista* aspects of the narrative all serve to delimit the status of the novel as an example embedded in the historical field. These strategies, however, do not claim the same level of authority for the veracity of novel as found in *Los periodistas*. Perhaps owing to the more privatized nature of the narrative, in contrast to the public resonance of *Los periodistas*, *La gota de agua* depends heavily on the need to construct a "thick description" of the narrator's experience of social reality.[12]

In contrast to both *Los periodistas* and *La gota de agua*, the third nonfiction novel, *Asesinato*, investigates the space between the public and the private. Except for the critical acclaim of *Los albañiles* and the polemics surrounding *Los periodistas*, no other novel of Vicente Leñero has attracted as much attention.[13] Although the public desire to understand the atrocities of the Flores Muñoz case in part explains this success, the novel has also evoked numerous responses to its status as a literary document.[14] In *Asesinato* Leñero explores the potentials of form in nonfiction and novelistic narration. Compared with the impassioned history of *Los periodistas* or the humorous, subjective narration of *La gota de agua*, *Asesinato* strives for a solemn objectivity. In many ways similar to *Los periodistas*, which is framed by a prologue and uses limited documentation in the novelistic transformation of a public event, *Asesinato* carries these techniques to an extreme. A collage of documentary materials--journalistic, historical, literary, and judicial--constitutes the novel and represents various aspects of the conviction of Gilberto Flores Alavez for the murder of his grandparents. The abundant use of such public records appears to minimalize the transformation between world and text. Likewise, the limitation of the narrator to the function of selecting and organizing the documentary materials seems almost to deny the transformation of text into novel.

The prefatory statement, "Aclaraciones y agradecimientos," begins with the following paragraphs:

> Reportaje o novela sin ficción--y sin literatura, quizás--este libro quiere ser el análisis detallado, minucioso, de un crimen ocurrido en la ciudad de México en octubre de 1978 y cuyas características, antecedentes y repercusiones permiten iluminar áreas significativas de la sociedad mexicana en esta segunda mitad del siglo veinte.

En un empeño por mantener el máximo grado de objetividad, todos los datos consignados a lo largo del libro tienen un apoyo documental que se ha hecho público de algún modo o que de algún modo consta en escritos de diversa especie. El autor no ha querido tomarse libertad alguna para imaginar, inventar o deducir hechos; ni siquiera ha utilizado materiales provenientes de entrevistas o investigaciones personales que no se encuentren avalados por una constancia escrita. Sólo los datos existentes en documentos o testimonios públicos forman parte de esta historia; con ello se pretende evitar cualquier sospecha de difamación o deformación de acontecimientos y personas contraria a los propósitos descriptivos de la investigación. (5)

Although the reviews of *Asesinato* readily concede its status as a nonfiction novel, Leñero begins the text by questioning its genre: "Reportaje o novela sin ficción--y sin literatura, quizás. . . ." The narrator thus underscores the difficulty of categorizing the text, and foregrounds its worldliness through his insistence on the intention of analyzing the public significance of a private event. Furthermore, the "empeño por mantener el máximo grado de objetividad" leads him to emphasize the neutral, non-transforming character of the text and to objectify himself as the linguistic third-person, the author: "El autor no ha querido tomarse libertad alguna para imaginar, inventar, o deducir hechos; ni siquiera ha utilizado materiales provenientes de entrevistas o investigaciones personales que no se encuentren avalados por una constancia escrita." In sum, the "celo documental" of *Asesinato* that proposes to avoid "cualquier sospecha de difamación o deformación de acontecimientos y personas" appears to minimalize the transformation of world into text, and hence, to emphasize its worldliness.

Whereas such an emphasis on the worldliness of *Asesinato* may explain the aside "y sin literatura, quizás," other overtly expressed intentions signal the transforming characteristics of the analysis. First, *Asesinato* presupposes a socio-historical intention beyond the simple descriptive purposes of the research: a search for the broader implications of the crime whose "características, antecedentes y repercusiones permiten iluminar áreas significativas de la sociedad mexicana en esta segunda mitad del siglo veinte." Furthermore, the prefatory statement concludes: ". . . esta aventura literaria que no obstante estar enfocada a un acontecimiento único y preciso ejemplifica la necia búsqueda, el empeño obsesivo--casi siempre infructuoso--por descubrir la verdad" (6). Although the novel is a literary adventure focused on a singular, precise event, *Asesinato* also exemplifies a transforming, philosophical obsession with the nature of truth. The "Aclaraciones y agradecimientos," then, form an integral part of the novel. On the one hand, the statement insists on the worldliness of the text, a constant characteristic of the novel with its abundant footnotes, photographs and collage of documents. On the other hand, and in contrast to the feigned elimination of the transformation between world and text, *Asesinato* presupposes the transforming principles of both a broad, socio-historical investigation, a "literary adventué," and a philosophical consideration of truth as mediations between the world and the text.

Taken as a group, these nonfiction novels manifest an empiricist import in their claims to authority. References to "los hechos verdaderos," "el máximo grado de objetividad," and "materiales . . . avalados por una constancia escrita" in *Los periodistas* and *Asesinato* establish a positive nexus with the historical field and an overt appelation to the authority of social reality. In addition, *Los periodistas* implicitly represents the narrator's growth into the authoritative position from which he writes. *La gota de agua*, although self-defined as an allegorical example, sets into play an implicit "nonfiction code" and exploits a *costumbrista* narrative style, all of which undergirds the historical reality of the text. In each of these novels, therefore, the narrator founds his authority on the empiricist affirmation of worldliness. Nevertheless, while such a movement does, in effect, make patent the worldly quality of these novels, it also attempts to mask the narrator's role as mediator and ingredient in the transformation of world into text. In each case the narrator moves toward a specific history--the "true" story of Echeverría's censoring *Excélsior*, the thick description of the personal dilemma of a water shortage, and the "objective" search for the dynamics of the public meaning of a private murder--and hence transforms the historical field. In the end, *Asesinato* makes problematic the "necia búsqueda" of this empiricist intent with its philosophical bent toward questioning the nature of truth. Before proceeding to that issue, however, and the general question of the contestatory force of the texts, a consideration of the organizational strategies in these novels will establish the particulars of the specific histories produced by the transformation of world into text.

II

Although one may discuss the organizational strategies of Leñero's nonfiction novels in many perspectives, a consideration of the technique of emplotment narrows the critical focus to the kind of story narrated in each text and, in turn, helps account for their contestatory force. Hayden White uses the basic plot patterns established by Northrop Frye in order to analyze the transformation of the historical field into a sequence of meaningful events in the historical work.[15] Similarly, in order to explain the dynamics of sequentiality and revealed meaning in the narrative (literary) text, Peter Brooks explores the interweaving of a code of action and a code of enigma (as delineated by Roland Barthes).[16] In both White and Brooks, critical attention emphasizes the importance of the linear representation of events in the text, their temporal unfolding as a structuring mechanism that establishes or reveals the significance of events and hence delimits the kind of story being narrated. Since events, the historical field, do not narrate themselves, the organizational device of emplotment makes manifest both the principles that regulate the transformation of world into text and the importance of novelistic techniques in Leñero's nonfiction novels.

As suggested in the prologue, *Los periodistas* employs a plot that predicates the global story of the triumph of the free press over government manipulation. The text is divided into three major parts--"Primera parte/*Excélsior*," "Segunda parte/El golpe," and "Tercera parte/*Proceso*"--all of which is followed by an "Indice de nombres." In addition to extending the self-defining function of the prologue (as discussed above), the first part of *Los periodistas* sets forth the "problemas internos" of *Excélsior* before the golpe. It generates interest in the individuals and groups involved in the overthrow and the enigma of their personal (re)actions. At the same time, such a focus suggests their vulnerability to government manipulation. Thus, the first part, through a juxtaposition of multiple temporal levels, provides the information necessary to understand the later development and manipulation of the internal conflicts in *Excélsior*: jealousy and ambition within the hierarchy of the cooperative, dissension over the administration and division of benefits from a real estate investment, and the financial viability of a subsidiary publishing endeavor.

After the multiple anachronies of the first part, *Los periodistas* adopts a more chronological ordering of events, an organizational strategy that drives home the thematic movement toward the triumph of the free press over unjust government manipulation. The second part, "El golpe," recounts in detail the consequences of the internal problems and how they were manipulated to orchestrate the *golpe* that ousted Julio Scherer García and his supporters; this second part concentrates specifically on the days around the overthrow. The third part, "*Proceso*," then describes the aftermath of the golpe: the vacuum of power in *Excélsior* and Scherer's successful struggle to establish an independent journal before the end of Echeverría's *sexenio* and thus defend the freedom of the press.

The importance of the chronological thematic movement notwithstanding, it is the figure of Julio Scherer García that unifies the novel. Throughout *Los periodistas* he is consistently characterized by his function: the defender and hero of uncompromised, critical journalism.[17] In contrast to Scherer (and the general emphasis on historical veracity and documentation), the oppositional group within *Excélsior*, first characterized by jealousy and mediocrity, is eventually caricatured in a ten-scene farce that culminates with its drowning in excrement. In sum, *Los periodistas* moves from the antecedents of the *golpe*, to the actual details of the overthrow, and ends with the triumph of free speech over the abuse of presidential power; simultaneously, it proceeds to characterize heroically those who defend the value of free speech while caricaturing the journalists who fail to protect their freedom and profession.[18]

In this respect, emplotment not only orders the sequence of events in *Los periodistas*, it also structures a specific version of events. Although the novel does exploit many other innovative narrative strategies, such as temporal anachronies, the use of various forms of discourse (like interrogations, interviews, transcription of dialogues from hidden tape recorders, scenic directions for camera), and the intercalation of documents, the sequential ordering of the text is at the service of a story that must justify the triumph of Scherer and his group over the unjust manipulation of the Echeverría administration. *Los periodistas* exploits techniques and structures characteristic of and available for novelistic narration in order to transform world into text and constitute a mediated version of the events. Moreover, as will become evident when considering the contestatory effect of the novel, the emplotment in *Los periodistas* produces a rather polarized or Manichean social representation that defines the ideological principles at work in the text and invests journalism with a power that certain aspects of *Asesinato* later renounce. In sum, emplotment in *Los periodistas* gives rise to a story that opposes the official version of events espoused by the government and by *Excélsior*.

In constrast to the directly confrontational drive that determines the organization of *Los periodistas*, *La gota de agua*, as a more privatized case, depends on the representation of the narrator as he changes during the course of the crisis and the search for its various tentative solutions. In general, the narrator is characterized in two major aspects: his unsuccessful attempts to write a traditional novel, *La situación*, and his thwarted efforts to purchase a water-storage tank and have it properly installed. The representation of the writer at work carries the mimetic tendency of Realism to an extreme: while the narrator corrects the first draft of the beginning pages of *La situación*, the text represents the process by including the initial version on the left side of the page and the correction on the right. Comparison of the two columns makes evident the mental process of the writer and the material product of his labor. Also, the juxtaposition of *La situación* to the surrounding text foregrounds the technical principles that constitute *La gota de agua*. The narrator describes *La situación* as "un experimento, un tour de force para mí. Por primera vez en la vida me había propuesto construir una historia lineal, cronológica, sin cambios de tiempo ni de puntos de vista y sin malabarismos formales. Una historia narrada en primera persona, al modo tradicional, como Dios manda" (26). Whereas the fragment of *La situación* imitates traditional narrative style, the surrounding text pushes the same techniques to an extreme; in opposition to the "reality effect" of the literary conventions used in *La situación*, its very inclusion in the novel presupposes an intensification and even rejection of the mimetic drive of Realism, a rejection that is further supported by the interweaving of the nonfiction code. In addition, the sporadic insertion of the double columns of *La situación* throughout the novel foregrounds the frustrations of the writer as worry over the water-storage tank competes for his undivided attention.

The story of the water-storage tank, the *tinaco*, controls the overall development of *La gota de agua* and manifests the changes in the narrator. The beginning of the novel sets the stage for the adventure of the *tinaco*. In the first three chapters, the narrator recounts the crisis of the water shortage and the decision to install a cistern. In the fourth, an analepsis dramatizes the narrator's "fobia ingenieril" (57) of plumbing.[19] Against this backdrop, the narrator of the first chapters of the novel maintains his faith in official statements that promise the rapid resolution of the shortage that began January 31, 1982. In the last chapter, on March 9, 1982, he declares: "Después de las que hemos pasado ya es difícil creer" (203). The movement from a believing to a wisely skeptical citizen responds to the development of the story of the *tinaco* throughout the novel: the choice of a *tinaco* instead of a cistern, the difficulty of purchasing a *tinaco*, the repeated delays in the delivery, the problems of having it installed, and finally, the repetition of the cycle with the leaking pump, the irreparably cracked *tinaco*, and the ever present leaks. In the linear progression of the text, the narrator ends each chapter with the heightened expectation of a promising solution, an expectation that is inevitably shattered in the following sequence of events.

Most importantly, the repeated pattern of heightened expectations--frustrated solution determines the significance of the outcome of the novel in progress and the *tinaco*. In the concluding chapter, the narrator finishes the correction of the draft and remarks: "No, no funcionaba. Definitivamente no funcionaba, maldita sea. Ni transcritas en limpio aquellas 23 cuartillas iniciales pintaban para una novela medianamente regular. Qué desastre. Carecían de chiste, eran sosas, insustanciales, vacías. Qué desastre" (202). Similarly, three days later, when the new *tinaco* is in place, "una víscera cardiaca funcionando con absoluta perfección," the narrator inspects it more closely and discovers "una pequeñísima grieta que hacía sudar el tinaco, con una especie de salpullido. Sudaba el tinaco, se estaba filtrando el agua, eso era evidente, oh Dios, me lleva la chingada, hijos de puta éstos de Eureka" (204). In a flash he imagines the unbearable repetition of the previous pattern of events and, without a second thought, he purchases a waterproofing cement and seals the leak. When Eureka's quality-control expert advises him that such a make-shift repair will probably not last, the narrator remembers "aquellos héroes de Salgari que se jugaban la vida en batallas terribles," "astronautas que se la jugaban también al aceptar ser lanzados al misterio del universo en tinacos espaciales," the horse races, the lottery, Las Vegas's roulette tables, and exclaims: "Me la juego . . . . Así se queda el remiendo, muchas gracias. ¡Me la juego!" (207). As soon as the expert leaves, the narrator runs to his study, finds the pages of the manuscript, "y agrupándolas en manojos las rompí por la mitad y las arrojé al bote de la basura. Hasta ese momento descansé" (207). In contrast to the virtue of enduring and insisting, both in the correction of the draft and the installation of a *tinaco*, the contrasting decisions of the conclusion suggest the wisdom of knowing when to give up, as with *La situación*, and when to take a risk, as with the *tinaco*.

In summary, *La gota de agua* is a domestic example of the crises produced by Mexico City's recurring water shortages. The novel, through its nonfiction code and experimental representation of the writer at work, exploits the flexibility of generic techniques to test the limits of mimetic Realism. Moreover, it employs a plot that moves from the virtue of patience to the wisdom of resignation and risk, a recognition that both in the midst of the crisis and even after its tentative solution, "Estábamos salvados, parcial y provisionalmente salvados" (140).[20] In brief, the mechanics of plot in *La gota de agua* produces a version of events that corresponds to the contradictions expressed in the epigraph taken from Alejando Aura: "Acepto la derrota,/ pero que la ciudad/ acepte también/ que la he vencido."

In constrast to *Los periodistas* and *La gota de agua*, Leñero's third nonfiction novel challenges the basic assumptions of a straightforward conception of emplotment. *Asesinato* consists of six parts that progress from the discovery of the crime in October, 1978, to the historico-biographical antecedents of the Flores family, and back to a linear reconstruction of events and analytical considerations from the date of the crime up to the narrator's interview with Gilberto Flores Alavez in June, 1984. Throughout the novel the organizational pattern produces two important yet distinct perspectives in which to evaluate the incident. First, the restricted focus and chronological ordering of material in each part serves to establish a specific version of the event, one that is not necessarily objective or neutral. For example, the first part, "Historia periodística," introduces the journalistic coverage of the crime and initial speculations. The juxtaposition and accumulation of materials demonstrates the many errors of "fact" and the guilt almost unanimously accredited to Gilberto by journalists even before his conviction. Similarly, the fifth part, "Investigación de las investigaciones," considers not only the judicial irregularities of Gilberto's trial, but also the differing versions of the prosecution and the defense and some of the internal inconsistencies in their respective arguments. At the level of individual parts, then, *Asesinato* concentrates on a limited theme that either adds complexity to the antecedents and motives of the murder (the second and third parts deal with the family past and personality conflicts, respectively) or makes patent certain injustices, as in the case of sensationalistic "yellow journalism" and dubious judicial proceedings.

The other evaluative perspective of *Asesinato* depends on the global accumulation and expansion of antecedents, motives and versions according to their order in the text. For example, the fourth part, "La novela del crimen," reconstructs events from October 4, two days before the discovery of the murder, through October 19, the day of Gilberto's sentencing. In six chapters the narrator constructs a version of the events in a rather traditional novelistic form that integrates into the narrative the multiple and conflicting testimonies of the characters involved. Although the order of events in "La novela del crimen" independently produces a growing dramatic intensity, especially with the focalization on the grandson, Gilberto Flores Alavez, the three preceding sections expand the implications of the murder, the investigation, the journalistic coverage and the judicial proceeding. "La carrera política de Gilberto Flores Muñoz" (Part 2, Chapter 1), for example, establishes the grandfather's importance and recent conflicts in the CNIA (Comisión Nacional de la Industria Azucarera); "Problemas familiares" (Part 3, Chapter 1) recounts the threats the family had received and alludes to the grandfather's missing "documentos sumamente comprometedores y un borrador de sus memorias que estaba escribiendo con el auxilio de su esposa" (205). Together all of this implies the possibility of a politically motivated murder. In addition, the use of a machete in the murders signals interests possibly associated with the sugar industry. In the third chapter of "La novela del crimen," however, when the investigation is beginning on the morning of the crime, captain Jesús Miyazawa, director of the Judicial Police of the Distrito Federal, orders Gilberto the grandson:

> --Es muy importante tranquilizar a la opinión pública--dijo Miyazawa--; luego los periódicos lo tergiversan todo. Diles a los periodistas que no se trata de un crimen político.
> --Ya lo dije.
> --Pues otra vez, para que quede bien claro. Que no es un crimen político, que no es nada contra el gobierno, que en momentos como éste debemos estar con el gobierno. Díselos. Es importante que lo oigan de ti para no dar lugar a confusiones que hagan más difícil la investigación. (281)

Beyond the manipulation of Gilberto and the lack of proof for such a declaration, the previously mentioned antecedents of the crime make patent that it could indeed have been a political crime. The implications of the exchange are further expanded when one recalls the journalistic coverage directed against Gilberto in "Primera parte: Historia periodística."

The confusing triangle of pressures among the police, the press, and Gilberto mounts when the fifth chapter of "La novela del crimen" introduces Gilberto's promise to confess to the crime. After resisting hours of pressure from reporters, Procuraduría (the Office of the Public Prosecutor) must give the press some information. The prosecutors grant Anacarsis Peralta, Gilberto's friend and alleged accomplice, immunity as witness for the state and they convince Gilberto's sister to pretend that she is being beaten in an adjoining room in order to force Gilberto to confess. While listening to his sister's screams, Gilberto is told:

> --¿Ya ves por no declarar? Le están dando una tranquiza a tu hermana y luego se la van a coger.
> El muchacho se puso lívido--era cierto, es Licha--; empezó a revolverse--no le pueden hacer esto a Licha, bandidos, no se lo pueden hacer--. En ese instante se quebró:
> --Ya. Está bien. Yo fui. (317)

Whereas the coerced confession itself foregrounds the injustice of Gilberto's plight and the unreliability of his admission of guilt, the preceding parts of *Asesinato* multiply the implications: the pressure of information-hungry reporters against the Procuraduría's need to appear professional and efficient; the negative bias of the press against Gilberto and its preference for sensationalism. And in the fifth part, "La investigación de las investigaciones," the accumulative effect of antecedents continues to expand as the narrator considers the political connections that allowed Anacarsis Peralta to negotiate his legal immunity. Throughout *Asesinato* the organization of the text constantly evokes greater complexity with the gradual accumulation of antecedents, testimonies, and motives. Such an accumulation expands the denunciatory quality of isolated episodes and events, and embeds them in a web of relationships, social and political, that illuminates "áreas significativas de la sociedad mexicana en esta segunda mitad del siglo veinte" (5).[21] Thus the novel becomes a cautionary tale about the manipulation of bureaucracy in contemporary Mexico.

This structural organization also gives rise to the philosophical questioning of truth suggested in the preface. As the linear progression throughout the text accumulates the antecedents and motives for the crime, the constant expansion of the network of social and political interests framing the incident denies arrival at an objective, absolute or "pure" truth. The constant insistence on the worldliness of the text, the narrator's supposedly objective, neutral role, and the abundance of conflicting, contradictory accounts create a web of voices in which each one has its own interests at stake. In the closing lines of the novel, when the narrator interviews Gilberto and asks, "Gilberto, ¿mataste tú a tus abuelos?" the response he receives can only continue to echo as one of the many limited, biased voices: "Por supuesto que no" (541). By carrying the "celo documental" to an extreme, while infinitely complicating the possible disentanglement of the events, Asesinato creates a text "de superficie objetiva para . . . minar esa superficie y hacernos comprender cuantos caminos parecen llevarnos a la verdad, sin jamás acercarnos a ella."[22] The apparent objectivity of Asesinato undermines the possibility of objectivity and an absolute truth because all versions of the events, and even the version(s) represented by the novel itself, are already partial, interested transformations of the world.

In addition to the mediatory function of organization in the transformation of world into text, the structure of the text also explores the potentials of novelistic form, the limits of emplotment. Sergio Gómez Montero has pointed out that Asesinato addresses the question of the plot "en términos de límites, de umbrales . . . ."[23] Whereas the fourth part, "La novela del crimen," most closely conforms to more traditional techniques of novelistic narration and conceptions of emplotment, its intercalation as a single part of the whole and its ironic title indicate the limitations and implicit rejection of such a form.[24] Indeed, all of *Asesinato* depends on the principle of intercalation and implicit rejection of various genres of discourse. The strategy of a distant and supposedly neutral narrator permits the interjection of multiple genres: journalism, biography, literary analysis, *curriculum vitae*, various forms of judicial discourse--arguments, decisions, testimonies, descriptions, psychological evaluation, etc.--, and the final interview. In each case, the juxtaposition and ordering of these genres makes patent their limited and biased concept of objectivity. Moreover, even the opening "Aclaraciones y agradecimientos" demonstrate the limits of objectivity in the genre of prefaces, given that the narrator overtly claims neutrality while he deftly states the transforming and interested purposes of socio-historical analysis, literary adventure, and philosophical speculation on truth. In formalist terms, the generic frame of *Asesinato* encompasses a multiplicity of genres that constitute the *récit*; and, through the multiple and unreconciliable *histoires* generated by such a *récit*, *Asesinato* explores the limits of plot(s).

The textual organization of *Asesinato* thus mediates the transformation of world into text. The emphasis on the worldliness of the text through extensive documentation claims to minimalize the distance between world and text. Nevertheless, the order of documentation in the text presupposes the transforming purposes of socio-historical analysis and a philosophical questioning of truth. In a different perspective, the strategy of an uninvolved, neutral narrator produces a novel that integrates a variety of genres. Although the dependence on public documents permits the narrator's denial of literary qualities, the ordering and juxtaposition of genres of discourse throughout the *récit* interrogates the limits and limitations of plot(s) within the frame of a novel by generating multiple, irreconcilable *histoires*. In sum, *Asesinato* represents the will to objectivity in the extreme in order to demonstrate both the web of interests that entangles the manipulation of objectivity and the impossibility of establishing truth as an achievable absolute.

In summary, emplotment as a strategy of narrative organization has an important function in each of Leñero's nonfiction novels. In *Los periodistas* the specific version of the oppositional encounter between the free press and the government, which ends with the triumph of the press, arises from the significance imbued in events by means of plot and characterization. *La gota de agua* predicates a more flexible although no less specific version of the agonies of a water shortage. And *Asesinato* explores the very nature of plot. Juxtaposition and accumulation of various versions of the events places in doubt the possibility of a totalizing plot that would determine the meaning of events. Instead, the linear organization of the text evokes a multiplicity of irreconcilable plots that serve the socio-historical interest of the narrator and his philosophical interrogation of truth. In each of these cases, moreover, the organizational strategies of the text demonstrate both the transformation of world into text and the intricacies of novelistic technique involved in such a narrative transformation.

III

A final consideration of the three novels must account for the combined effect of the authority of nonfiction and the specific version of events produced by emplotment: the contestatory force of the texts and the production of a specific ideological position. First, it must be recognized that the empiricist quality of authority in the novels is, to a certain degree, an illusion. Indeed, the historical field to which the novels refer (i.e., the events themselves) may have existed theoretically, yet as a narrated plot any historical record is always already a transformed version of events. Moreover, such a transformation responds to the need to produce an interesting novelistic narrative and a convincing representation of events. Analysis, therefore, must account for the rhetorical force of the nonfiction novels, a recognition both of the versions of reality that the texts contest and of the hierarchization of values designed to estrange readers from received interpretations and to gain their acceptance of the version proposed by the text. In each case, however, there are certain contradictions in such a project.

Los periodistas, of all of the nonfiction novels, depends most heavily on a closed hierarchy of values and somewhat manipulative rhetorical structure. Although the final chapter strives to avoid this closure by opening the situation to future changes and by referring to the continual divisions, even among the journalists ousted with Scherer, the transformation of world into text and the strategies of textual organization inscribe a determinate system of values: the absolute value of freedom of the press against the undesirable machinations of government censorship (whether by covert manipulation or overt retaliation). At first such an oppositional hierarchy seems to be completely justified, and even necessary, given that *Los periodistas* contests government denial of involvement in the affair.

Nevertheless, Jean Franco has noted that the ideological positioning of readers in *Los periodistas*, by both plot and characterization, also implies another hierarchy: "the novel appears to set the demand for free expression against the demand (however manipulated) for social justice . . . ." Hence, one may adduce the additional hierarchy of free expression over social justice (i.e., the demand for a more equitable distribution of wealth). Consequently, Franco notes, this second hierarchy "unwittingly reproduces the very conditions which allow the state to manipulate so effectively."[25] But such a hierarchization also narrows the implications of the ideological position promoted by *Los periodistas*. In contrast to a more radical theory of social change that would demand equitable distribution of wealth before freedom of expression, *Los periodistas* represents a liberal imagination that would use free expression to correct social inequities.[26] Indeed, it is precisely the unrelentless tendency of *Excélsior* to criticize and make known various forms of social injustice that eventually incurs the wrath of Echeverría.

The emplotment of *Los periodistas*, then, positions readers to privilege the value of free expression as an instrument of change that can intervene in the contradictions between the notion of justice and the concrete system of the state in order to transform society. The techniques of emplotment and characterization construct a story that defends such values on the basis of the Scherer group as "good guys" and the opposition as either idiots or bandits. The constant appeal to the authority of empirical reality by the use of documents and lack of "disguise" attempts to promote Leñero's version of events over the government's official denials of any manipulation. Nevertheless, empirical reality is only a function of the rhetorical structure in *Los periodistas*: in the case of both the government and Leñero's novel, versions of reality are pitted against each other, both sides claim empirical truth for their version, and acceptance (or failure) depends on the success of the appeal to liberal notions of truth, justice, and social change.

In *La gota de agua* the rhetorical force and internal contradiction of the text arise from its classification as an "example." Although humorous and more lighthearted than *Los periodistas*, in the end it positions readers ideologically as "el primer grito literario de alarma para autoridades y ciudadanos."[27] Principally, the novel is at odds with itself to reconcile the example as a form with the greater social injustice caused by the inadequate material conditions of existence affecting millions in the vast metropolis of Mexico City. First, *La gota de agua* includes the narrator's guilt when he juxtaposes the power of his influences to the majority that has no voice:

> . . . iba a vanagloriarme ante las hijas de mis poderosas influencias con los funcionarios públicos, cuando oí que en el comedor mi hija Estela hablaba de su amigo Mario Zambrano. Decía que Mario Zambrano había tomado muy en serio

186

> aquello del compromiso con los pobres, y en
> concordancia con sus ideas se había ido a vivir a un
> cuartucho en una colonia proletaria . . . para luchar
> por los derechos de los marginados. Ellos sí que
> están jodidos --decía mi hija Estela--: sin títulos de
> propiedad, sin servicios sanitarios, sin agua
> potable. Jodidos jodidos. (17)

The only solution to the disparity between the example of the Leñero household and the *marginados* is to leave the guilt of the social contradiction unresolved throughout the novel.

In contrast, when the narrator later insists that *Proceso* publish an exposé on the problem of the Mexico City water supply, *La gota de agua* includes material that allows readers to evaluate scientifically the monumental proportions of the situation and confront the quality of the Leñero household as an isolated example among "técnicos, urbanistas, funcionarios, ingenieros, arquitectos, economistas, sociólogos, antropólogos, médicos, biólogos agrónomos, historiadores, campesinos, ejidatarios, paracaidistas, intelectuales, obreros, líderes de opinión, políticos, empleados, amas de casa, maestros, catedráticos, artistas y gente, mucha gente común . . ." (151). In sum, whereas *La gota de agua* is written as an allegorical, nonfiction example, the form has its limitations in the focus on the household of an influential journalist. Most importantly, then, the novel acknowledges and leaves unresolved the contradictions between the example and the masses in order to ask and implicit question noted by Marco Antonio Campos: "Hoy me sucede a mí, dirá Leñero, pero mañana será a usted, a aquellos, a los otros, a la ciudad entera. ¿No leyó las noticias del pasado diez de enero sobre la angustiosa carestía del líquido? Bueno, déle una revisada a los periódicos. ¿Y qué va a pasar cuando una ciudad de veinte millones de personas no tenga agua? Nada más, piénselo."[28] In this manner *La gota de agua* exploits its own internal contradiction as a privatized version of a social problem affecting millions and positions readers ideologically to consider all of the versions excluded from the example.

In contrast to the function of emplotment and characterization in *Los periodistas* and the tension between privatized example and public injustice in *La gota de agua*, the social and philosophical values investigated by *Asesinato* produce a base of incommensurate categories: the distance between the desire to *iluminar* a socio-historical reality and the "empeño obsesivo . . . por descubrir la verdad" opens a problematic space in the ideological values presupposed by *Asesinato*. In the socio-historical perspective, the individual parts of *Asesinato* function as a denunciation of biased "yellow journalism" and improper police-judicial proceedings. Although the novel itself depends, in part, on the public fascination with a sensational crime, the denunciations imply the possibility of a more objective, informative press and an impartial system of justice. Nevertheless, the philosophical import of *Asesinato* and the lack of a totalizing plot, which undermine the notion of objectivity and place in doubt the concept of truth, make problematic the contestatory implications of these denunciations. In this respect, *Asesinato* inscribes a complex series of values: on the one hand, the urgent need to strive for truth in both journalism and judicial process; on the other, the interminable necessity to analyze the mechanisms by which truth is always embedded in the worldly circumstance of interests and deformed by the limitations of perspective.

In a final consideration of the contestatory function of nonfiction, taken as a group these novels interrogate the ideology and power of journalism. Indeed, the question of journalism and its powers thematically enters into each of the novels. As Roberto González Echevarría has pointed out, journalism not only lies at the origins of the documentary novel but is also a part of Western literary tradition, particularly given the importance of *crónicas* in the *Quijote* and the dynamics of journalism and censorship that produced Spanish America's first novel, *El Periquillo Sarniento*. More pointedly, the importance of journalism for the nonfiction novel resides in the way that the genre of journalistic writing "tends to diffuse the question of authorship. Since facts determine the content, the author becomes a neutral conductor, not the generator of the text. Journalism fosters the illusion that incidents write themselves into history."[29] To a large extent the rhetorical force of *Los periodistas* depends on this illusion and the supposed authority of an objective, empirical truth in the events. With the publication of *Asesinato*, however, such a project falls apart, for the multitude of plots and the lack of a totalizing plot demonstrate how all versions of reality are limited interpretations that manipulate the concepts of "truth" and "justice" according to specific ideological interests. Similarly, *La gota de agua* alludes to the manipulative power of journalism in the public arena when bureaucrats offer prompt and deferential treatment to the narrator *qua* subdirector of *Proceso*. Although in isolation the texts deal with particular facets of journalism, as a group the three nonfiction novels demonstrate the contradictions of the powers of journalism: subject to repressive manipulation by the state, capable of sensationalistically manipulating public opinion against the state, and theoretically available to mediate between the state and society as a tool for effective social change.

IV

In this chapter, I have placed in the foreground two aspects of Leñero's nonfiction novels. First, the references to the nonfictional status of *Los periodistas*, *La gota de agua*, and *Asesinato* emphasize the worldliness of the texts, the series of relationships that embed each novel in its circumstances. Second, the texts all depend upon and often surprisingly exploit narrative stategies characteristic of the novel. As an effect of these aspects, the narrative transformation in each novel attempts to convince readers that a certain interpretation of the world, usually at variance with or simply omitted from either official or popular interpretations, is indeed a better representation of reality.

Terms such as transformation, interpretation, and representation, however, make patent the problematic status of the dichotomy between fiction and nonfiction. Although *Los periodistas* and *Asesinato* explicitly reject "fiction" as disguise and deformation and all three of the novels strive for immediacy through references to real persons, places, public documents and historical events, they are nevertheless linguistic constructions, and hence, mediated representations of the world. In this respect, nonfiction itself is also a disguise, deformation, or as I prefer, a transformation, for the events do not write themselves. Instead, by using the same narrative techniques available for and associated with fiction, the nonfiction novel represents the world in a manner that endows the events with meaning. This is not to deny the change of directors in *Excélsior*, the shortage of water in Mexico City, or the experiences of the Flores family. Rather, as the philosophical speculation on truth in *Asesinato* demonstrates, meaningful representations are both enmeshed in worldly interests and limited by worldly perspectives. Therefore, the significance of these events--the incident in *Excélsior* as a political *golpe* against free expression, the potentially catastrophic and actually unjust dimensions of Mexico City's water problems, and the socio-historical implications of the Flores Muñoz murders together with the abuse of Gilberto Flores Alavez by the press, police, and judiciary system--are all effects produced and limited by the strategic use of novelistic narrative techniques as set into play by a specific series of worldly interests. In this perspective, the self-referential emphasis on the nonfictional status of the novels, rather than ontologically separate them from fiction, functions as a literary convention that endows the texts with greater urgency; it creates the illusion of the empirical authority of the novelistic representation, and in turn, seeks to hold greater persuasive powers over readers. In sum, the nonfiction novels of Vicente Leñero extend his dual critical practice of novelization: they participate in the utility of the Mexican novel to comprehend history, to create history, and to explore the real by transforming, representing, and interpreting specific facets of contemporary Mexican reality.

Conclusion:

Vicente Leñero: The Novelist as Critic

> . . . la literatura no se hace con fragmentos de realidad, ni
> con estupideces ni con cinta grabadora; la literatura es
> algo tan serio, tan serio, tan serio, tan serio.

> --Vicente Leñero

Throughout his career as a novelist, Vicente Leñero has explored the formal flexibility and the worldly potential of the novel in a variety of manners. The psychoanalytic dialogue of *A fuerza de palabras*, the socio-epistemological detective work in *Los albañiles*, the metafictional constructs of *Estudio Q* and *El garabato*, the cultural and religious commentary of *Redil de ovejas* and *El evangelio de Lucas Gavilán*, and the contestatory practice of the nonfiction novels, *Los periodistas*, *La gota de agua*, and *Asesinato*, all of these specific manifestations of Leñero's practice of novelistic writing attest to the protean critical uses of the genre. First, each of Leñero's novels may be read against canonic notions about the genre in order to account for exploration of various literary conventions, an implicit critique of the practices of writing novels. And second, the novels all establish important connections to contemporary reality and function as critical comments on the state of human existence. Taken as a whole, the constant, double-edged critical movement that characterizes these texts also constitutes repetitive patterns of values that attach to the phrase "Leñero's novels."

The evolving changes in this body of novels, both in their critique of generic form and of social representation, emerge from the interaction among a series of constant concerns, a core of interests that are not necessarily unified, coherent, or noncontradictory. In general terms, Leñero's use of the novel and his social criticism move in the interstices of the issues of redemption and the communal constitution of the world. The constellation of problems surrounding redemption takes on many forms: social redemption in the denunciation and correction of injustice; spiritual or religious redemption for both the individual and society through a search for meaning in existence; and quite often, an intellectual redemption expressed as a need to understand the possible existence and significance of the concept of truth. Likewise, Leñero's interest in the social constitution of reality conforms to a variety of questions: the conditions that allow for the production and recognition of knowledge; and the different manifestations of power relationships in society, especially in terms of the State (as government, police, and judicial system), journalism, the Church as a social institution, and, more broadly, the communal constraints governing the definition of the natural or the normal in social and psychological behavior. The determining factor in the movement of these concerns throughout Leñero's novels is not the possible, coherent unification of this group of interests, but the various syntheses of them, in which the attention given to a predominant topic modifies, filters, or supresses the working of the others.[1]

According to the chronology of their publication, Leñero's novels emerge as two sequential groups with one text serving as a transitional moment between the two. The "first cycle" of Leñero's novels includes *A fuerza de palabras* (originally *La voz adolorida*), *Los albañiles*, *Estudio Q*, and *El garabato*. Central to all of these novels is the epistemological interrogation of knowledge. To a certain degree, the structure of each novel responds to the problematic nature of knowledge, truth, and the search for definite answers: Enrique's "dialogue" with his therapist manifests his desire for freedom and regeneration in *A fuerza de palabras*; the detective (or anti-detective) structure of *Los albañiles* foregrounds Munguía's search for truth and the resolution of an enigma; and the metafictional strategies of *Estudio Q* and *El garabato* make patent the arbitrariness of the socially and institutionally defined boundaries of reality.

Moreover, the structural interrogation of the limits of knowledge is repeated in the interaction between text and readers. A profound asymmetry between addresser and addressee lies at the base of these novels, and readers are constantly placed in the difficult position of wrestling with the problematic production of knowledge through the act of reading. Thus, while the significance of the first cycle of novels may ultimately depend on readers' frustrations, such a meaning arises from a basically noncooperative interaction between text and readers.[2] Just as the principal characters or narrator(s) of the first cycle of novels grapple with the problem of knowledge in their search for various kinds of redemption, so do readers similarly confront the problematic place of knowledge in the attempt to explain and justify interpretations.

At the base of this asymmetry resides another aspect of Leñero's practice of the novel: power relationships. Each of the texts thematically explores the hierarchy of power relationships: Enrique's insufficiency and subnormalcy vis-a-vis his therapeutic interlocutor and "normal" society in *A fuerza de palabras*; Munguía's official power to demand answers from the murder suspects versus their tactics of resistance, and also the internal hierarchies that both unify and divide all of the social groups in *Los albañiles*; and finally, the characters' struggles to establish identity and autonomy in worlds that continually collapse into the shadow-box of a master puppeteer in *Estudio Q* and *El garabato*. The hierarchical order sustained by these power relations provokes antagonistic behavior that is metaphorically demonstrated in one of the least commented passages of *Los albañiles*. When one of the suspects, the ex-seminarian Sergio, attends a night-school class in English, he is called upon to read:

> --The mice in council. Some little mice, who lived in
> the walls of house, met together one night, to talk of
> the wicked cat and to consider what could be done to
> get ride (sic) of her. The head mice were Brown-back,

> Gray-ear, and White-whisker. "There is no comfort
> in the house", said Brown-back. "What can we do?"
> asked Gray-ear. "Shall we all run at her at once and
> bite he (sic), and frighten her away?"[3]

Throughout the early novels power relations arise from
hierarchical social orders in which the underlings continually
strive to unite themselves against the power from above, and, as
the "reading" from *Los albañiles* suggests, such a plan usually
implies various forms of violence.

Similarly, the problem of power relations at the thematic level
recurs in the interaction between text and readers: the witholding
of knowledge, viewed in one perspective as an epistemological
problem for interpretation, not only thwarts the desire incited in
readers for greater knowledge and the resolution of enigmas, but
also it provokes a certain frustration and requires greater
participation on the part of readers in the production of meaning.
On the one hand, such a relationship may have quite positive
effects. The intense and overt deployment of novelistic techniques
in these texts places in the foreground their process of
composition and, in a parallel movement, encourages readers to
occupy more active interpretive positions. Terry Eagleton judges
such activity to be ultimately beneficial; texts openly display their
own becoming "so that they will not be mistaken for absolute
truth--so that the reader will be encouraged to reflect critically on
the partial, particular ways they construct reality, and so to
recognize how it might all have happened differently."[4]

On the other hand, Leñero's novels of the 1960s and a great
number of the novels of the Boom all bear the hallmark of a
constant search for originality, and hence an ever-increasing
exploitation of literary pyrotechnics. In the context of the Spanish
American novel, the abundance of extremely self-conscious or
metafictional texts in these years comes to constitute a norm
rather than an exception. In the case of Leñero, however, the
intense interrogation of the limits of novelistic structure led him to

the practice of self-parody.[5]   According to Leñero's autobiographical statements, self-parody implied a certain loss of
relevance, an entrapment within the pages of a purely literary or
textual world that often seemed to have little to do with social
reality.[6] In a similar manner, the difficulty of a novel as complex as
Estudio Q has led few readers to applaud enthusiastically its
structural perfection.   In this perspective, the asymmmetry of
textual power relations eventually gave rise not only to rejection or
lack of attention from readers but also to "burn out" for Leñero.

Indeed, after the first cycle of novels Vicente Leñero turned
his creative energies toward the theater and journalistic endeavors.
In both his drama and journalism, the emphasis on documentary
and historical discourse seems to underscore a search for a
different kind of communication that was not satisfied by the
writing of novels.   Moreover, the events at Tlatelolco in 1968
perhaps served to confirm Leñero's need to redirect his expressive
energies toward different readerships.   Finally, in 1973 Leñero
published another novel, *Redil de ovejas*. Although Leñero began
this text as early as 1966, he did not complete it until the early
1970s.[7] Perhaps because of the prolonged interruption in its
composition, *Redil de ovejas* occupies a place as a transitional text
into his "second cycle" of novels.

In *Redil de ovejas* readers encounter a combination of the
predominant preoccupations of Leñero's first cycle of novels--
problems of knowledge about society and the search for
redemption--combined with an entrance into the principal
concerns of his later novels: the workings of power in social
institutions such as the Church and journalism, and the
ideological implications of the aesthetic representation of social
reality in general. The structural patterns and repetitive identities
in *Redil de ovejas* serve to explore the socio-historical context of
institutional changes in Catholicism. In the chapters that produce
a questioning of the nature of identity, Leñero returns to the
structural innovations of his earlier novels and readers confront
the epistemological difficulty of separating parallel generations of

identically named characters. The problematic identity/knowledge structure, in turn, is alternated among another series of chapters dealing with specific moments in Mexican history. Through this progression of historical frames, *Redil de ovejas* traces the use of religious symbols in Mexican culture and the liberalizing movement of Vatican II that culminates in a negative reaction on the part of conservative Mexican Catholicism. Such a combination of themes and techniques in *Redil de ovejas* begins the shift away from the intricacies of the literary experimentation with novel form and moves toward the historical dynamics of forces that constitute the dominant interpretations of social reality in Mexican culture.

Throughout the second cycle, Leñero's novels respond in a direct manner to the forces at work in the social constitution of reality. This group includes: *El evangelio de Lucas Gavilán* and the three nonfiction novels, *Los periodistas*, *La gota de agua*, and *Asesinato*. The kinds of power relationships considered in these novels include the function of the Church (not as a spiritual institution but as a social institution with concrete, material interests), the State (with its powers to censor, to police, and to judge), and journalism. Moreover, these novels are much more easily read than the previous ones, a strategy that perhaps derives from the need to respond more directly to issues relevant to contemporary Mexican society. Although the importance of structure and the interest in the potential uses of the genre never diminish, such an exploration adopts quite different guises in these texts.

Of all Leñero's novels, *El evangelio de Lucas Gavilán* most overtly confronts the issue of the power relations among social groups and it does so in terms of class conflict. As a translation of the Gospel of Luke into a contemporary Mexican context, the novel emphasizes Christ's interest in the liberation of the poor and marginal in the original text (the outcast Other of the dominant classes), and it also "deconstructs" the received interpretations that control the social significance of the biblical text. In brief, *El evangelio de Lucas Gavilán* explores the possibility of a socially responsible and critical Christianity according to the insights of liberation theology. Although the novel structurally follows the organization of the biblical pre-text, *El evangelio de Lucas Gavilán* demands a reading attentive both to the novel itself and to the decomposition of received interpretations. Such activity does not require that readers become theologians but rather that they participate in an act of imagination that reveals what Christianity could become.

In contrast to the imaginative hermeneutics of *El evangelio de Lucas Gavilán* and its emphasis on social redemption, the nonfiction novels exploit a different strategy. These novels presuppose the necessity of convincing readers that a certain interpretation of events is correct, even though it may have been excluded from either official or popular accounts. Indeed, the narrative strategies in these nonfiction texts strive to constitute a convincing representation of reality. First, the novels all depend on the integration of documents from the "real world" in order to establish an empirical authority for the text. In the case of *Los periodistas* and *Asesinato*, introductory statements make explicit the claim to have constructed a true representation of the events. *La gota de agua*, by comparison, depends on a variety of intensified Realism that integrates multiple, commonplace elements of the "real world" into the text. In this way the nonfiction novels set into play their subversive communicative purpose, that is, they attempt to debunk prior versions of the events.

Moreover, in each of these novels, the use of structure and narrative strategies is determined by the specific version of events that Leñero has chosen to represent. In *Los periodistas* the movement of the novel from problem to crisis to resolution is coupled with a dichotomous characterization that shows how honest journalists won out over the under-handed manipulation of a government that wanted to censor critical expression. *La gota de agua* similarly exploits the momentum of a linear development from the beginning of a crisis, through its rising action, and to its end in order to make patent the different lessons that the narrator learned in the experience. *Asesinato*, in contrast, eschews any traditional formulation of textual structuring as narrative plot. In general terms, *Asesinato* recounts the story of a murder and an investigation from several points of view: the sensationalistic news coverage, the biographical past of the family involved in the crime, a novelization of the night of the crime itself with its consequences, a reconsideration of all of the legal data, and an interview with the convicted murderer. In the final analysis, the ordering and juxtaposition of versions of the crime moves the novel away from establishing a single truth and instead stages truth as an element enmeshed in social interests and controlled by the power of the dominant class in Mexican society. *Asesinato* thus manifests a return to issues similar to those confronted in *Los albañiles*: a quasi-detective structure that contemplates the impossibility of absolute knowledge; a consideration of the power relations that allow a dominant class to control justice in society; and the almost mystic faith of the fervently Catholic grandson convicted for the murder of his grandparents.

In summary, the second cycle of novels questions primarily the working of power in contemporary Mexican society. In these novels, however, structure is not necessarily at the service of a search for originality in terms of new generic configurations; rather it is a rhetorical device that, on the one hand, serves to translate effectively the Gospel of St. Luke in terms of contemporary Mexican social problems, and on the other, endows the nonfiction texts with authority and power to convince readers of a certain representation of the world. In addition, the confrontations among the State, journalism, and society at large is a central thematic concern in all of the nonfiction novels. Whereas *Los periodistas* denounces government attempts to censor critical, liberal journalism, and *La gota de agua* indirectly demonstrates the power socially attributed to journalists in the form of deferential treatment from State bureaucrats, *Asesinato* reconsiders the power of journalism to manipulate unjustly the

State and society by fomenting a misinformed public opinion. In other words, the nonfiction novels as a group suppose the vulnerability of journalism to State manipulation, the power of journalism to manipulate the State and society, and finally, the possibility of a positive and transforming journalism that could mediate between the State and society in the correction of social injustice. In the end, however, any optimism implicit in such a project is tempered by a strong degree of skepticism in *Asesinato*, which demonstrates that truth and justice are not abstract notions to be strived for in isolated purity, but pragmatic concepts embedded in the power relations of social reality and hence subject to all kinds of distortions according to the interests of the controlling powers.

Throughout Leñero's novels readers confront a constant emphasis on both the formal aspects of the genre and the importance of social criticism. With regard to these facets, his texts evolve in principally two stages. In the first cycle of novels, the production of knowledge about society is the predominant concern. Similarly, the early novels depend on narrative structures that create a deep asymmetry between text and readers and hence repeat the epistemological thematics in the process of their reading. The second cycle of novels, in contrast, moves toward a more direct consideration of contemporary social reality, especially of the power relations at work in society. Whereas Redil de ovejas serves as a transition between the two cycles of novels, the later group predicates a fundamentally different approach to literary communication. First, given the variance between the latter novels and official, popular, or received interpretations of reality and religion, they must each strive to convince readers, to subvert persuasively the hold of previous versions or interpretations. And second, structure serves to produce a specific kind of story, a cogent representation of a different version of events. In sum, the textual practice of Leñero's novels has constantly exploited the flexibility of the genre and its possible uses for social criticism. As a result of this double, critical focus,

Leñero's novels stand among the most formally protean and culturally aware novels in contemporary Mexican and Spanish American literature.

NOTES

Introduction: Vicente Leñero and the Contemporary Mexican Novel

1 Michel Foucault, *Language, Counter-Memory, Practice*, ed. Donald F. Bouchard, trans. Donald F. Bouchard and Sherry Simon (Ithaca: Cornell UP, 1977) 123.

2 Edward W. Said, *The World, the Text, and the Critic* (Cambridge, Massachusetts: Harvard UP, 1983) 35.

3 Said 157.

4 Context is a problematic concept for it has no closure: it extends backward throughout the past history of society and language, and forward up to the present in which readers attempt to interpret a specific text. See, for example, T. K. Seung, *Semiotics and Thematics in Hermeneutics* (New York: Columbia UP, 1982) 17-50. Consequently, the observations in this introduction synthetically reduce the context to a series of basic frames or trends that impinge upon the evaluation of Leñero's novelistic production.

5 John S. Brushwood, *The Spanish American Novel: A Twentieth-Century Survey* (Austin: U of Texas P, 1975) 157.

6 Although I will emphasize the nature of such innovation below, it bears pointing out that this experimentation is not an *ex nihilo* novelty in the history of either the Mexican or the Spanish American novel. Indeed, it is a moment of synthesis in which the vanguardist interests characteristic of some prose fiction of the late 1920s and 1930s come into contact with the more socially oriented and regionalistic veins of Spanish American letters. See Brushwood, *Spanish American Novel* 157-60, 211-13, and José M. Promis, "En torno a la Nueva Novela Hispanoamericana: reubicación de un concepto," *Chasqui* 7.1 (1976): 15-27.

7 Roland Barthes, *S/Z*, trans. Richard Howard (New York: Hill and Wang, 1974) 4-5.

8 Joseph P. Sommers, *After the Storm: Landmarks of the Modern Mexican Novel* (Albuquerque: U of New Mexico P, 1968) 166.

9 Margarita Vargas, *Grupo "Revista Mexicana de Literatura" y sus coetáneos*, diss., University of Kansas, 1985 (Ann Arbor: UMI, 1986), provides detailed treatment of the predominant group associated with the "universalizing" tendency in Mexican literature. Although there is thematic similarity between the early novels of Vicente Leñero and the production of the group from *Revista Mexicana de Literatura*, particularly in their questioning of the nature of reality, Leñero never formed a part of this association of writers, in spite of their generational link.

10 John S. Brushwood, *México en su novela: Una nación en busca de su identidad*, trans. Fracisco González Aramburo (Mexico: Fondo de Cultura Económica, 1973) 78.

11 Brushwood, *México en su novela* 92-93.

12 John S. Brushwood, *La novela mexicana (1967-1982)* (Mexico: Grijalbo, 1985) 17-33.

13 Vicente Leñero, *Vicente Leñero: Nuevos escritores mexicanos del siglo XX presentados por sí mismos* (Mexico: Empresas Editoriales, 1967) 24, 42-43, 54.

14 George R. McMurray, "Current Trends in the Mexican Novel," *Hispania* 51 (1986): 536.

15 Brushwood, *México en su novela* 76-121; Brushwood, *Novela mexicana* 17-33.

16 Brushwood, *México en su novela* 83.

17 Brushwood, *Spanish American Novel* 211; Angel Rama, "El 'boom' en perspectiva," *Más allá del boom: Literatura y mercado* (Mexico: Marcha Editores, 1981) 51-110.

18 José Miguel Oviedo, "Una discusión permanente," *América Latina en su literatura*, ed. César Fernández Moreno (Mexico: Siglo XXI and UNESCO, 1972) 436-437.

19 Fernando Alegría, "Antiliteratura," *América Latina en su literatura* 243-258.

20 Brushwood, *Novela mexicana* 17-33.

21 Brushwood, *Novela mexicana* 35.

22 Nostalgia tends to characterize the novels of younger writers who begin to publish in the 1970s. Alice Reckley, *Looking*

Ahead Through the Past: Nostalgia in the Recent Mexican Novel,
diss., University of Kansas, 1985 (Ann Arbor: UMI, 1986), offers a
critical examination of the various kinds of nostalgia in selected
contemporary Mexican novels.

23 Brushwood, *Novela mexicana* 98-100.

24 See John S. Brushwood, "Mexican Fiction in the Seventies:
Author, Intellect, and Public," *Ibero-American Letters in a
Comparative Perspective,* eds. Wolodymyr T. Zyla and Wendell M.
Aycock (Lubbock: Texas Tech P, 1978) 35-47, for a consideration of
the difficulties readers confront in self-referential novels.

25 Angel Rama, "Los contestatarios del poder," *Novísimos
narradores hispanoamericanos en marcha 1964-1980* (Mexico:
Marcha Editores, 1981) 9-48, underscores the importance of the
"reingreso de la historia" (15).

26 Although *modernismo* in Hispanic literary studies has
traditionally suggested *modernista* poetry, the movement has
deep links with journalism and prose fiction. Two studies by Aníbal
González, *La crónica modernista hispanoamericana* (Madrid:
Ediciones José Porrúa Turranzas, 1983) and *La novela modernista
hispanoamericana* (Madrid: Editorial Gredos, 1987), indicate the
lines along which the exclusive identification of *modernismo* with
poetry errs.

27 In addition to the studies cited above in note 6, see Gustavo
Pérez Firmat, *Idle Fictions* (Durham, North Carolina: Duke UP,
1982) for a sustained account of vanguard prose fiction in Hispanic
literatures.

28 Carol Clark D'Lugo, *Fragmentation and Reader Response:
A Study of Anti-Classical Strategies in the Mexican Novel: 1947-
1965,* diss., Brown University, 1983 (Ann Arbor: UMI, 1984),
provides a provocative study of the relationship between narrative
strategies and the experience of reading. Generally, she identifies
the possibility of a "passive" reading with classical strategies,
which I refer to as the conventions of nineteenth-century Realism,
and similarly, she notes the imperative of an "active" experience
because of anti-classical strategies that come to the fore after 1947.

One: Epistemology and Interpretation:
The Contradictions of Narrative in *A fuerza de palabras*

1 Vicente Leñero, *La voz adolorida* (Xalapa: Universidad Veracruzana, 1961) and *A fuerza de palabras* (Buenos Aires: Centro Editor de América Latina, 1967). Throughout the study I will refer to the most recent edition, *A fuerza de palabras* (Mexico: Grijalbo, 1976). Page numbers for quoted passages will appear within parentheses.

In reference to the differences between the versions of the novel Lois Sherry Grossman, *Las novelas de Vicente Leñero: El primer ciclo (1961-1967)*, diss., Rutgers University, 1972 (Ann Arbor: UMI, 1973), states: "Los cambios entre una y otra edición son significativos pero no radicales. Sirven para reforzar la continuidad del monólogo, insistir más en ella; pero el concepto de continuidad ya quedó bien claro aún en la forma más tradicional" (22-23); see also 29-30. In a later study Miguel Angel Niño, *Religión y sociedad en la obra de Vicente Leñero*, diss., Michigan State University, 1977 (Ann Arbor: UMI, 1978), refers to Grossman's analysis and concludes that *A fuerza de palabras* is a stylistically better novel but that the characterization of Enrique becomes weaker (49-50). Although consideration of the differences between the two editions does provide an evolutionary perspective on literary creation, this chapter confronts solely the question of signifying structures in the definitive version of the text, *A fuerza de palabras*.

2 M. M. Bakhtin, *The Dialogic Imagination*, trans. Caryl Emerson and Michael Holquist (Austin: U of Texas P, 1981) 15.

3 Emile Benveniste, "Subjectivity in Language," *Problems in General Linguistics*, trans. Mary Elizabeth Meek (Coral Gables, Florida: U of Miami P, 1971) 223-30, outlines the role of language in establishing human "subjectivity." See also his essays "Relationships of Person in the Verb" (195-204) and "The Nature of Pronouns" (217-22).

4 The critic Iris Josefina Ludmer, "Vicente Leñero, *Los albañiles*. Lector y actor," *Nueva novela latinoamericana I*, ed. Jorge Lafforgue (Buenos Aires: Editorial Paidós, 1969), 194-208, has observed that all of Leñero's novels of the 1960s are based on a communicative imbalance:

> . . . se estructuran en base a una relación asimétrica. Por un lado un interlocutor, una persona que gana información a costa de otra, sin que la gane a costa de ella: es el receptor que escucha, organiza, piensa, lee. Por otro lado el actor, el hablante que actúa, vive, siente, comunica, se expresa sobre sí mismo y constituye la ficción. La función del receptor es ordenar, dar forma, interpretar el material dado y recrear imaginativamente los hechos; la función del locutor es simplemente emitir una narración, tratando de dejar de lado toda conciencia y toda racionalización. (197)

Although Ludmer refers to *La voz adolorida* in her comments, this asymmetry remains constant in *A fuerza de palabras*. In fact, it is perhaps even more noteworthy in the later version given that the interlocutor previously called *doctor* has become simply *usted*.

Also, Seminario de Semiótica: Ana Guadalupe Martínez, et al., "La organización temporal del relato en *A fuerza de palabras*," *Semiosis* 7-8 (1981-82): 35-63, considers many aspects related to Enrique's speaking. Seminario de Semiótica: Reina América Pulido, et al., "*A fuerza de palabras*: Una decodificación," *Semiosis* 7-8 (1981-82): 3-34, takes into account the aspect of speaking, although in a manner somewhat more tangential than in the previous article.

5 Lucía Garavito, "La narración y la focalización como bases para un análisis de la novelística de Vicente Leñero," *Semiosis* 4 (1980): 61-82, characterizes the distortion of Enrique's subjectivity by noting that

> . . . el relato está a cargo de Enrique. Se trata pues, según la terminología de Bal, de un narrador autodiegético, es decir, un narrador homodiegético, que cuenta una historia en la que él es el protagonista principal. A más de ser narrador, el protagonista es simultáneamente focalizador, puesto que selecciona los eventos y personajes a presentar y la manera de hacerlo. La totalidad del *récit* está contado de acuerdo con su punto de vista y el énfasis recae por lo tanto en la forma en que el narrador-focalizador interpreta la realidad que lo rodea. (62-63)

Garavito refers to the narratological theories of Mieke Bal, *Narratologie: Les instances du récit* (Paris: Editions Klincksieck, 1977). Although Garavito makes the quoted observation with respect to *La voz adolorida*, the remarks still hold true for *A fuerza de palabras*.

[6] For a detailed analysis of the opening phrases of the novel, see the Seminario de Semiótica, "La organización temporal del relato en *A fuerza de palabras*" 45.

[7] Benveniste, "Remarks on the Function of Language in Freudian Theory," *Problems in General Linguistics* 65.

[8] In more technical terms, this is the process of formulating *implicatures*: the various deductions and inferences one makes in order to attribute meaning to a certain use of language. See H. P. Grice, "Logic and Conversation," *Syntax and Semantics: Volume 3 Speech Acts*, eds. Peter Cole and Jerry L. Morgan (New York: Academic P, 1975) 41-58. Although formulated for the analysis of speech acts in conversational exchange, Mary Louise Pratt, *Toward a Speech-Act Theory of Literary Discourse* (Bloomington: Indiana UP, 1977) extends the function of implicatures to the understanding of the literary text.

[9] T. K. Seung, *Semiotics and Thematics in Hermeneutics* (New York: Columbia UP, 1982) 33.

[10] Seung 34.

[11] The terms *histoire* and *récit* serve to establish the relationship between discourse and the events that it recounts; they refer to ordering of the temporal aspects of the text. The *récit* consists of the printed text as it is presented to readers, the events as rendered in the discourse including possible temporal inversions or *anachronies*, principally *analepses* (flashbacks) and *prolepses* (flashforwards). The *histoire*, in contrast, is a reconstruction of the events in their linear, chronological sequence; that is to say, a "history" of events prior to their representation, a history before it is transformed by the act of narrating, the technical sense of *narration*, in order to produce the *récit*. See Gérard Genette, *Narrative Discourse: An Essay in Method*, trans. Jane E. Lewin (Ithaca: Cornell UP, 1980) 27, 25-86.

[12] Seminario de Semiótica, "*A fuerza de palabras*: Una decodificación" 5-13.

[13] Niño 39-50.

[14] R. Díaz-Guerrero, *Psychology of the Mexican* (Austin: U of Texas P, 1975) 56. Cited Niño 50.

[15] Niño 53.

[16] Bakhtin 49.

[17] The terms refer to the theoretical elements of the literary communication act as proposed by Seymour Chatman, *Story and Discourse: Narrative Structures in Fiction and Film* (Ithaca: Cornell UP, 1978), Roman Jakobson, "Linguistics and Poetics," *Style in Language*, ed. T. A. Sebeok (Cambridge, Massachusetts: M. I. T. P, 1960), Wayne Booth, *The Rhetoric of Fiction* (Chicago: U of Chicago P, 1961), and M. M. Bakhtin, *The Dialogic Imagination*, trans. Caryl Emerson and Michael Holquist (Austin: U of Texas P, 1975).

[18] Naomi Schor, "Fiction as Interpretation/Interpretation as Fiction," *Reading in Detail: Aesthetics and the Feminine* (New York: Methuen, 1987) 120-30, provides an account of how characters who interpret in a text, *intepretants* in her terminology, provide

models that guide readers of a text in their own interpretive activity.

19 I will be using the word "transference" in two senses. First, I am signaling the apparent shift or exchange in the location of critical power and interpretive authority. Secondly, I am alluding to the more technical sense of transference as it is used in psychoanalysis, specifically along Lacanian lines. In brief, this latter technical meaning of transference establishes the place of knowledge in the relationship between analyst and analysand. As Michel de Certeau, in "Lacan: An Ethics of Speech," *Heterologies: Discourses on the Other*, trans. Brian Massumi (Minneapolis: U of Minnesota P, 1986), explains:

> At the beginning, the analyst is "presumed" by his patients to "know": he functions as the object of their belief. As for these patients, they expect from him what at heart they do not want to know (the secret of their "trouble"), and they instead want only an ear to hear their symptoms. . . .
>
> What, then, is an analyst? Lacan answers that, "Whoever it may be," he is put in the position of "supposed knowledge," he has grasped and does not forget the state of this knowledge; thereafter, he becomes capable of "operating" with this hand of cards, if and only if he does not identify with this position and does not turn what is given to him into an object of pleasure. (54-55)

20 In exploring the implications of a Lacanian notion of transference for literary interpretation, Shoshana Felman, "To Open the Question," *Literature and Psychoanalysis: The Question of Reading: Otherwise*, ed. Shoshana Felman (Baltimore: Johns Hopkins UP, 1982) 5-10, notes the "odd status of what is called a 'literary critic'" (7). She explains that this odd status owes to a paradox of literature for two reasons:

1) the work of literary analysis resembles the work of the psychoanalyst; 2) the status of what is analyszed--the text--is, however, not that of a patient, but rather that of a master: we say of the author the he is a master; the text has for us authority--the very type of authority by which Jacques Lacan indeed defines the role of the psychoanalyst in the structure of transference. Like the psychoanalyst viewed by the patient, the text is viewed by us as "a subject presumed to know"--as the very place where meaning, and *knowledge* of meaning, reside. With respect to the text, the literary critic occupies thus at once the place of the psychoanalyst (in the relation of interpretation) *and* the place of the patient (in the relation of transference). (7)

In the same volume, Shoshana Felman, "Turning the Screw of Interpretation" (94-207), performs a brilliant reading of transference in the interpretation of Henry James's *The Turn of the Screw*.

21 The subnormalcy of the represented speech situation notwithstanding, Pratt points out that in written texts, understanding arises from the conventionally accepted fact that the text as a whole is meaningful (201-223). Whereas the represented speech acts among characters may not be meaningful, one must assume that the literary speech act itself is an expression commensurate with the author's intention. Hence the "hyperprotected" (215) convention of meaningfulness and also the opposition between the "represented speech act/situation" and the "literary speech act." See also, Jonathan Culler, "Problems in the Theory of Fiction," *Diacritics* 14.1 (1984): 2-11.

22 Shoshana Felman, "Psychoanalysis and Pedagogy: Teaching Terminable and Interminable," *Teaching as a Literary*

Genre, ed. Barbara Johnson (Baltimore: Johns Hopkins UP, 1982), 29-30.

23 Peter Brooks, "Fictions of the Wolfman: Freud and Narrative Understanding," *Diacritics* 9.1 (1979): 77. Peter Brooks, *Reading for the Plot: Design and Intention in Narrative* (New York: Alfred A. Knopf, 1984), includes a revised version of this essay. Notably, in the quoted passage Brooks is referring to the epistemological binds that Freud encountered when interpreting the famous case history of the "Wolfman."

24 Various critics have recognized the epistemological dilemma yet no one has confronted its importance as an integral aspect of the meaning of *A fuerza de palabras.* For example, Grossman indicates:

> Al terminar la novela el lector se da cuenta de que la narrativa del enfermo ha sido la reconstrucción de una vida que existe tanto novelísticamente como realmente en sus palabras. Es decir, Enrique existe sólo en función de su habilidad de comunicar su existencia al interlocutor mudo que le escucha: sea psiquiatra, el lector de la novela o la sociedad en general. Hacerse entender para conseguir la ayuda que ansía sería conseguir la comprensión que necesita. . . . (17)

Yet Grossman feels the need to explain Enrique's narrative because "se crea en la novela el retrato de un ambiente real que refleja un segmento de la sociedad mexicana contemporánea" (18). In this case, to move from text to world too rapidly collapses the difference between Enrique's act of representing his life through discourse and the novel's status as a representation of discourse. Such a collapse obscures the difficult referential value of Leñero's novel, and by imposing meaningfulness it also forecloses consideration of the transferences that catch up readers in the play of interpretive power.

Two: Risk and Responsibility: Detective, Readers, and the Postmodern in *Los albañiles*

[1] Vicente Leñero, *Los albañiles* (Barcelona: Seix Barral, 1964). The page numbers for quotations from this edition will appear within parentheses after the cited passage.

[2] Tzvetan Todorov, *The Poetics of Prose*, trans. Richard Howard (Ithaca: Cornell UP, 1977) 44.

[3] Todorov 45. On the basis of these characteristics, Todorov elaborates a more detailed description of the whodunit:

> We are concerned then in the whodunit with two stories of which one is absent but real, the other present but insignificant. This presence and this absence explain the existence of the two in the continuity of the narrative. The first involves so many conventions and literary devices (which are in fact the "plot" aspects of the narrative) that the author cannot leave them unexplained. These devices are, we may note, of essentially two types, temporal inversions and individual "points of view": the tenor of each piece of information is determined by the person who transmits it, no observation exists without an observer; the author cannot, by definition, be omniscient as he was in the classical novel. The second story then appears as a place where all these devices are justified and "naturalized": to give them a "natural" quality, the author must explain that he is writing a book! And to keep this second story from becoming opaque, from casting a useless shadow on the first, the style is to be kept neutral and plain, to the point where it is rendered imperceptible. (46-7)

4 Michael Holquist, "Whodunit and Other Questions: Metaphysical Detective Stories in Post-War Fiction," *New Literary History* 3 (1971): 151.

5 Peter Brooks, *Reading for the Plot: Design and Intention in Narrative* (New York: Alfred A. Knopf, 1984) 316.

6 Holquist 155.

7 Iris Josefina Ludmer, "Vicente Leñero, *Los albañiles*. Lector y actor," *Nueva novela latinoamericana: I*, ed. Jorge Lafforgue (Buenos Aires: Paidós, 1969) 194-196; Lois Sherry Grossman, *Las novelas de Vicente Leñero: El primer ciclo (1961-1967)*, diss., Rutgers U, 1972 (Ann Arbor: UMI, 1973) 11, 40-41; Neil Jay Devereaux, *Tres escritores representativos de la novelística mexicana reciente*, diss., U of Texas-Austin, 1973 (Ann Arbor: UMI, 1973) 37-8; John M. Lipski, "Vicente Leñero: Narrative Evolution as Religious Search," *Hispanic Journal* 3.2 (1982): 43.

8 Brooks 287.

9 Grossman 57, considers three temporal levels: the investigation, the murder (Monday night), and the nine months preceeding the crime. Before this period, she speaks of prehistory. I prefer to divide the temporal levels into two groups: before the murder and after the murder. The actual night of the murder is a void not included in either of the divisions. Whereas the investigation, after the crime, seeks to know what happened in the void, the period before the crime is the sequence of events leading up to it, which I divide into two categories: the nine months of work at the construction site, and the individual past of each character before their coming together as a group. All temporal levels either lead up to or attempt to return to the murder, but as an enigma, the time of the murder is the absence around which *Los albañiles* is organized.

10 The verisimilitude of social details in *Los albañiles* is documented in Mary L. Seale, "Two Views of Contemporary Mexico," *South Atlantic Bulletin* 41.4 (1976): 48-55, and Miguel Angel Niño, *Religión y sociedad en la obra de Vicente Leñero*, diss., Michigan State U, 1977 (Ann Arbor: UMI, 1977) 66-74.

[11] This technique of representation resembles Oscar Lewis's innovative anthropological reporting in *The Children of Sánchez* (London: Penguin Books, 1964). In Lewis's study the composite picture of the social group arises from a thrice-repeated pattern of accounts given by four children of Jesús Sánchez, framed within a prologue and an epilogue in the words of Jesús Sánchez. This unusual style of anthropological reporting supposedly includes the data necessary for formulating a more objective view of reality as readers must organize and evaluate the subjective versions of each speaker. In this regard, see the comparison Seale makes between *Los alabañiles* and *The Children of Sánchez*.

[12] In this regard, see the comparison Seale makes between *Los albañiles* and *The Children of Sánchez*.

[13] Ludmer 196-97.

[14] Ludmer, Grossman, Niño, and Lipski all allude to the importance of *el hombre de la corbata a rayas*. See also Humberto Robles, "Aproximaciones a *Los albañiles* de Vicente Leñero," *Revista Iberoamericana* 73 (1970):579-99.

[15] Jacques Derrida, "Plato's Pharmacy," *Dissemination*, trans. Barbara Johnson (Chicago: U of Chicago P, 1981) 61-171; Rene Girard, *Violence and the Sacred*, trans. Patrick Gregory (Baltimore: Johns Hopkins UP, 1977); and Northrop Frye, *Anatomy of Criticism* (Princeton: Princeton UP, 1957), all include various interpretations of the "figure" of the scapegoat or *pharmakos*.

[16] Jean-François Lyotard, *The Postmodern Condition: A Report on Knowledge*, trans. Geoff Bennington and Brian Massumi (Minneapolis: U of Minnesota P, 1984) xxiii.

[17] Lyotard xxiii-xxiv.

[18] Lyotard 40.

[19] Lyotard 32-33.

[20] Lyotard 46.

[21] Brooks 287.

[22] Brooks 287.

23 Lucía Garavito, "La narración y la focalización como base para un análisis de la novelística de Vicente Leñero," *Semiosis* 4 (1980): 71-2.

24 For example, Ludmer writes:

> . . . el verdadero enigma de *Los albañiles*: no quién fue el asesino, sino qué mitos y qué símbolos en movimiento; el lector debe realizar la misma operación del detective pero en segundo grado, debe estructurar el mito religioso, la figura ética y psicológica. El enigma que plantea Leñero son los múltiples sentidos de sus símbolos, que remiten a un trabajo de interpretación: la ambigüedad del símbolo, la indeterminación de los varios sentidos, la equivocidad de las palabras y la anfibología de los enunciados es lo que el detective sabe que tiene que resolver. No caben lecturas a un solo nivel: el intérprete de Leñero es justamente el que da forma igualmente a todas las posibles lecturas; todas las interpretaciones son igualmente necesarias. (206-7)

Indeed, all interpretations are equally necessary, but as Ludmer fails to note, all interpretations according to such mythic and archetypal models are also equally frustrated.

25 Deveraux 34-5.

26 Lipski 45. Joseph Sommers, *After the Storm: Landmarks of the Modern Mexican Novel* (Albuquerque: U of New Mexico P, 1968), while recognizing the importance of the cultural context in *Los albañiles*, labels it "deceptive" (177) and proceeds to note:

> The basic puzzles with which the author confounds the reader make it clear that the Mexican setting, sharply delineated as it is, is merely the vehicle for philosophic examination of universal problems

inherent in modern society. *Los albañiles*, remarkably sure in style and sophisticated in its narrative structure, takes the post-Revolution for granted and assumes that literature must explore the limitations of human nature, human knowledge, and morality. (178)

[27] Mario Benedetti, "México en el pantógrafo de Vicente Leñero," *El ejercicio del criterio* (Mexico: Nueva Imagen, 1981) 285-88, emphasizes the pessimism of *Los albañiles*, stating his dislike for its inherent nihilism.

[28] Julio Cortázar, *Rayuela* (Buenos Aires: Sudamericana, 1963) 453, chapter 79.

[29] Cortázar 454, chapter 79.

[30] Jonathan Culler, *On Deconstruction: Theory and Criticism after Structuralism* (Ithaca: Cornell UP, 1982) 79.

[31] Jacuqes Derrida, *Positions*, trans. Alan Bass (Chicago: U of Chicago P, 1981) 41-42, explains the nature of hierarchies, their inversion, and the interval between binary oppositions.

Three: The Boudaries of Metafiction: *Estudio Q* and *El garabato*

[1] Vicente Leñero, *Estudio Q* (Mexico: Joaquín Mortiz, 1965) and *El garabato* (Mexico: Joaquín Mortiz, 1967). The page numbers that identify the cited passages from these editions will be indicated in parentheses within the text of the chapter.

[2] Robert C. Spires, *Beyond the Metafictional Mode: Directions in the Modern Spanish Novel* (Lexington: UP of Kentucky, 1984) 4.

[3] Gérard Genette, *Narrative Discourse: An Essay in Method*, trans. Jane E. Lewin (Ithaca: Cornell UP, 1980); Mieke Bal, *Narratologie: Les instances du récit* (Paris: Editions Klincksieck, 1977); Seymour Chatman, *Story and Discourse: Narrative*

Structure in Fiction and Film (Ithaca: Cornell UP, 1978); and Shlomith Rimmon-Kenan, *Narrative Fiction: Contemporary Poetics* (London: Methuen, 1983).

4 Spires 15.

5 Genette 236.

6 Spires 15.

7 Lucía Garavito, "La narración y la focalización como base para un análisis de la novelística de Vicente Leñero," *Semiosis* 4 (1980): 61-82, offers a detailed consideration of the use of focalization and narration in the transgression of narrative levels. Ellen Marie McCracken, *The Mass-Media and the Latin American New Novel: Vicente Leñero and Julio Cortázar*, diss., U of California--San Diego, 1977 (Ann Arbor: UMI, 1978), also considers the circularity of the structure of *Estudio Q.*

8 Jorge Luis Borges, "Magias parciales del Quijote," *Prosa completa, II* (Barcelona: Editorial Bruguera, 1980) 172.

9 Luciana Figuerola, "Los códigos de veridicción en *El garabato* de Vicente Leñero," *Semiosis* 4 (1980): 31-59.

10 Roland Barthes, "L'éffet de réel," *Communications* 11 (1968): 84-89.

11 Julio Ortega, "Un ejercicio narrativo de Vicente Leñero," *La contemplación y la fiesta: Notas sobre la novela hispanoamericana* (Caracas: Monte Avila, 1969) 183-88, considers *El garabato* to be fundamentally a questioning of the nature of the novelistic genre.

12 Lois S. Grossman, *Las novelas de Vicente Leñero: El primer ciclo (1961-1967)*, diss., Rutgers U, 1972 (Ann Arbor: UMI, 1973), analyzes *El garabato* as a work of self-parody. Grossman comments: "En *El garabato* Leñero se ha propuesto no la creación sino la parodia de una realidad: la suya, la de un autor de ficción" (107). In this perspective, she views *El garabato* as both a novel and an autobiographical exercise.

13 Spires 16.

14 McCracken also recognizes a similar effect on readers although she posits a consequent movement of self-containment

that always keeps reading at the margin of the textual implications (50-51).

15 Grossman examines the slave-master relation in *Estudio Q* as a question of alienation (87-89). Her commentary manifests great insight into the theme, yet as I demonstrate here, it is not a subordinate aspect of the novel but an integral element of the textual structure.

16 Although John M. Lipski, "Vicente Leñero: Narrative Evolution as Religious Search," *Hispanic Journal* 3.2 (1982): 41-59, considers the religious implications of Leñero's novels, his treatment of *Estudio Q* and *El garabato* in terms of epistemology (47-49) supports the thesis of the arbitrary nature of textual boundaries and the ungrounded nature of an absolute standard of judgment. In addition see, John M. Lipski, "Reading the Writers: Hidden Meta-Structures in the Modern Spanish American Novel," *Perspectives on Contemporary Literature* 6 (1980): 117-24.

17 Throughout this analysis I am indebted to the writings of Jacques Derrida. In reference to the folding and unfolding of the textual surface, Derrida writes about the notion of *invagination* in "Living On * Border Lines," trans. James Hulbert, *Deconstruction and Criticism*, eds. Harold Bloom, et al. (New York: Seabury P, 1979) 75-176. Also of interest are the interviews in Jacques Derrida, *Positions*, trans. Alan Bass (Chicago: U of Chicago P, 1981). Jonathan Culler, *On Deconstruction: Theory and Criticism after Structuralism* (Ithaca: Cornell UP, 1982) gives an evaluation of Derrida's writings. In particular, the section of chapter two titled "Grafts and Graft" (134-55) pertains to the question of self-referentiality.

Four: *Redil de ovejas*:
The Novel as Cultural Criticism

[1] Vicente Leñero, *Redil de ovejas* (Mexico: Joaquín Mortiz, 1973). Page references to the novel will be indicated within parentheses.

[2] Lois S. Grossman, *Las novelas de Vicente Leñero: El primer ciclo* (1961-1967), diss., Rutgers U, 1972 (Ann Arbor: UMI, 1973).

[3] Edward W. Said, *The World, the Text, and the Critic* (Cambridge, Massachusetts: Harvard UP, 1983) 35.

[4] Said 157.

[5] Miguel Angel Niño, *Religión y sociedad en la obra de Vicente Leñero*, diss., Michigan State U, 1977 (Ann Arbor: UMI, 1977). Niño enumerates the various Catholic mentalities portrayed in *Redil de ovejas* (141-53).

[6] Lois S. Grossman, "*Redil de ovejas*: A New Novel from Vicente Leñero," *Romance Notes* 17.2 (1976): 127-30, considers the "flaws" of the novel. See also, Niño 155.

[7] Lucía Garavito, "La narración y la focalización como base para un análisis de la novelística de Vicente Leñero," *Semiosis* 4 (1980): 79-82. In brief, the term focalization refers to the locus of perceptions in narrative. According to Gérard Genette, *Narrative Discourse: An Essay in Method*, trans. Jane E. Lewin (Ithaca: Cornell UP, 1980), 185-211, focalization serves to refine the more traditional concept of "point of view." Whereas *voice*, according to Genette, answers the question "Who speaks?", *focalization* responds to the question "Who sees or who perceives?" This separation of the two aspects of point of view makes evident the narrative possibility that a narrator can report what one of the characters perceives.

Since Genette's work on focalization, others have refined the notion to an opposition between external and internal focalization. In brief, *external focalization* designates a narrative situation in which the source of the perceptions, the focalizer, does not participate in the events of the narrative. *Internal focalization*, in contrast, defines a situation in which characters (participants in the events) serve as the source of perceptions, that is, the character is focalizer. Shlomith Rimmon-Kenan, *Narrative Fiction: Contemporary Poetics* (London: Methuen, 1983), 71-85, provides a concise overview of the diverse aspects associated with focalization.

8 Ana María Amar Sánchez, "Leñero: confesar, contar, escribir," *Texto Crítico* 24-25 (1982): 239.

9 Amar Sánchez 239.

10 John S. Brushwood, "La novela mexicana (1967-1982): Los que siguieron narrando," *Symposium* 37.2 (1983): 94. Rpt. in John S. Brushwood, *La novela mexicana (1967-1982)* (Mexico: Grijalbo, 1985).

11 John M. Lipski, "Vicente Leñero: Narrative Evolution as Religious Search," *Hispanic Journal* 3.2 (1982): 50.

12 Lipski 50.

13 Niño 153-54.

14 Victor Turner, *Dramas, Fields, and Metaphors: Symbolic Action in Human Society* (Ithaca: Cornell UP, 1974) 98-155.

15 Eric R. Wolf, "The Virgin of Guadalupe: A Mexican National Symbol," *Journal of American Folklore* 71 (1958): 34-35.

16 Grossman, "*Redil de ovejas*" 129.

17 For example, Gustavo Gutiérrez, *A Theology of Liberation: History, Politics, and Salvation* (Maryknoll, New York: Orbis Books, 1973), first published in Spanish in 1971, is a ground-breaking formulation of the "new" Latin American theology, which has its origins in the social changes of the 1960s. More general references to the changes in Mexican Catholicism are found in Niño.

18 Amar Sánchez 239.

222

Five: Effective Translation, Effective Intervention:
Demystification as Textual Process in
El evangelio de Lucas Gavilán

1 Vicente Leñero, *El evangelio de Lucas Gavilán* (Barcelona: Seix Barral, 1979). Page numbers for cited passages appear in parentheses in the text of the chapter.

2 John M. Lipski, "Vicente Leñero: Narrative Evolution as Religious Search," *Hispanic Journal* 3.2 (1979): 52-53.

3 Beginning in the late 1960s and throughout the 1970s, theology has asserted the discovery of the ideological implications of religious faith and practices. Principally a Third World phenomenon, this theological discovery has not proceeded from a series of theoretical formulations to a revised set of religious practices. On the contrary, after experimentation in alternative organization of Christian communities, writers began to conceive of a theology based on precisely those social experiments. Although many now practice the "new" theology, especially in Asia and Africa, it began in Latin America, and finally received its label with the publication of Gustavo Gutiérrez's *Teología de la liberación: Perspectivas* (Lima: CEP, 1971). The other theologians mentioned in Lucas Gavilán's prologue also have contributed major works, especially to the theological discipline of Christology: Leonardo Boff, *Jesus Cristo Libertador. Ensaio de Cristologia Crítica para o nosso Tempo* (Petrópolis, Brazil: Editora Vozes, 1972), and Jon Sobrino, *Cristología desde América Latina (esbozo a partir del seguimiento del Jesús histórico)* (Mexico: Centro de Reflexión Teológica, 1976).

4 Edward W. Said, *The World, the Text, and the Critic* (Cambridge, Massachusetts: Harvard UP, 1983) 157.

5 Harvey Cox, *Religion in the Secular City: Toward a Postmodern Theology* (New York: Simon and Schuster, 1984) 160.

6 The term "translation" at this point acquires a wide range of connotations. First, the Jerusalem Bible cited in the novel is already a translation into Spanish and into a prior series of logical

equivalents. Similarly, the traditional interpretations often evoked by the novel constitute another level of translations institutionalized as the practices and beliefs of Mexican Catholicism. Leñero's novel, then, is yet another in a series of translations that sets into play a radical reevalution of the many versions.

7 Cox 176.

8 Mary Douglas, "The Effects of Modernization on Religious Change," *Daedalus* 111 (1982): 1-19; Cox, "The Gelding of God and the Birth of Modern Religion," *Religion in the Secular City* 191-204.

9 Cox 234.

10 Cox 204.

11 Said 292.

12 Said 26.

13 Jorge von Ziegler, "La buena nueva de Leñero," *La Semana de Bellas Artes* 118 (May 5, 1980): 14.

14 Cox 141.

15 Cox 235.

16 José Luis Martínez Morales, "Vicente Leñero: un autor evangélico," *Revista de la Facultad de Letras, Universidad Veracruzana* 1 (1985): 6-13, considers the possible interpretations of Christ figures in the literary text. Although I shall continue to use the term *imitatio Christi*, Martínez Morales specifies the particular import of Jesucristo Gómez as a "transfiguración ficcional" (7-8).

17 Lipski 53.

18 As an example of the "equivalencia lógica" in Lucas Gavilán's translation, the phrase *pescadores de hombres* becomes *pepenadores de hombres*, referring to the poverty-stricken scavengers who make their living by combing through garbage heaps in search of salvageable goods.

19 Jacques Derrida, *Positions*, trans. Alan Bass (Chicago: U of Chicago P, 1981) 41.

20 Derrida 42.

21 Derrida 42.

22 See Cox's comments on Eberhard Jungel, *The Doctrine of the Trinity: God's Being is Becoming* (Grand Rapids: Eerdmans, 1976), for a similar consideration of the nature of God (229).

23 In addition to the proliferation of studies relating deconstruction to theology, G. Douglas Atkins, "Partial Stories: Hebraic and Christian Thinking in the Wake of Deconstruction," *Notre Dame English Journal* 15.3 (1983): 7-21, suggests that liberation theology in and of itself bears a close resemblance to deconstructive interpretation. Following Atkins's thinking, there is room for considerable investigation along deconstructive lines into christological formulations such as found in *El evangelio de Lucas Gavilán*. The proposal of Christ's being as a becoming decenters traditional Christology, and proposes the possibility of the "presence" of Christ as an "absence" or "freeplay" in the world.

24 Said 29.

Six: Narrative Transformations in *Los periodistas*, *La gota de agua*, and *Asesinato*: World, Text, and Nonfiction Novels

1 Jorge Ruffinelli, "Notas sobre la novela en México (1975-1980)" *Cuadernos de Marcha* 2a época 14 (1981): 48.

2 In this perspective, the utility of the nonfiction novel in the post-Tlatelolco context parallels the rise of the nonfiction novel in the United States, which critics generally perceive to be a response to the profound social upheavals of the 1960s. For studies on the nonfiction novel in the United States see: John Hellmann, *Fables of Fact: The New Journalism as New Fiction* (Urbana: U of Illinois P, 1981); John Hollowell, *Fact and Fiction: The New Journalism and the Nonfiction Novel* (Chapel Hill: U of North Carolina P, 1977); Robert A. Smart, *The Nonfiction Novel* (New York: UP of America, 1985); Ronald Weber, *The Literature of Fact: Literary Nonfiction in American Writing* (Ahtens: Ohio UP, 1980); and Mas'ud

Zavarzadeh, *The Mythopoeic Reality: The Postwar American Nonfiction Novel* (Urbana: U of Illinios P, 1976).

Although critics have made numerous references to the importance of 1968 in Mexican literature, the following articles and books confront the issue directly: Jean Franco, "The Critique of the Pyramid and Mexican Narrative after 1968," *Latin American Fiction Today: A Symposium*, ed. Rose S. Minc (Takoma Park, Maryland: *Hispamérica* and Montclair State College, 1979) 49-59; Luis Leal, "Tlatelolco, Tlatelolco," *Denver Quarterly* 14.1 (1979): 3-13; Carlos Monsiváis, "Con las confrontaciones del '68 empezó todo: Un proceso opuesto al nacionalismo cultural," *Siempre* 20 June 1982: 12-13; Jaime Labastida, "Literatura del '68," *Excélsior* 19 Oct. 1982: 7-8; Dolly Young, "Mexican Literary Reactions to Tlatelolco 1968," *Latin American Research Review* 20.2 (1985): 71-85; Gonzalo Martré, "El '68 en la novela mexicana" and Alejandro Toledo, "Anotaciones: El '68 en la novela mexicana," *La Palabra y el Hombre* (nueva época) 53-54 (1985): 17-26; Christopher Domínguez, "La muerte de la literatura política," *Casa del tiempo* 49-50 (1985): 37-42; John S. Brushwood, *La novela mexicana* (1967-1982) (Mexico: Grijalbo, 1985); and Marco Antonio Campos, prologue, *Narraciones sobre el movimiento estudiantil de 1968*, eds. Marco Antonio Campos and Alejandro Toledo (Xalapa: Universidad Veracruzana, 1986) 7-14.

3 I have in mind the formulation of "repressive powers" and "ideological apparatuses" set forth in Louis Althusser, "Ideology and Ideological State Apparatuses (Notes towards and Investigation)," *Lenin and Philosophy and Other Essays*, trans. Ben Brewster (London: NLB, 1971) 121-73.

4 David William Foster, "Latin American Documentary Narrative," *PMLA* 99 (1984): 42; article rpt. in David William Foster, *Alternate Voices in the Contemporary Latin American Narrative* (Columbia: U of Missouri P, 1985) 1-44.

5 Hayden White, *Metahistory: The Historical Imagination in Nineteenth-Century Europe* (Baltimore: Johns Hopkins UP, 1973)

and *Tropics of Discourse: Essays in Cultural Criticism* (Baltimore: Johns Hopkins UP, 1978).

6 Vicente Leñero, *Los periodistas* (Mexico: Joaquín Mortiz, 1978). Page numbers for all quotations are indicated in parentheses in the text of this chapter.

7 *Sexenio* refers to the six-year term of office to which a Mexican president is elected.

8 Jean Franco reads the narrator's insistence on the term "novel" as an ironic reference to the relationship between the official, government versions and *Los periodistas*, for "if the official version claimed to be truth, then other versions could only be fictions" (52-53). Moreover, according to Franco, the manipulation of a "real" space in juxtaposition of an "fantasy" space produces the ideological positioning of the reader. Norma Klahn, "Vicente Leñero: De *Los albañiles* a *Los periodistas*; de la ficción a la verificación," *Requiem for the "Boom"--Premature?*, eds. Rose S. Minc and Marilyn R. Frankenthaler (Montclair, New Jersey: Montclair State College, 1980), comments on the usefulness of the term novel both as a statement on the impossibility of an objective history and as a technique for representing reality unavailable in other genres (166).

9 Throughout this chapter I refer to the character named Vicente Leñero in the three nonfiction novels as the narrator. Although the communicative norms governing referentiality point to the repetition between the author Leñero and the textual Leñero, the narrator/character functions as a linguistic position of enunciation, or more precisely writing, and is not to be taken as the equivalent of a "real" Vicente Leñero. In other words, my analyses here all presuppose the role of the narrator in the production of meaning, his participation in the structuring of the text, his participation as a structure of the text, and the convergence of structuring and structure in the meanings of each text.

10 Vicente Leñero, *La gota de agua* (Mexico: Plaza y Janés, 1984). Page numbers for all quotations are indicated in parentheses in the text of the chapter.

11 Indeed, there may be even greater similarities between Defoe's text and Leñero's. A tradition of critical debate surrounds the evaluation of the "factual" qualities of Defoe's account, the question of the belatedness of his actual writing of the text (Zavarzadeh 102-13). Similarly, close attention to *La gota de agua* will reveal the belated nature of the text in spite of its journal-like tone and organization.

12 I have in mind Clifford Geertz, "Thick Description: Toward an Interpretive Theory of Culture," *The Interpretation of Cultures* (New York: Basic Books, 1973), 3-30. In brief, Geertz's "thick description" serves as a critique of the claims to methodological objectivity. Instead of such reductivism, Geertz emphasizes a semiotic concept of culture:

> Believing, with Max Weber, that man is an animal suspended in webs of significance he himself has spun, I take culture to be those webs, and the analysis of it to be therefore not an experimental science in search of a law but an interpretive one in search of meaning. It is explication I am after, construing social expressions on their surface enigmatical. (5)

Thick description, then, is Geertz's approach to an anthropological analysis, an interpretive approach that emphasizes the local or microscopic focus of ethnographic study. Similarly, the nonfiction code and *costumbrista* traits of *La gota de agua* provide Leñero with an entry into the problems involved in the representation of a specific social milieu. In sum, just as Geertz's thick description combats the reductive methodological dogmas of cultural anthropology, so also does Leñero's experiment in nonfictional representation serve as an interpretive antidote to both the ideology of historical objectivity and the inherited, nineteenth-century Realism that has predominated throughout the evolution of the Spanish American novel. Moreover, it does so in much the same spirit of Geertz's thick description by means of its focus on the local or microscopic details of contemporary social reality.

13 Vicente Leñero, *Asesinato: El doble crimen de los Flores Muñoz* (Mexico: Plaza y Janés, 1985). Page numbers for all quotations are indicated in parentheses in the text of this chapter.

14 The label "novel" manifests its value as a double-edged sword in the reviews of *Asesinato*; in some contexts, the generic label serves to emphasize the creativity and innovation of Leñero's text, while in others, it seems to disparage the book as a work of "yellow journalism" by implying that it is "only a novel" (i.e., not "truth"). See, for example, Carlos Marín, "*Asesinato*: La ficción de la vida pública," *Proceso* 10 June 1985: 58; Francisco Prieto, rev. of *Asesinato*, *Proceso* 10 June 1985: 58-59; Fabienne Bradu, rev. of *Asesinato*, *Vuelta* 107 (1985): 47-48; Federico Patán, "*Asesinato*: Novela sin ficción de Vicente Leñero," *México en el arte* (Nueva época) 11 (1985-86): 84-85; Sergio Gómez Montero, rev. of *Asesinato*, *Sábado*, supp. of *Uno más uno*, 10 May 1986: 4.

15 See White, "Introduction: The Poetics of History," *Metahistory* 1-42, especially 5-11. Northrop Frye, *Anatomy of Criticism* (Princeton: Princeton UP, 1957).

16 Peter Brooks, *Reading for the Plot: Design and Intention in Narrative* (New York: Knopf, 1984), 3-36 and 287-88. Roland Barthes, *S/Z*, trans. Richard Miller (New York: Hill and Wang, 1974).

17 Indeed, there is an extensive interweaving of characterization and linguistic metaphors with respect to Julio Scherer García, "corazón de esta historia" (7). Whereas Julio Sherer comments, "Que escriban libremente, yo paro los golpes . . ." (42), he must later suffer the literal consequences of his function when one of Echeverría's bodyguards stikes him, a "golpe de karate" (128). Moreover, the entire second part of *Los periodistas* is a political *golpe*. Finally, in the third part of the novel, Julio Scherer directly

invokes the allegory of his defending role when he points out the comparison between a vicious dog that is about to attack and the strong-arm tactics of Echeverría's manipulation of the press (305).

[18] See Klahn for a consideration of the characterization of opposing groups and the heroic structure of the text in terms of Northrop Frye's *mythos* of summer, "la estructura de la búsqueda lograda" (168). Unlike Klahn, however, who conceptualizes the conflict in terms of "la fuerza de los trabajadores contra la clase dominante" (168), I would underscore that the conflict is between the journalists and the dominant political group, both of which occupy similar "class" positions. In contrast, the lowest members of the journalistic hierarchy and a group of land-squatters constitute the true social underdogs, the "class" instruments that are open to manipulation and that, in turn, can manipulate either the controlling journalists of the cooperative or the dominant political group.

[19] In brief, a *cisterna* is a buried water-storage device whereas a *tinaco* is a prefabricated tank installed above ground, usually beside or on top of a house.

[20] José Luis Martínez Morales, "Leñero: ficción de la realidad, realidad de la ficción," *Texto Crítico* 29 (1984): 173-87, is the only critical study of *La gota de agua*. In brief, Martínez Morales's study supports my approach to *La gota de agua* through his insistence on the Model Reader required to recognize what I have characterized as a nonfiction code and a *costumbrista* import. Martínez Morales also underscores exaggeration as the transforming principle that informs the narrator's point of view with respect to his household as an example.

[21] Bradu contends that *Asesinato* fails as a socio-political investigation because the actions of the novel "no son sintomáticos de ninguna situación nacional, de ningún sector o 'clase' social, de ninguna decadencia de la institución familiar." Thus, Bradu states, the risk incurred by *Asesinato* is the selection of "un termómetro demasiado pequeño y trivial para medir una situación más amplia y compleja" (48). Marín, Prieto, and Gómez Montero, in contrast,

emphasize the political facets of *Asesinato*. Indeed, Marín writes: ". . . *Asesinato* es, por encima y por debajo, un libro político" (58). In the end, *Asesinato* does perhaps consider only "áreas significativas" of Mexican society, the affluent and power-controlling classes, but such a consideration extends outward as it impinges upon the more modest economic classes employed and accused by the elite, the relative "blindness" of justice depending upon family wealth, social position, and politics, and the journalistic manipulation of the literate masses.

22 Patán 84.

23 Gómez Montero 4.

24 In this perspective, the project of a nonfiction, non-transforming account makes manifest the irony of the title of the fourth part, the "novel" of the crime. Indeed, it is the strategy of novelization as disguise and deformation, to use terms from the prologue of *Los periodistas*, that the narrator implicitly critiques in the first part of *Asesinato* when he refers to *Mitad oscura* (1982) by Luis Spota and *Los cómplices* (1983) by Luis Guillermo Piazza (85-86).

25 Franco 55.

26 Ellen McCracken, "Vicente Leñero's Critical Contribution to the Boom: From *Telenovela* to *Novela-Testimonio*," *Requiem for the "Boom"--Premature?*, eds. Rose S. Minc and Marilyn R. Frankenthaler (Montclair, New Jersey: Montclair State College, 1980) 174-185, emphasizes the importance of *Los periodistas* as a positive critique of the "breakdown in the smooth functioning of the media. . ." (182).

27 Marco Antonio Campos, rev. of *La gota de agua*, by Vicente Leñero, *Proceso* 23 January 1984: 60.

28 Campos 60.

29 Roberto González Echevarría, *The Voice of the Masters: Writing and Authority in Modern Latin American Literature* (Austin: U of Texas P, 1985) 115.

Conclusion: Vicente Leñero: The Novelist as Critic

1 I must clarify that by "synthesis" I do not refer to an always coherent combination of two distinct yet equal elements. T. K. Seung, *Semiotics and Thematics in Hermeneutics* (New York: Columbia UP, 1982), cogently argues that in dialectics the movement toward synthesis constitutes a variety of possible relationships between the initial terms of the process, and that a unified or balanced combination of such terms is not necessarily the prerequisite for a synthesis. Synthesis may maintain varying degrees of imbalance between terms, or even of repression and supression. See particularly chapter eleven in Seung's text, "Thematic Dialectic" (192-217).

2 I have in mind here Mary Louise Pratt, "Ideology and Speech-Act Theory," *Poetics Today* 7.1 (1986): 59-72, where she points out the fallacy of supposing that texts must be cooperative. She argues that a seriously critical account of literary communication must work beyond the ideologically limited and limiting assumptions of the Gricean Cooperative Principle: "One must be able to talk about reader/text/author relations that are coercive, subversive, conflictive, submissive, as well as cooperative, and about relations that are some or all of these simultaneously or at different points in a text" (70). Although this study moves far beyond some of her previous statements in *Toward a Speech-Act Theory of Literary Discourse*, especially with regard to the Cooperative Principle and its relation to the convention of meaningfulness, Pratt's insights should go a long way toward opening up a reconsideration of readerships in contemporary Spanish American narrative. Rather than simply discussing the quantitative increase in readers' participation in the production of meaning in contemporary Spanish American novels, the goal must be to interrogate the qualitatively different and possibly contradictory roles of readerships.

3 Vicente Leñero, *Los albañiles* (Barcelona: Seix-Barral, 1964) 196.

4 Terry Eagleton, *Literary Theory: An Introduction* (Minneapolis: U of Minnesota P, 1983) 170. With respect to the positive role of such texts in Latin American literature, Fernando Alegría, "Antiliteratura," *América Latina en su literatura*, ed. César Fernández Moreno (México: Siglo XXI and UNESCO, 1972) 243-258.

5 John M. Lipski, "Reading the Writters: Hidden Meta-Structures in the Modern Spanish American Novel," *Perspectives on Contemporary Literature* 6 (1980): 117-24, suggests this direction in the first cycle of Leñero's novels.

6 See Vicente Leñero, *Vicente Leñero: Nuevos escritores mexicanos del siglo XX presentados por sí mismos* (Mexico: Empresas Editoriales, 1967), especially 23, 42-43, and 54-55.

7 Vicente Leñero, "Vicente Leñero," *Los narradores ante el público* (1st series) (Mexico: Joaquín Mortiz, 1966) 179-188, refers to a work in progress that meets the description of *Redil de ovejas* (188).

BIBLIOGRAPHY

Bibliography

Novels of Vicente Leñero

Leñero, Vicente. *La voz adolorida.* Xalapa: Universidad Veracruzana, 1961.

---. *Los albañiles.* Barcelona: Seix Barral, 1964.

---. *Estudio Q.* Mexico City: Joaquín Mortiz, 1965.

---. *El garabato.* Mexico City: Joaquín Mortiz, 1967.

---. *A fuerza de palabras.* Buenos Aires: Centro Editor de América Latina, 1967; Mexico City: Grijalbo, 1976.

---. *Redil de ovejas.* Mexico City: Joaquín Mortiz, 1973.

---. *Los periodistas.* Mexico City: Joaquín Mortiz, 1978.

---. *El evangelio de Lucas Gavilán.* Barcelona: Seix Barral, 1979.

---. *La gota de agua.* Mexico City: Plaza y Janés, 1983.

---. *Asesinato: El doble crimen de los Flores Muñoz.* Mexico City: Plaza y Janés, 1985.

Other Narrative, Journalism, and Cited Works of Vicente Leñero

Leñero, Vicente. *La polvareda y otros cuentos.* Mexico City: Editorial Jus, 1959.

---. "Vicente Leñero." *Los narradores ante el público.* 1st series. Mexico City: Joaquín Mortiz, 1966. 179-188.

---. *Vicente Leñero: Nuevos escritores mexicanos del siglo XX presentados por sí mismos.* Mexico City: Empresas Editoriales, 1967.

---. *Cajón de sastre.* Puebla: Editorial UAP, 1981.

---. *Justos por pecadores: Tres guiones cinematográficos.* Mexico City: Marcha Editores, 1982.

---. *Teatro completo.* 2 vols. Mexico City: Universidad Nacional Autónoma de México, 1982.

---. *Vivir del teatro.* Mexico City: Joaquín Mortiz, 1982.

---. *Talacha periodística.* Mexico City: Diana, 1983.

---. *¡Pelearán diez rounds!*. Mexico City: Editores Mexicanos Unidos, 1985.

---. *La ruta crítica de Martirio de Morelos*. Mexico City: Océano, 1985.

Leñero, Vicente, and José Revueltas. *Los albañiles: un guión rechazado*. Mexico City: Premiá Editores, 1983.

Critical Studies of the Novels of Vicente Leñero

Amar Sánchez, Ana María. "Leñero: Confesar-contar-escribir: espacio del enfrentamiento." *Texto Crítico* 24-25 (1982): 229-41.

Benedetti, Mario. "México en el pantógrafo de Vicente Leñero." *El ejercicio del criterio*. Mexico City: Nueva Imagen, 1981. 285-88.

Bradu, Fabienne. Rev. of *Asesinato*, by Vicente Leñero. *Vuelta* 107 (1985): 47-48.

Campos, Marco Antonio. Rev. of *La gota de agua*, by Vicente Leñero. *Proceso* 23 January 1984: 60.

Clark, Lucie. "*Los albañiles*." *Cuadernos Americanos* 162.1 (1969): 219-23.

Devereaux, Neil Jay. *Tres escritores representativos de la novelística mexicana reciente*. Diss. U of Texas-Austin, 1973. Ann Arbor: UMI, 1973. 73-25,998.

Figuerola, Luciana. "Los códigos de la veredicción en *El garabato* de Vicente Leñero." *Semiosis* 4 (1980): 31-59.

Garavito, Lucía. "La narración y la focalización como base para un análisis de la novelística de Vicente Leñero." *Semiosis* 4 (1980): 61-82.

Gómez Montero, Sergio. Rev. of *Asesinato*, by Vicente Leñero. *Sábado* 10 May 1986: 4.

Grossman, Lois S. "*Los albañiles*, Novel and Play: A Two-Time Winner." *Latin American Theatre Review* 9.2 (1976): 5-12.

---. *Las novelas de Vicente Leñero: El primer ciclo (1961-1967)*. Diss. Rutgers U, 1972. Ann Arbor: UMI, 1973. 73-4750.

---. "*Redil de ovejas*: A New Novel from Leñero." *Romance Notes* 17.2 (1976): 127-30.

Kellerman, Owen L. "*Los albañiles* de Vicente Leñero: Estudio de la víctima." *Hispanófila* 70 (1980): 45-55.

Klahn, Norma. "Vicente Leñero: De *Los albañiles* a *Los periodistas*; de la ficción a la verificacción." *Requiem for the "Boom"--Premature?*. Eds. Rose S. Minc and Marilyn R. Frankenthaler. Montclair, New Jersey: Montclair State College, 1980. 162-73.

Langford, Walter M. "Vicente Leñero--a Mexican Graham Greene?" *The Mexican Novel Comes of Age*. Notre Dame: U of Notre Dame P, 1971. 151-67.

Lipski, John M. "Vicente Leñero: Narrative Evolution as Religious Search." *Hispanic Journal* 3.2 (1982): 41-59.

Ludmer, Iris Josefina. "Vicente Leñero, *Los albañiles*. Lector y actor." *Nueva novela latinoamericna* I. Ed. Julio Lafforgue. Buenos Aires: Paidós, 1969. 194-208.

Marín, Carlos. "*Asesinato:* La ficción de la vida pública." *Proceso* 10 June 1985: 58.

Martínez Morales, José Luis. "Leñero: ficción de la realidad y realidad de la ficción." *Texto Crítico* 29 (1984): 173-87.

---. "Vicente Leñero: un autor evangélico." *Revista de la Facultad de Letras de la Universidad Veracruzana* 1 (1985): 6-13.

McCracken, Ellen Marie. *The Mass Media and the Latin American New Novel: Vicente Leñero and Julio Cortázar*. Diss. U of California-San Diego, 1977. Ann Arbor: UMI, 1978. 7732818.

---. "Vicente Leñero's Critical Contribution to the Boom: From *Telenovela* to *Novela-testimonio*." *Requiem for the "Boom"--Premature?*. Eds. Rose S. Minc and Marilyn R. Frankenthaler. Montclair, New Jersey: Montclair State College, 1980. 174-85.

McMurray, George R. "The Novels of Vicente Leñero." *Critique: Studies in Modern Fiction* 8.3 (1966): 55-61.

238

Niño, Miguel Angel. *Religión y sociedad en la obra de Vicente Leñero*. Diss. Michigan State U, 1977. Ann Arbor: UMI, 1977. 77-25,273.

Ortega, Julio. "Un ejercicio narrativo de Leñero." *La contemplación y la fiesta: Notas sobre la novela latinoamericana actual*. Caracas: Monte Avila, 1969. 183-88.

Patán, Federico. "*Asesinato*: Novela sin ficción de Vicente Leñero." *México en el arte* 11 (1985-86): 84-85.

Prieto, Francisco. Rev. of *Asesinato*, by Vicente Leñero. *Proceso* 10 June 1985: 58-59.

Robles, Humberto E. "Aproximaciones a *Los albañiles* de Vicente Leñero." *Revista Iberoamericana* 73 (1970): 579-99.

Seale, Mary L. "Two Views of Contemporary Urban Mexico." *South Atlantic Bulletin* 41.4 (1976): 48-55.

Seminario de Semiótica: Reina América Pulido, et al. "*A fuerza de palabras*: Una decodificación." *Semiosis* 7-8 (1981-82): 3-34.

Seminario de Semiótica: Ana Guadalupe Martínez, et al. "La organización temporal del relato en *A fuerza de palabras*." *Semiosis* 7-8 (1981-82): 35-63.

von Ziegler, Jorge. "La buena nueva de Leñero." *La Semana de Bellas Artes* 5 March 1980: 14-5.

General Reference: Literary History, Culture, and Literary Theory

Althusser, Louis. "Ideology and Ideological State Apparatuses (Notes towards an Investigation)." *Lenin and Philosophy*. Trans. Ben Brewster. London: NLB, 1971. 121-73.

Atkins, G. Douglas. "Partial Stories: Hebraic and Christian Thinking in the Wake of Deconstruction." *Notre Dame English Journal* 15.3 (1983): 7-21.

---. *Reading Deconstruction: Deconstructive Reading*. Lexington: UP of Kentucky, 1983.

Bakhtin, M. M. *The Dialogic Imagination.* Trans. Caryl Emerson and Michael Holquist. Austin: U of Texas P, 1981.

Bal, Mieke. *Narratologie: Les instances du récit.* Paris: Editions Klincksieck, 1977.

Barthes, Roland. "L'éffet de réel." *Communications* 11 (1968): 84-9.

---. *S/Z.* Trans. Richard Howard. New York: Hill and Wang, 1974.

Benavides, Ricardo. "Mito, mímesis y manierismo: la novela hispanoamericana del siglo XX." *Chasqui* 7.3 (1977): 5-26.

---. "Sobre el realismo en la narrativa hispanoamericana." *Chasqui* 7.1 (1976): 5-16.

Benveniste, Emile. *Problems in General Linguistics.* Trans. Mary Elizabeth Meek. Coral Gables, Florida: U of Miami P, 1971.

Blanco, José Joaquín. "Aguafuertes de narrativa mexicana, 1950-1980." *Nexos* August 1982: 23-39.

Boff, Leonardo. Jesus Cristo Libertador. *Ensaio de Cristologia Crítica para o nosso Tempo.* Petrópolis, Brazil: Editora Vozes, 1972.

Booth, Wayne C. *The Rhetoric of Fiction.* Chicago: U of Chicago P, 1961.

Borges, Jorge Luis. *Prosa completa.* Barcelona: Bruguera, 1980.

Brooks, Peter. "Fictions of the Wolfman: Freud and Narrative Understanding." *Diacritics* 9.1 (1979): 72-81.

---. *Reading for the Plot: Design and Intention in Narrative.* New York: Alfred A. Knopf, 1984.

Brushwood, John S. "Importancia de Faulkner en la novela latinoamericana." *Letras nacionales, literatura comparada* 31 (1976): 7-14.

---. "Literary Periods in Twentieth-Century Mexico: The Transformation of Reality." *Contemporary Mexico.* Eds. James W. Wilkie, Michael C. Meyer, and Edna Monzón de Wilkie. Los Angeles: UCLA Latin American Center, 1976. 671-83.

---. "Mexican Fiction in the Seventies: Author, Intellect, and Public." *Ibero-American Letters in a Comparative*

240

Perspective. Eds. Wolodymyr T. Zyla and Wendell M. Aycock. Proc. of a Comparative Literature Symposium, Texas Tech U. Lubbock: Texas Tech P, 1978. 35-47.

---. *México en su novela: Una nación en busca de su identidad.* Trans. Francisco González Aramburo. Mexico City: Fondo de Cultura Económica, 1973.

---. *La novela mexicana* (1968-1982). Mexico City: Grijalbo, 1985.

---. *The Spanish American Novel: A Twentieth-Century Survey.* Austin: U of Texas P, 1975.

Campos, Marco Antonio, and Alejandro Toledo. Prologue. *Narraciones sobre el movimiento estudiantil de 1968.* Xalapa: Universidad Veracruzana, 1986. 7-14.

Certeau, Michel de. *Heterologies: Discourses on the Other.* Trans. Brian Massumi. Minneapolis: U of Minnesota P, 1986.

Chatman, Seymour. *Story and Discourse: Narrative Structure in Fiction and Film.* Ithaca: Cornell UP, 1978.

Cockcroft, James D. *Mexico: Class Formation, Capital Accumulation, and the State.* New York: Monthly Review P, 1983.

Cortázar, Julio. *Rayuela.* Buenos Aires: Editorial Sudamericana, 1963.

Cox, Harvey. *Religion in the Secular City: Toward a Postmodern Theology.* New York: Simon and Schuster, 1984.

Culler, Jonathan. *On Deconstruction: Theory and Criticism after Structuralism.* Ithaca: Cornell UP, 1982.

---. "Problems in the Theory of Fiction." *Diacritics* 14.1 (1984): 2-11.

---. *The Pursuit of Signs: Semiotics, Literature, and Deconstruction.* Ithaca: Cornell UP, 1981.

---. *Structuralist Poetics: Structuralism, Linguistics, and the Study of Literature.* Ithaca: Cornell UP, 1975.

Derrida, Jacques. *Dissemination.* Trans. Barbara Johnson. Chicago: U of Chicago P, 1981.

---. "Living On * Borderlines." Trans. James Hulbert. *Deconstruction and Criticism.* Eds. Harold Bloom, et al. New York: Seabury P, 1979. 75-176.

---. *Margins of Philosophy.* Trans. Alan Bass. Chicago: U of Chicago P, 1982.

---. *Of Grammatology.* Trans. Gayatri Chakravorty Spivak. Baltimore: Johns Hopkins UP, 1974.

---. *Positions.* Trans. Alan Bass. Chicago: U of Chicago P, 1981.

---. *Writing and Difference.* Trans. Alan Bass. Chicago: U of Chicago P, 1978.

Díaz-Guerrero, R. *Psychology of the Mexican.* Austin: U of Texas P, 1975.

D'Lugo, Carol Clark. *Fragmentation and Reader Response: A Study of Anti-Classical Strategies in the Mexican Novel: 1947-1965.* Diss. Brown U, 1983. Ann Arbor: UMI, 1983. 8325968.

Domínguez, Christopher. "La muerte de la literatura política." *La Casa del Tiempo* 49-50 (1985): 37-42.

Douglas, Mary. "The Effects of Modernization on Religious Change." *Daedalus* 111.1 (1982): 1-19.

Duncan, J. Ann. "Innovations in Mexican Prose Fiction since 1970." *Hispanic Journal* 5.1 (1983): 117-27.

Eagleton, Terry. *Literary Theory: An Introduction.* Minneapolis: U of Minnesota P, 1983.

Eco, Umberto. *The Role of the Reader: Explorations in the Semiotics of Texts.* Bloomington: Indiana UP, 1979.

Fell, Claude. "Destrucción y poesía en la novela latinoamericana contemporánea." *III Congreso Latinoamericano de Escritores.* Caracas: Ediciones del Congreso de la República Sesquicentenario de la Batalla de Carabobo, 1971. 207-13.

Felman, Shoshana, ed. *Literature and Psychoanalysis: The Question of Reading: Otherwise.* Baltimore: Johns Hopkins UP, 1982.

---. "Psychoanalysis and Pedagogy: Teaching Terminable and Interminable." *Teaching as a Literary Genre.* Ed. Barbara Johnson. Baltimore: Johns Hopkins UP, 1982. 21-44.

Fernández Moreno, César, ed. *América Latina en su literatura.* Mexico: Siglo XXI and UNESCO, 1972.

Fish, Stanley. *Is There a Text in this Class?: The Authority of Interpretive Communities.* Cambridge: Harvard UP, 1980.

Foster, David William. "Latin American Documentary Narrative." *PMLA* 99 (1984): 41-55.

---. *Alternate Voices in the Contemporary Latin American Narrative.* Columbia: U of Missouri P, 1985.

Foucault, Michel. *Language, Counter-Memory, Practice.* Ed. Donald F. Bouchard. Trans. Donald F. Bouchard and Sherry Simon. Ithaca: Cornell UP, 1977.

Franco, Jean. "The Critique of the Pyramid and Mexican Fiction after 1968." *Latin American Fiction Today: A Symposium.* Ed. Rose S. Minc. Takoma Park, Maryland: Hispamérica and Montclair State College, 1979. 49-59.

---. "Trends and Priorities for Research on Latin American Literature." *Ideologies and Literature* 4 (1983): 107-120.

Frye, Northrop. *Anatomy of Criticism.* Princeton: Princeton UP, 1957.

Geertz, Clifford. *The Interpretation of Cultures.* New York: Basic Books, 1973.

---. *Local Knowledge.* New York: Basic Books, 1983.

Genette, Gérard. *Narrative Discourse: An Essay in Method.* Trans. Jane E. Lewin. Ithaca: Cornell UP, 1980.

Girard, René. *Violence and the Sacred.* Trans. Patrick Gregory. Baltimore: Johns Hopkins UP, 1977.

Glantz, Margo. *Repeticiones: ensayos sobre literatura mexicana.* Xalapa: Universidad Veracruzana, 1979.

González, Aníbal. *La crónica modernista hispanoamericana.* Madrid: Ediciones José Porrúa Turranzas, 1983.

---. *La novela modernista hispanoamericana.* Madrid: Gredos, 1987.

González Echevarría, Roberto. *The Voice of the Masters: Writing and Authority in Modern Latin American Literature.* Austin: U of Texas P, 1985.

Grice, H. P. "Logic and Conversation." *Syntax and Semantics: Volume 3 Speech Acts.* Eds. Peter Cole and Jerry L. Morgan. New York: Academic P, 1975. 41-58.

Gutiérrez, Gustavo. *Teología de la liberación: Perspectivas.* Lima: CEP, 1971.

Harss, Luis, and Barbara Dohmann. *Los nuestros.* Buenos Aires: Sudamericana, 1966.

Hellmann, John. Fables of Fact: *The New Journalism as New Fiction.* Urbana: U of Illinois P, 1981.

Herrnstein Smith, Barbara. *On the Margins of Discourse: The Relation of Literature to Language.* Chicago: U of Chicago P, 1978.

---. "Narrative Versions, Narrative Theories." *On Narrative.* Ed. W. J. T. Mitchell. Chicago: U of Chicago P, 1980. 209-32.

Hollowell, John. *Fact and Fiction: The New Journalism and the Nonfiction Novel.* Chapell Hill: U of North Carolina P, 1977.

Holquist, Michael. "Whodunit and Other Questions: Metaphysical Detective Stories in Post-War Fiction." *New Literary History* 3.1 (1971): 135-56.

Hutcheon, Linda. *Narcissistic Narrative: the Metafictional Paradox.* London: Methuen, 1984.

Iser, Wolfgang. *The Act of Reading: A Theory of Aesthetic Response.* Baltimore: Johns Hopkins UP, 1978.

Jakobson, Roman. "Linguistics and Poetics." *Style in Language.* Ed. Thomas A. Sebeok. Cambridge, Massachusetts: M.I.T. P, 1960. 350-77.

Jungel, Eherhard. *The Doctrine of the Trinity: God's Being is Becoming.* Grand Rapids: Eerdmans, 1976.

Labastida, Jaime. "Literatura del 68." *Excelsior* 19 October 1982: 7.

Leal, Luis. "Tlatelolco, Tlatelolco." *Denver Quarterly* 14.1 (1979): 3-13.

Lewis, Oscar. *The Children of Sánchez.* 1961. London: Penguin Books, 1964.

Lipski, John M. "Reading the Writers: Hidden Meta-Structures in the Modern Spanish American Novel." *Perspectives on Contemporary Literature* 6 (1980): 117-24.

Lyotard, Jean-Francois. *The Postmodern Condition: A Report on Knowledge.* Trans. Geoff Bennington and Brian Massumi. Minneapolis: U of Minnesota P, 1984.

Matré, Gonzalo. "El '68 en la novela mexicana." *La Palabra y el Hombre* 53-54 (1985): 17-22.

McMurray, George R. "Current Trends in the Mexican Novel." *Hispania* 51 (1968): 532-37.

Miller, J. Hillis. *Fiction and Repetition: Seven English Novels.* Cambridge: Harvard UP, 1982.

Minc, Rose S., and Marilyn R. Frankenthaler, eds. *Requiem for the "Boom" --Premature?: A Symposium.* Montclair, New Jersey: Dept. of Spanish and Italian, School of Humanities, Latin American Area Studies Program, Latin American Student Association, Montclair State College, 1980.

Mitchell, W. J. T., ed. *On Narrative.* Chicago: U of Chicago P, 1981.

Monsiváis, Carlos. "Con las confrontaciones del 68 empezó todo un proceso opuesto al nacionalismo cultural." *Siempre* 20 June 1982: 12-13.

Ocampo, Aurora M., ed. *La crítica de la novela mexicana contemporánea.* Mexico City: UNAM, 1981.

Ocampo de Gómez, Aurora M., and Ernesto Prado Velázquez. *Diccionario de escritores mexicanos.* Mexico City: UNAM and Centro de Estudios Literarios, 1967.

Pérez Firmat, Gustavo. *Idle Fictions: The Hispanic Vanguard Novel, 1926-1934.* Durham: Duke UP, 1982.

Pratt, Mary Louise. "Ideology and Speech Act Theory." *Poetics Today* 7.1 (1986): 59-72.

---. "Interpretive Strategies/Strategic Interpretations: On Anglo-American Reader Response Criticism." *boundary 2* (1983): 201-231.

---. *Toward a Speech Act Theory of Literary Discourse.* Bloomington: Indiana UP, 1977.

Promis, José M. "En torno a la nueva novela hispanoamericana: Reubicación de un concepto." *Chasqui* 7.1 (1976): 16-27.

Rama, Angel. "El 'boom' en perspectiva." *Más allá del boom: literatura y mercado.* Mexico City: Marcha Editores, 1981. 51-110.

---. "Los contestatarios del poder." *Novísimos narradores hispanoamericanos en marcha 1964-1980.* Mexico City: Marcha Editores, 1981. 9-48.

Reckley, Alice Ruth. *Looking Ahead Through the Past: Nostalgia in the Recent Mexican Novel.* Diss. U of Kansas, 1985. Ann Arbor: UMI, 1986. 8608439.

Rimmon-Kenan, Shlomith. *Narrative Fiction: Contemporary Poetics.* London: Methuen, 1983.

Ruffinelli, Jorge. "Notas sobre la novela en México (1975-1980)." *Cuadernos de Marcha* ns 14 (1981): 47-59.

Said, Edward W. *Beginnings: Intention and Method.* 1975. New York: Columbia UP, 1985.

---. "Opponents, Audiences, Constituencies, and Community." *Critical Inquiry* 9 (1982): 1-26.

---. *Orientalism.* New York: Vintage Books, 1979.

---. *The World, the Text, and the Critic.* Cambridge: Harvard UP, 1983.

Schor, Naomi. *Reading in Detail: Aesthetics and the Feminine.* New York: Methuen, 1987.

Schwartz, Kessel. *A New History of Spanish American Fiction II: Social Concern, Universalism, and the New Novel.* Coral Gables: U of Miami P, 1971.

Seung, T. K. *Semiotics and Thematics in Hermeneutics.* New York: Columbia UP, 1982.

---. *Structuralism and Hermeneutics.* New York: Columbia UP, 1982.

Sklodowska, Elzbieta. "Aproximaciones al discurso histórico en la nueva novela hispanoamericana." *Plural* January 1985: 11-19.

Smart, Robert A. *The Nonfiction Novel.* New York: UP of America, 1985.

Sobrino, Jon. *Cristología desde América Latina (esbozo a partir del seguimiento del Jesús histórico).* Mexico City: Centro de Reflexión Teológica, 1976.

Sommers, Joseph. *After the Storm: Landmarks of the Modern Mexican Novel.* Albuquerque: U of New Mexico P, 1968.

Souza, Raymond D. "Language vs. Structure in the Contemporary Spanish American Novel." *Hispania* 52 (1969): 833-39.

Spires, Robert C. *Beyond the Metafictional Mode: Directions in the Modern Spanish Novel.* Lexington: U of Kentucky P, 1984.

Todorov, Tzvetan. *The Poetics of Prose.* Trans. Richard Howard. Ithaca: Cornell UP, 1977.

Toledo, Alejandro. "Anotaciones: El '68 en la novela mexicana." *La Palabra y el Hombre* 53-54 (1985): 23-26.

Turner, Victor. *Dramas, Fields, and Metaphors: Symbolic Action in Human Society.* Ithaca: Cornell UP, 1974.

Vargas, Margarita. *Grupo "Revista Mexicana de Literatura" y sus coetáneos.* Diss. U of Kansas, 1985. Ann Arbor: UMI, 1986. 8608454.

Weber, Ronald. *Literature of Fact: Literary Nonfiction in American Writing.* Athens: Ohio UP, 1980.

White, Hayden. *Metahistory: The Historical Imagination in Nineteenth-Century Europe.* Baltimore: Johns Hopkins UP, 1973.

---. *Tropics of Discourse: Essays in Cultural Criticism.* Baltimore: Johns Hopkins UP, 1978.

Wolf, Eric R. "The Virgin of Guadalupe: A Mexican National Symbol." *Journal of American Folklore* 71 (1958): 34-9.

Young, Dolly. "Mexican Literary Reactions to Tlatelolco 1968." *Latin American Research Review* 20.2 (1985): 71-85.

Zavarzadeh, Mas'ud. *The Mythopoeic Reality: The Postwar American Nonfiction Novel.* Urbana: U of Illinois P, 1976.

INDEX

Index

254

University of Texas Studies
in Contemporary Spanish-American Fiction

Robert Brody
General Editor

This new series welcomes original critical studies (200-350 pp.) in English or Spanish on any aspect of the narrative literature in Spanish America from its formative period in the 1930s and 1940s to the present. No methodological approach will be excluded, provided the manuscript does not contain excessive technical terminology that might tend to obscure rather than illuminate.

Chiles, Frances

OCTAVIO PAZ
The Mythic Dimension

American University Studies: Series 2 (Romance Languages and Literature). Vol. 6
ISBN 0-8204-0079-3   224 pp.   hardback US $ 33.50/sFr. 56.00

Recommended prices – alterations reserved

Octavio Paz: The Mythic Dimension is a study of myth and mythmaking in the eminent Mexican writer's poetry based on an archetypal analysis of the central theme of the dialectic of solitude and communion. The author also attempts to illustrate Paz's mission to redeem the positive values of biblical, classical, pre-Columbian, and oriental mythologies by re-creating and enriching them in new forms and meanings more appropriate to a contemporary world view. Poems are selected from both early and recent collections to illustrate the continuity of Paz's works; quoted passages are in the original Spanish with English translations. In addition to mythological sources, significant contributions of certain literary sources to Paz's thought and poetry are also discussed to demonstrate his place in the modern literary tradition.

Contents: *The Wasteland* and *The Garden* deal with the poet's vision of contemporary reality as the demonic world. *Love and the Beloved* and *The Poetic Revelation* explore eroticism and poetry as communion experiences. *The End of the Circuitous Journey* is a synthesis and epilogue.
Dr. Chiles has done a superlative job of exposing the indebtedness to myth and the mythopoetic contribution of a man whom consensus now considers the world's greatest poetic talent.
(Eugen E. Reed, The University of Idaho)

PETER LANG PUBLISHING, INC.
62 West 45th Street
USA – New York, NY 10036